Mastering IPython 4.0

Get to grips with the advanced concepts of interactive computing to make the most out of IPython

Thomas Bitterman

[PACKT] open source ✿
PUBLISHING   community experience distilled

BIRMINGHAM - MUMBAI

Mastering IPython 4.0

First published: May 2016

Production reference: 1240516

Published by Packt Publishing Ltd.
Livery Place
35 Livery Street
Birmingham B3 2PB, UK.

ISBN 978-1-78588-841-0

www.packtpub.com

Credits

Author
Thomas Bitterman

Reviewers
James Davidheiser

Dipanjan Deb

Commissioning Editor
Veena Pagare

Acquisition Editor
Manish Nainani

Content Development Editor
Deepti Thore

Technical Editor
Tanmayee Patil

Copy Editor
Vikrant Phadke

Project Coordinator
Shweta H. Birwatkar

Proofreader
Safis Editing

Indexer
Monica Ajmera Mehta

Graphics
Disha Haria

Production Coordinator
Nilesh Mohite

Cover Work
Nilesh Mohite

About the Author

Thomas Bitterman has a PhD from Louisiana State University and is currently an assistant professor at Wittenberg University. He previously worked in the industry for many years, including a recent stint at the Ohio Supercomputer Center. Thomas has experience in such diverse areas as electronic commerce, enterprise messaging, wireless networking, supercomputing, and academia. He also likes to keep sharp, writing material for Packt Publishing and O'Reilly in his copious free time.

I would like to thank my girlfriend for putting up with the amount of time this writing has taken away.

The Ohio Supercomputer Center has been very generous with their resources. The AweSim infrastructure (`https://awesim.org/en/`) is truly years ahead of anything else in the field. The original architect must have been a genius.

And last (but by no means least), I would like to thank Deepti Thore, Manish Nainani, Tanmayee Patil and everyone else at Packt, without whose patience and expertise this project would have never come to fruition.

About the Reviewer

Dipanjan Deb is an experienced analytics professional with about 16 years of cumulative experience in machine/statistical learning, data mining, and predictive analytics across the healthcare, maritime, automotive, energy, CPG, and human resource domains. He is highly proficient in developing cutting-edge analytic solutions using open source and commercial packages to integrate multiple systems to provide massively parallelized and large-scale optimization.

He has extensive experience in building analytics teams of data scientists that deliver high-quality solutions. Dipanjan strategizes and collaborates with industry experts, technical experts, and data scientists to build analytic solutions that shorten the transition from a POC to commercial release.

He is well versed in overarching supervised, semi-supervised, and unsupervised learning algorithm implementations in R, Python, Vowpal Wabbit, Julia, and SAS; and distributed frameworks, including Hadoop and Spark, both in-premise and in cloud environments. He is a part-time Kaggler and IoT/IIoT enthusiast (Raspberry Pi and Arduino prototyping).

www.PacktPub.com

eBooks, discount offers, and more

Did you know that Packt offers eBook versions of every book published, with PDF and ePub files available? You can upgrade to the eBook version at www.PacktPub. com and as a print book customer, you are entitled to a discount on the eBook copy. Get in touch with us at customercare@packtpub.com for more details.

At www.PacktPub.com, you can also read a collection of free technical articles, sign up for a range of free newsletters and receive exclusive discounts and offers on Packt books and eBooks.

https://www2.packtpub.com/books/subscription/packtlib

Do you need instant solutions to your IT questions? PacktLib is Packt's online digital book library. Here, you can search, access, and read Packt's entire library of books.

Why subscribe?

- Fully searchable across every book published by Packt
- Copy and paste, print, and bookmark content
- On demand and accessible via a web browser

Table of Contents

Preface

Welcome to the world of IPython 4.0, which is used in high performance and parallel environments. Python itself has been gaining traction in these areas, and IPython builds on these strengths.

High-performance computing (HPC) has a number of characteristics that make it different from the majority of other computing fields. We will start with a brief overview of what makes HPC different and how IPython can be a game-changing technology.

We will then start on the IPython command line. Now that Jupyter has split from the IPython project, this is the primary means by which the developer will interface with the language. This is an important enough topic to devote two chapters to. In the first, we will concentrate on basic commands and gaining an understanding of how IPython carries them out. The second chapter will cover more advanced commands, leaving the reader with a solid grounding in what the command line has to offer.

After that, we will address some particulars of parallel programming. IPython parallel is a package that contains a great deal of functionality required for parallel computing in IPython. It supports a flexible set of parallel programming models and is critical if you want to harness the power of massively parallel architectures.

Programs running in parallel but on separate processors often need to exchange information despite having separate address spaces. They do so by sending messages. We will cover two messaging systems, ZeroMQ and MPI, and in relation to both how they are used in already existing programs and how they interact with IPython.

We will then take a deeper look at libraries that can enhance your productivity, whether included in IPython itself or provided by third-parties. There are far too many tools to cover in this book, and more are being written all the time, but a few will be particularly applicable to parallel and HPC projects.

An important feature of IPython is its support for visualization of datasets and results. We will cover some of IPython's extensive capabilities, whether built-in to the language or through external tools.

Rounding off the book will be material on testing and documentation. These oft-neglected topics separate truly professional code from also-rans, and we will look at IPython's support for these phases of development. Finally, we will discuss where the field is going. Part of the fun of programming is that everything changes every other year (if not sooner), and we will speculate on what the future might hold.

What this book covers

Chapter 1, Using IPython for HPC, discusses the distinctive features of parallel and HPC computing and how IPython fits in (and how it does not).

Chapter 2, Advanced Shell Topics, introduces the basics of working with the command line including debugging, shell commands, and embedding, and describes the architecture that underlies it.

Chapter 3, Stepping Up to IPython for Parallel Computing, explores the features of IPython that relate directly to parallel computing. Different parallel architectures will be introduced and IPython's support for them will be described.

Chapter 4, Messaging with ZeroMQ and MPI, covers these messaging systems and how they can be used with IPython and parallel architectures.

Chapter 5, Opening the Toolkit – The IPython API, introduces some of the more useful libraries included with IPython, including performance profiling, AsyncResult, and View.

Chapter 6, Works Well with Others – IPython and Third-Party Tools, describes tools created by third-parties, including R, Octave, and Hy. The appropriate magics are introduced, passing data between the languages is demonstrated, and sample programs are examined.

Chapter 7, Seeing Is Believing – Visualization, provides an overview of various tools that can be used to produce visual representations of data and results. Matplotlib, bokeh, R, and Python-nvd3 are covered.

Chapter 8, But It Worked in the Demo! – Testing, covers issues related to unit testing programs and the tools IPython provides to support this process. Frameworks discussed include unittest, pytest, and nose2.

Chapter 9, Documentation, discusses the different audience for documentation and their requirements. The use of docstrings with reStructuredText, docutils, and Sphinx is demonstrated in the context of good documentation standards.

Chapter 10, Visiting Jupyter, introduces the Jupyter notebook and describes its use as a laboratory notebook combining data and calculations.

Chapter 11, Into the Future, reflects on the current rapid rate of change and speculates on what the future may hold, both in terms of the recent split between IPython and the Jupyter project and relative to some emerging trends in scientific computing in general.

What you need for this book

This book was written using the IPython 4.0 and 4.0.1 (stable) releases from August 2015 through March 2016; all examples and functions should work in these versions. When third-party libraries are required, the version used will be noted at that time. Given the rate of change of the IPython 4 implementation, the various third-party libraries, and the field in general, it is an unfortunate fact that getting every example in this book to run on every reader's machine is doubtful. Add to that the differences in machine architecture and configuration and the problem only worsens. Despite efforts to write straightforward, portable code, the reader should not be surprised if some work is required to make the odd example work on their system.

Who this book is for

This book is for IPython developers who want to make the most of IPython and perform advanced scientific computing with IPython, utilizing the ease of interactive computing.

It is ideal for users who wish to learn about the interactive and parallel computing properties of IPython 4.0, along with its integration with third-party tools and concepts such as testing and documenting results.

Conventions

In this book, you will find a number of text styles that distinguish between different kinds of information. Here are some examples of these styles and an explanation of their meaning.

Code words in text, database table names, folder names, filenames, file extensions, pathnames, dummy URLs, user input, and Twitter handles are shown as follows: "These methods must be named setUpClass and tearDownClass and must be implemented as class methods."

A block of code is set as follows:

```
def setUp(self):
    print("Doing setUp")
    self.vals = np.zeros((10), dtype=np.int32)
    self.randGen = myrand.MyRand( )
```

Any command-line input or output is written as follows:

```
pip install pytest
```

New terms and **important words** are shown in bold. Words that you see on the screen, for example, in menus or dialog boxes, appear in the text like this: "At a finer level of detail are the bugs listed under the **Issues** tag and the new features under the **Pulls** tag."

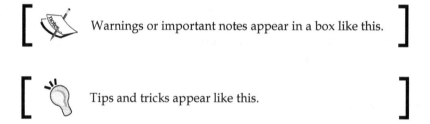

Warnings or important notes appear in a box like this.

Tips and tricks appear like this.

Reader feedback

Feedback from our readers is always welcome. Let us know what you think about this book—what you liked or disliked. Reader feedback is important for us as it helps us develop titles that you will really get the most out of.

To send us general feedback, simply e-mail feedback@packtpub.com, and mention the book's title in the subject of your message.

If there is a topic that you have expertise in and you are interested in either writing or contributing to a book, see our author guide at www.packtpub.com/authors.

Customer support

Now that you are the proud owner of a Packt book, we have a number of things to help you to get the most from your purchase.

Downloading the example code

You can download the example code files for this book from your account at `http://www.packtpub.com`. If you purchased this book elsewhere, you can visit `http://www.packtpub.com/support` and register to have the files e-mailed directly to you.

You can download the code files by following these steps:

1. Log in or register to our website using your e-mail address and password.
2. Hover the mouse pointer on the **SUPPORT** tab at the top.
3. Click on **Code Downloads & Errata**.
4. Enter the name of the book in the **Search** box.
5. Select the book for which you're looking to download the code files.
6. Choose from the drop-down menu where you purchased this book from.
7. Click on **Code Download**.

You can also download the code files by clicking on the **Code Files** button on the book's webpage at the Packt Publishing website. This page can be accessed by entering the book's name in the **Search** box. Please note that you need to be logged in to your Packt account.

Once the file is downloaded, please make sure that you unzip or extract the folder using the latest version of:

- WinRAR / 7-Zip for Windows
- Zipeg / iZip / UnRarX for Mac
- 7-Zip / PeaZip for Linux

The code bundle for the book is also hosted on GitHub at `https://github.com/PacktPublishing/Mastering-IPython-4`. We also have other code bundles from our rich catalog of books and videos available at `https://github.com/PacktPublishing/`. Check them out!

Downloading the color images of this book

We also provide you with a PDF file that has color images of the screenshots/diagrams used in this book. The color images will help you better understand the changes in the output. You can download this file from `https://www.packtpub.com/sites/default/files/downloads/MasteringIPython40_ColorImages.pdf`.

Errata

Although we have taken every care to ensure the accuracy of our content, mistakes do happen. If you find a mistake in one of our books — maybe a mistake in the text or the code — we would be grateful if you could report this to us. By doing so, you can save other readers from frustration and help us improve subsequent versions of this book. If you find any errata, please report them by visiting `http://www.packtpub.com/submit-errata`, selecting your book, clicking on the **Errata Submission Form** link, and entering the details of your errata. Once your errata are verified, your submission will be accepted and the errata will be uploaded to our website or added to any list of existing errata under the Errata section of that title.

To view the previously submitted errata, go to `https://www.packtpub.com/books/content/support` and enter the name of the book in the search field. The required information will appear under the **Errata** section.

Piracy

Piracy of copyrighted material on the Internet is an ongoing problem across all media. At Packt, we take the protection of our copyright and licenses very seriously. If you come across any illegal copies of our works in any form on the Internet, please provide us with the location address or website name immediately so that we can pursue a remedy.

Please contact us at `copyright@packtpub.com` with a link to the suspected pirated material.

We appreciate your help in protecting our authors and our ability to bring you valuable content.

Questions

If you have a problem with any aspect of this book, you can contact us at `questions@packtpub.com`, and we will do our best to address the problem.

1
Using IPython for HPC

In this chapter, we are going to look at why IPython should be considered a viable tool for building high-performance and parallel systems.

This chapter covers the following topics:

- The need for speed
- Fortran as a solution
- Choosing between IPython and Fortran
- An example case — the Fast Fourier Transform
- High-performance computing and the cloud
- Going parallel

The need for speed

Computers have never been fast enough. From their very beginnings in antiquity as abaci to the building-sized supercomputers of today, the cry has gone up "Why is this taking so long?"

This is not an idle complaint. Humanity's ability to control the world depends on its ability to model it and to simulate different courses of action within that model. A medieval trader, before embarking on a trading mission, would pull out his map (his model of the world) and plot a course (a simulation of his journey). To do otherwise was to invite disaster. It took a long period of time and a specialized skill set to use these tools. A good navigator was an important team member. To go where no maps existed was a perilous journey.

The same is true today, except that the models have become larger and the simulations more intricate. Testing a new nuclear missile by actually launching it is ill-advised. Instead, a model of the missile is built in software and a simulation of its launching is run on a computer. Design flaws can be exposed in the computer (where they are harmless), and not in reality.

Modeling a missile is much more complex than modeling the course of a ship. There are more moving parts, the relevant laws of physics are more complicated, the tolerance for error is lower, and so on and so forth. This would not be possible without employing more sophisticated tools than the medieval navigator had access to. In the end, it is our tools' abilities that limit what we can do.

It is the nature of problems to expand to fill the limits of our capability to solve them. When computers were first invented, they seemed like the answer to all our problems. It did not take long before new problems arose.

FORTRAN to the rescue – the problems FORTRAN addressed

After the initial successes of the computer (breaking German codes and calculating logarithms), the field ran into two problems. Firstly, the machine itself was slow – or at least slower than desired – for the new problems at hand. Secondly, it took too long to write the instructions (code) that the machine would execute to solve the problem.

Making the machine itself faster was largely an engineering problem. The underlying substrate went from steam and valves to electromechanical relays to vacuum tubes to integrated circuits. Each change in the substrate improved the rate at which instructions could be executed. This form of progress, while interesting, is outside of the scope of this book.

Once computers evolved past needing their programs to be wired up, programmers were free to start expressing their algorithms as text, in a programming language. While typing is faster than running wires, it has its own issues. Fortran was one of the first languages to address them successfully.

Readability

Early languages were generally not very human-friendly. It took specialized training to be able to write (and read) programs written in these languages. Programmers would often add comments to their code, either within the code itself or in external documentation, but the problem was deeper. The languages themselves were cryptic.

For example, the following code in x86 assembly language determines whether a year is a leap year or not (from `http://rosettacode.org/wiki/Leap_year#X86_Assembly`):

```
        align 16
; Input year as signed dword in EAX
IsLeapYear:
        test eax,11b
        jz .4
        retn ; 75% : ZF=0, not a leap year
.4:
        mov ecx,100
        cdq
        idiv ecx
        test edx,edx
        jz .100
        cmp edx,edx
        retn ; 24% : ZF=1, leap year
.100:
        test eax,11b
        retn ; 1% : ZF=?, leap year if EAX%400=0
```

This is the first problem Fortran addressed. Fortran set out to be more readable. An important goal was that mathematical equations in code should look like mathematical expressions written by human beings. This was an important step in enabling coders to express algorithms in terms that they themselves understood, as opposed to a format the machine could directly work with. By comparison, a Fortran function to determine whether a year is a leap year reads easily (from `http://rosettacode.org/wiki/Leap_year#Fortran`):

```
pure elemental function leap_year(y) result(is_leap)
   implicit none
   logical :: is_leap
   integer,intent(in) :: y

   is_leap = (mod(y,4)==0 .and. .not. mod(y,100)==0) .or.
(mod(y,400)==0)

end function leap_year
```

Portability

The first languages were specific to the machine they were meant to run on. A program written on one machine would not run on another. This led to the wheel being reinvented often. Consider a sorting algorithm. Many programs need to sort their data, so sorting algorithms would be needed on many different computers. Unfortunately, an implementation of quicksort on one machine, in that machine's language, would not run on another machine, in its language. This resulted in many, many reimplementations of the same algorithm.

Also, a programmer who knew how to write code on one machine had to relearn everything to use another. Not only was it difficult for talented individuals to go where they were needed, but also buying a new machine meant retraining the entire staff. The first thing the staff then did was rewrite all the existing (working) code so that it would run on the new machine. It was a tremendous waste of talent and time.

This is the second problem Fortran addressed — how can a program be expressed so that it runs on more than one machine (that is, how can programs be made portable)? The goal was that if a program was written in Fortran on one machine, then it would run on any other machine that supported Fortran.

To this end, Fortran compilers were developed. A compiler translates a program in one language (Fortran in this case) to another language (the language of the machine the program would run on).

Efficiency

While readability and portability were important, no one was going to use Fortran if the resulting program ran slowly on their computer. Early coders expended immense amounts of time and effort making their code run as quickly as possible. Problems were big and computers were slow and time was money.

This is the third problem Fortran addressed — and its solution — is the primary reason Fortran is still in use today: Fortran programs run fast. The details are out of the scope of this book but the result is clear. Algorithms expressed in Fortran run quickly. Fortran was designed that way. Implementations are judged on their efficiency, compilers generate clean code, and coders always have an eye on performance. Other languages have surpassed it in terms of readability, portability, and other measures of quality, but it is a rare language that measures up in terms of efficiency.

The computing environment

It is important to understand some of the environment that Fortran programs were running in when it was first developed. While we are used to a computer running multiple programs simultaneously today (multitasking), early computers ran only one program at a time. The programs would sit in a queue, in order. The operating system would take the first program, run it from beginning to end, then do the same for the next program, and so on. This form of job scheduling is known as a batch system.

Batch systems are very efficient. At the very bottom of things, a processor can only do one thing at a time. A multitasking system just switches what the processor is doing from one thing to another very quickly, so it looks like multiple things are happening at once. This makes for a smoother user experience; however, multitasking systems can spend a lot of time doing this switching.

Batch systems can devote this switching time to running the program. In the end, the program runs faster (although the user experience is degraded). Fortran, with its emphasis on speed, was a natural fit for batch systems.

Choosing between IPython and Fortran

We will start by taking a look at each language in general, and follow that with a discussion on the cost factors that impact a software project and how each language can affect them. No two software development projects are the same, and so the factors discussed next (along with many, many others) should serve as guidelines for the choice of language. This chapter is not an attempt to promote IPython at the expense of Fortran, but it shows that IPython is a superior choice when implementing certain important types of systems.

Fortran

Many of the benefits and drawbacks of Fortran are linked to its longevity. For the kinds of things that have not changed over the decades, Fortran excels (for example, numerical computing, which is what the language was originally designed for). Newer developments (for example, text processing, objects) have been added to the language in its various revisions.

The benefits of Fortran are as follows:

- Compilation makes for efficient runtime performance
- Existence of many tested and optimized libraries for scientific computing
- Highly portable

- Optimized for scientific computing (especially matrix operations)
- Stable language definition with a well-organized system for revisions

The drawbacks of Fortran are as follows:

- Text processing is an add-on
- Object-orientation is a recent addition
- Shrinking pool of new talent

IPython

IPython/Python is the new kid in town. It began in 2001 when Fernando Perez decided that he wanted some additional features out of Python. In particular, he wanted a more powerful command line and integration with a lab-notebook-style interface. The end result was a development environment that placed greater emphasis on ongoing interaction with the system than what traditional batch processing provided.

The nearly 45-year delay between the advent of Fortran and IPython's birth provided IPython the advantage of being able to natively incorporate ideas about programming that have arisen since Fortran was created (for example, object-orientation and sophisticated data structuring operations). However, its relative newness puts it behind in terms of installed code base and libraries. IPython, as an extension of Python, shares its benefits and drawbacks to a large extent.

The benefits of IPython are as follows:

- Good at non-numeric computing
- More concise
- Many object-oriented features
- Ease of adoption
- Useful libraries
- Sophisticated data structuring capabilities
- Testing and documentation frameworks
- Built-in visualization tools
- Ease of interaction while building and running systems

The drawbacks of IPython are as follows:

- Its interpreted nature makes for slower runtime
- Fewer libraries (although the ones that exist are of high quality)

Some of these benefits deserve more extensive treatment here, while others merit entire chapters.

Object-orientation

Object-oriented programming (OOP) was designed for writing simulations. While some simulations reduce to computational application of physical laws (for example, fluid dynamics), other types of simulation (for example, traffic patterns and neural networks) require modeling the entities involved at a more abstract level. This is more easily accomplished with a language that supports classes and objects (such as Python) than an imperative language.

The ability to match a program structure to a problem's structure makes it easier to write, test, and debug a system. The OOP paradigm is simply superior when simulating a large number of individually identifiable, complex elements.

Ease of adoption

It is easy to learn Python. It is currently the most popular introductory programming language in the United States among the top 39 departments (`http://cacm.acm.org/blogs/blog-cacm/176450-python-is-now-the-most-popular-introductory-teaching-language-at-top-us-universities/fulltext`):

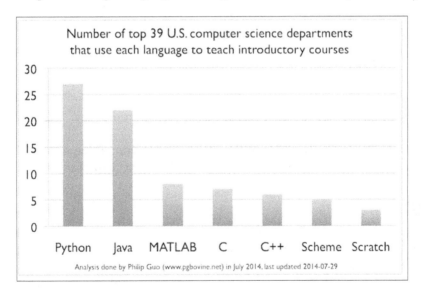

Note that Fortran is not on the list.

This is no accident, nor is Python limited to a "teaching language." Rather, it is a well-designed language with an easy-to-learn syntax and a gentle learning curve. It is much easier to learn Python than Fortran, and it is also easier to move from Fortran to Python than the reverse. This has led to an increasing use of Python in many areas.

Popularity – Fortran versus IPython

The trend toward teaching Python has meant that there is a much larger pool of potential developers who know Python. This is an important consideration when staffing a project.

TIOBE Software ranks the popularity of programming languages based on skilled engineers, courses, and third-party vendors. Their rankings for October 2015 put Python in the fifth place and growing. Fortran is 22nd (behind COBOL, which is 21st).

IEEE uses its own methods, and they produced the following graph:

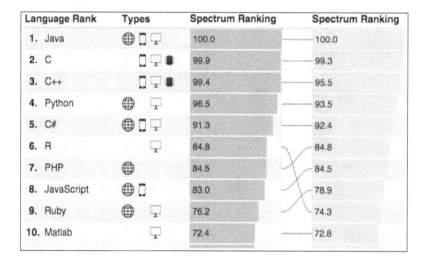

The column on the left is the 2015 ranking, and the column on the right is the 2014 ranking, for comparison. Fortran came in 29th, with a Spectrum ranking of 39.5.

Useful libraries

The growing number of Python coders has led to an increasing number of libraries written in/for Python. SciPy, NumPy, and sage are leading the way, with new open source libraries coming out on a regular basis. The usefulness of a language is heavily dependent on its libraries, and while Python cannot boast the depth in this field that Fortran can, the sheer number of Python developers means that it is closing the gap rapidly.

The cost of building (and maintaining) software

If developers were all equal in talent, they worked for free, development time were no object, all code were bug-free, and all programs only needed to run once and were then thrown away, Fortran would be the clear winner given its efficiency and installed library base.

This is not how commercial software is developed. At a first approximation, a software project's cost can be broken down into the cost of several parts:

- Requirements and specification gathering
- Development
- Execution
- Testing and maintenance

Requirements and specification gathering

There is no clear differentiation between IPython and Fortran in the difficulty of production, good requirements, and specifications. These activities are language-independent. While the availability of prewritten software packages may impact parts of the specification, both languages are equally capable of reducing requirements and specifications to a working system.

Development

As discussed previously, Python code tends to be more concise, leading to higher programmer productivity. Combine this with the growing numbers of developers already fluent in Python and Python is the clear winner in terms of reducing development time.

Execution

If it is costly to run on the target system (which is true for many supercomputers), or the program takes a long time to run (which is true for some large-scale simulations such as weather prediction), then the runtime efficiency of Fortran is unmatched. This consideration looms especially large when development on a program has largely concluded and the majority of the time spent on it is in waiting for it to complete its run.

Testing and maintenance

There are many different styles of testing: unit, coverage, mocks, web, and GUI, to name just a few. Good tests are hard to write and not very the effort put into them is often unappreciated. Most programmers will avoid writing tests if they can. To that end, it is important to have a set of good, easy-to-use testing tools.

Python has the advantage in this area, particularly because of such quality unit testing frameworks such as unit test, nose, and Pythoscope. The introspection capabilities of the Python language make the writing and use of testing frameworks much easier than those available for Fortran.

You could always just skip testing (it is, after all, expensive and unpopular), or do it the old-fashioned way; try a few values and check whether they work. This leads to an important consideration governing how much testing to do: the cost of being wrong. This type of cost is especially important in scientific and engineering computing. While the legal issues surrounding software liability are in flux, moral and practical considerations are important. No one wants to be the developer who was responsible for lethally overdosing chemotherapy patients because of a bug. There are types of programming for which this is not important (word processors come to mind), but any system that involves human safety or financial risk incurs a high cost when something goes wrong.

Maintenance costs are similar to testing costs in that maintenance programming tends to be unpopular and allows new errors to creep into previously correct code. Python's conciseness reduces maintenance costs by reducing the number of lines of code that need to be maintained. The superior testing tools allow the creation of comprehensive regression testing suites to minimize the chances of errors being introduced during maintenance.

Alternatives

There are alternatives to the stark IPython/Fortran choice: cross-language development and prototyping.

Cross-language development

Python began as a scripting language. As such, it was always meant to be able to interoperate with other languages. This can be a great advantage in several situations:

- **A divided development team**: If some of your developers know only Fortran and some know only Python, it can be worth it to partition the system between the groups and define a well-structured interface between them. Functionality can then be assigned to the appropriate team:
  - ° Runtime-intensive sections to the Fortran group
  - ° Process coordination, I/O, and others to the Python group

- **Useful existing libraries**: It always seems like there is a library that does exactly what is needed but it is written in another language. Python's heritage as a scripting language means that there are many tools that can be used to make this process easier. Of particular interest in this context is F2Py (part of NumPy), which makes interfacing with Fortran code easier.

- **Specialized functionality**: Even without a pre-existing library, it may be advantageous to write some performance-sensitive modules in Fortran. This can raise development, testing, and maintenance costs, but it can sometimes be worth it. Conversely, IPython provides specialized functionality in several areas (testing, introspection, and graphics) that Fortran projects could use.

Prototyping and exploratory development

It is often the case that it is not clear before writing a program how useful that program will turn out to be. Experience with the finished product would provide important feedback, but building the entire system would be prohibitively costly.

Similarly, there may be several different ways to build a system. Without clear guidelines to start with, the only way to decide between alternatives is to build several different versions and see which one is the best.

These cases share the problem of needing the system to be complete before being able to decide whether to build the system in the first place.

The solution is to build a prototype—a partially functional system that nevertheless incorporates important features of the finished product as envisioned. The primary virtue of a prototype is its short development time and concomitant low cost. It is often the case that the prototype (or prototypes) will be thrown away after a short period of evaluation. Errors, maintainability, and software quality in general are not important insofar as they are important to evaluating the prototype (say, for use in estimating the schedule for the entire project).

Python excels as a prototyping language. It is flexible and easy to work with (reducing development time) while being powerful enough to implement sophisticated algorithms. Its interpreted nature is not an issue, as prototypes are generally not expected to be efficient (only quick and cheap).

It is possible to adopt an approach known as **Evolutionary Prototyping**. In this approach, an initial prototype is built and evaluated. Based on this evaluation, changes are decided upon. The changes are made to the original prototype, yielding an improved version. This cycle completes until the software is satisfactory. Among other advantages, this means that a working version of the system is always available for benchmarking, testing, and so on. The results of the ongoing evaluations may point out functionality that would be better implemented in one language or another, and these changes could be made as described in the section on cross-language development.

An example case – Fast Fourier Transform

In this section, we will look at a small test program for a common scientific algorithm as written in Fortran and Python. Issues related to efficiency and general software engineering will be addressed.

Fast Fourier Transform

Rosetta Code (http://rosettacode.org/wiki/Rosetta_Code) is an excellent site that contains solutions to many problems in different programming languages. Although there is no guarantee that the code samples contained on the site are optimal (in whatever sense the word "optimal" is being used), its goal is to present a solution usable by visitors who are learning a new language. As such, the code is generally clear and well-organized. The following examples are from the site. All code is covered under the GNU Free Documentation License 1.2.

Fortran

From http://rosettacode.org/wiki/Fast_Fourier_transform#Fortran:

```
module fft_mod
  implicit none
  integer,       parameter :: dp=selected_real_kind(15,300)
  real(kind=dp), parameter :: pi=3.141592653589793238460_dp
contains
```

```fortran
! In place Cooley-Tukey FFT
recursive subroutine fft(x)
  complex(kind=dp), dimension(:), intent(inout)  :: x
  complex(kind=dp)                               :: t
  integer                                        :: N
  integer                                        :: i
  complex(kind=dp), dimension(:), allocatable    :: even, odd

  N=size(x)

  if(N .le. 1) return

  allocate(odd((N+1)/2))
  allocate(even(N/2))

  ! divide
  odd =x(1:N:2)
  even=x(2:N:2)

  ! conquer
  call fft(odd)
  call fft(even)

  ! combine
  do i=1,N/2
      t=exp(cmplx(0.0_dp,-2.0_dp*pi*real(i-1,dp)/ &
real(N,dp),kind=dp))*even(i)
      x(i)     = odd(i) + t
      x(i+N/2) = odd(i) - t
  end do

  deallocate(odd)
  deallocate(even)

  end subroutine fft

end module fft_mod

program test
  use fft_mod
  implicit none
  complex(kind=dp), dimension(8) :: data = (/1.0, 1.0, 1.0, 1.0, &
0.0, 0.0, 0.0, 0.0/)
  integer :: i
```

```
    call fft(data)

    do i=1,8
        write(*,'("(", F20.15, ",", F20.15, "i )")') data(i)
    end do

end program test
```

Python

From http://rosettacode.org/wiki/Fast_Fourier_transform#Python:

```python
from cmath import exp, pi

def fft(x):
    N = len(x)
    if N <= 1: return x
    even = fft(x[0::2])
    odd =  fft(x[1::2])
    T= [exp(-2j*pi*k/N)*odd[k] for k in xrange(N/2)]
    return [even[k] + T[k] for k in xrange(N/2)] + \
           [even[k] - T[k] for k in xrange(N/2)]

print( ' '.join("%5.3f" % abs(f)
for f in fft([1.0, 1.0, 1.0, 1.0, 0.0, 0.0, 0.0, 0.0])) )
```

Performance concerns

It would be difficult to compare the performance of these programs. The time required to run a program can be influenced by many things outside of the inherent properties of the language:

- Skilled Fortran and Python programmers could find optimizations at the code level
- Optimizing compilers vary in quality
- Underlying libraries (for example, numpy) could be substituted in and affect performance
- Critical sections could be coded in a compiled language (for example, Cython) or even assembly language, yielding a major speedup without affecting most of the lines of code
- The architecture of the machine itself could have an impact

Software engineering concerns

The question of how fast code runs is independent of the question of how long it takes to write, debug, and maintain. It is notoriously difficult to estimate how much time / how much effort will be required to write a program before the development has started. This uncertainty remains throughout the development cycle, with many projects going well over time and budget. Even when coding is complete, it can be difficult to tell how efficient the entire process was. A means to measure effort would help answer these questions.

There are two primary ways to measure the amount of effort required to write software, mentioned as follows.

Complexity-based metrics

Complexity-based metrics focus on either of these two:

- Code-level complexity (number of variables, loop nesting, branching complexity, and cyclomatic complexity)
- Functionality (based on intuitive ideas of how difficult implementing different pieces of functionality might be)

Complexity-based measures have the advantage that they tend to match intuitive ideas of what complexity is and what types of code are complex (that is, difficult to write and debug). The primary drawback is that such measures often seem arbitrary. Especially before a project is started, it can be difficult to tell how much effort will be required to write a particular piece of functionality. Too many things can change between project specification and coding. This effect is even greater on large projects, where the separation between specification and implementation can be years long.

Size-based metrics

Size-based metrics focus on a property that can be expressed on a linear scale, for example:

- Lines of code (LOC, or thousands of LOC, also known as KLOC)
- Lines of machine code (post-compilation)
- Cycles consumed (code that uses more cycles is probably more important and harder to write)

Size-based metrics have the advantage that they are easy to gather, understand, and objectively measure. In addition, LOC seems to be a decent correlate of project cost—the more the lines of code in a project, the more it costs to write it. The most expensive part of a software project is paying the coders, and the more lines of code they have to write, the longer it probably takes them to write. If the lines of code could be estimated upfront, they would be a tool for estimating the cost.

The primary drawback of this is that it is unclear whether they are very valid. It is often the case that better (clearer, faster, and easier to maintain) code will grade out as "smaller" under a size-based metric. In addition, such code is often easier to write, making the development team look even more productive. Bloated, buggy, and inefficient code can make a team look good under these metrics, but can be a disaster for the project overall.

As for the class of projects this book is concerned with, much of it involves taking mathematics-based models and translating them into executable systems. In this case, we can consider the complexity of the problem as fixed by the underlying model and concentrate on size-based measures: speed and lines of code. Speed was addressed previously, so the main concern left is LOC. As illustrated previously, Python programs tend to be shorter than Fortran programs. For a more detailed look, visit `http://blog.wolfram.com/2012/11/14/code-length-measured-in-14-languages/`.

Admittedly, such measures are fairly arbitrary. It is possible to write programs in such a way as to minimize or maximize the number of lines required, often to the detriment of the overall quality. Absent such incentives, however, any programmer tends to produce the same number of lines of code a day regardless of the language being used. This makes the relative conciseness of Python an important consideration when choosing a language to develop in.

Where we stand now

In the past, most HPC and parallel programming were done on a limited number of expensive machines. As such, the most important criteria by which programs were measured was execution speed. Fortran was an excellent solution to the problems of writing fast, efficient programs. This environment was acceptable to the community, which needed to perform these types of calculations, and it gradually separated from mainstream commercial computing, which developed other concerns.

The birth of cloud computing (and cheaper hardware in general) and the evolution of big data has caused some in the commercial mainstream to reconsider using large, parallel systems. This reconsideration has brought commercial concerns to the fore: development and maintenance costs, testing, training, and other things. In this environment, some (small) trade-off in speed is worth it for significant gains in other areas. Python/IPython has demonstrated that it can provide these gains with a minimal runtime performance cost.

High Performance Computing

At this point, we have to leave consumer computing aside for a while. As computing hardware became more affordable, the need for most people to have programs run as efficiently as possible diminished. Other criteria entered the picture: graphical interfaces, multitasking, interactivity, and so on. Usability became more important than raw speed.

This, however, was not true for everybody. There remained a small (but devoted) group of users/programmers for whom efficiency was not just the most important thing. It was the only thing. These groups hung out in nuclear labs and intelligence agencies and had money to spend on exotic hardware and highly skilled coders. Thus was shaped **High Performance Computing** (HPC).

True to the nature of HPC, its implementations have been chosen with efficiency in mind. HPC systems are highly parallel, are batch type, and run Fortran. It is important enough to the users of HPC systems that their programs run quickly, so much so that they have ignored any and all advances in the field which did not result faster programs.

The HPC learning curve

This was a satisfactory relationship for some time. The types of problems of interest to the HPC community (complicated physical modeling and advanced mathematics) had little overlap with the rest of computer science. HPC was a niche with a very high barrier to entry. After all, there were just not that many massively parallel computers to go around.

In a sense then, programming HPC systems was an island. On the island, there were ongoing research programs centered on important HPC-centric questions. Tools were built, skills were developed, and a community of practice developed to the point that approaching HPC from the outside could be daunting. Advances occurred outside of HPC also, but those inside it had their own concerns.

As time passed, the HPC island drifted further and further from mainstream computing. New areas opened up: web computing, mobile computing, agile methods, and many others. HPC took what it needed from these areas, but nothing really affected it. Until something finally did…

Cloudy with a chance of parallelism (or Amazon's computer is bigger than yours)

Amazon had a problem. During the Christmas season, it used a lot of computer power. For the rest of the year, these computers would sit idle. If there were some way to allow people to rent time on these idle machines, Amazon could make money. The result was an API that allowed people to store data on those machines (the Amazon **Simple Storage Service**, or **S3**) and an API that allowed people to run programs on the same machines (the Amazon **Elastic Compute Cloud**, or **EC2**). Together, these made up the start of the Amazon Cloud.

While not the first system to rent out excess capacity (CompuServe started off the same way several decades earlier), Amazon Cloud was the first large-scale system that provided the general public paid access to virtually unlimited storage and computing power.

It is not clear whether anybody realized what this meant at first. There are a lot of uses of clouds — overflow capacity, mass data storage, and redundancy, among others — that have a wide appeal. For our purposes, the cloud meant one thing: now everybody has access to a supercomputer. HPC will never be the same again.

HPC and parallelism

The current relationship between HPC and highly parallel architectures is relatively new. It was only in the 1990s that HPC left the realm of very fast single-processor machines for massively parallel architectures. In one sense, this was unfortunate, as the old Cray machines were aesthetic marvels:

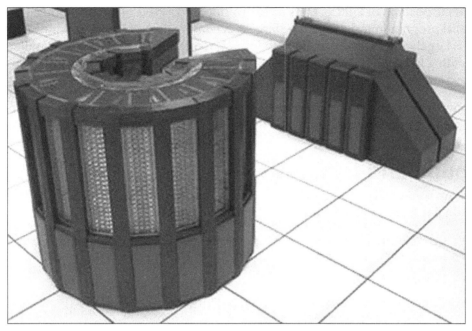

The image is taken from a public domain: `https://commons.wikimedia.org/wiki/File:Cray2.jpeg`

It was largely inevitable, however, as single-processor systems were bumping up against physical limitations involving transistor density and cooling.

The change in architecture did not bring with it a change in the problems to be solved. To this end, the generic supercomputer physical architecture evolved toward:

- Commodity processors—not custom-fast but top-of-the-line and homogeneous
- Commodity RAM—ditto
- High-end hard drives—lots of smaller, low-latency models (now turning into solid state drives)
- Super-fast interconnected networks

Moving from single to multiple processors brought issues with locality. Every time a program running on one processor needed data from another processor (or disk), processing could come to a halt as the data was being retrieved. The physical architecture of the supercomputer is meant to minimize the latency associated with non-local data access.

Given the position of HPC centers as early adopters of parallel architectures, "parallel programming" came to be largely synonymous with "HPC programming." This is largely a historical accident, and new paradigms have opened up parallel computing to constituencies outside of the HPC world. As such, this book will use the two terms interchangeably.

We now turn to one of the new paradigms, cloud computing, and discuss its similarities and differences from standard HPC.

Clouds and HPC

There are some differences between a "real" supercomputer and what most clouds offer. In particular, a cloud's physical architecture will contain:

- Commodity processors — not necessarily fast, but they make up for it in sheer numbers
- Commodity RAM — ditto
- Commodity hard drives — smaller, but larger in aggregate
- Slow(er) interconnected networks

In addition, clouds are generally heterogeneous and easily scaled. While an initial cloud is likely to have many subsystems with the same processor, RAM, hard drives, and so on, over time new subsystems will be added, with newer (or at least different) technology. The loose coupling of cloud systems encourages this sort of organic growth.

Differences in architecture mean that some algorithms will run well on supercomputers versus others that favor clouds. A lot of software that runs on supercomputers will not run on clouds; period (and vice versa)! This is not always just a matter of recompiling for a new target platform or using different libraries. The underlying algorithm may not be suited for a particular paradigm.

If speed is imperative and you have the budget, there is still no substitute for a special-purpose HPC system. If cost, ease of access, redundancy, and massive parallelism are desired, a cloud fits the bill.

That is not to say the two worlds (HPC and cloud) are completely distinct. Despite these architectural differences, it is worth noting that an Amazon EC2 C3 instance cluster is listed at 134 on the top 500 list of fastest HPC systems as of June 2015. Even on HPC's own terms, cloud computers offer respectable performance.

The core audience for this book then consists of members of both of these groups:

- Python programmers looking to expand into HPC/parallel-style programming
- HPC/parallel programmers looking to employ Python

Each group has the skills the other wants. HPC programmers understand scientific computing, efficiency, and parallelism. Python programmers are skilled in interactivity, usability, correctness, powerful development tools, ease of debugging, and other capabilities that mainstream computing values. New technology means that future systems will need to incorporate elements from both skill sets.

Going parallel

The previous sections are applicable to either serial or parallel computing. Even in the most parallelizable number crunching program, a great deal of serial code is written, so these observations are very applicable. After a certain point, however, parallel concerns come to dominate. We will start this section by introducing some terminology, before looking at a simple example.

Terminology

Wall-clock time is the amount of time that passes from the beginning of execution of a program to the end of its execution, as measured by looking at a clock on the wall. Wall-clock time is the measure people usually care about.

Cycle time is the time obtained by summing up the number of cycles taken by the program during its execution. For example, if a CPU is running at 1 MHz, each cycle takes 0.000001 seconds. So if it takes 2,500,000 cycles for a program to run, then it means the program took up 2.5 seconds of cycle time.

In a batch system with a single processor, the times are always the same. In a multitasking system, wall-clock time is often longer than cycle-time as the program may spend wall-clock time waiting to run without using any cycles.

With more than one processor, comparing the two times for an algorithm became more complicated. While not always true, many programs could be divided into pieces, such that running the program on two or more processors simultaneously reduced the wall-clock time, even if the cycle-time went up. Since wall-clock time is the important measure, for these algorithms, the answer was "Yes."

One can quantify this effect as follows:

Given a particular algorithm A

Call the wall-clock time for A when using n processors $W(A, n)$.

Similarly, the cycle time for A using n processors is $C(A, n)$.

We can define the speedup of $W(A, n)$ as $S_W(A,n) = \dfrac{W(A,1)}{W(A,n)}$

Similarly, we can define the speedup of $C(A, n)$ as $S_C(A,n) = \dfrac{C(A,1)}{C(A,n)}$

In general, when using a batch system:

For most algorithms, $W(A, n) < C(A, n)$ when $n > 1$.

For most algorithms, $S_W(A,n) < n$ when $n > 1$. For example, using two processors does not make the program run twice as fast. In general, adding more processors to run a program yields diminishing returns.

There are some algorithms for which $S_W(A,n) = n$. These are known as *embarrassingly parallel* algorithms. In this case, adding more processors results in linear speedup, which is where machines with many processors really shine.

In summary, the answer to the question, "Are more processors better?" is that it depends on the algorithm. Luckily for parallel computing, many algorithms show some amount of speedup and many important problems can be solved using these algorithms.

A parallel programming example

Consider the Collatz conjecture. Given the following function:

$$f(n) = \begin{cases} \dfrac{n}{2} & if\ n = 0\ mod\ 2 \\ 3n+1 & if\ n = 1\ mod\ 2 \end{cases}$$

The conjecture is: for any positive integer, repeated application of *f(n)* will always reach the number 1. It is believed that the conjecture is true, but there is currently no proof. We are concerned with how long it takes to reach 1, that is, how many applications of *f(n)* are required for a given *n*. We would like to find the average for all *n*, 1 to 100.

The term for the sequence of numbers generated for any *n* is **hailstone sequence**. For example, the hailstone sequence for *n* = 6 is 6, 3, 10, 5, 16, 8, 4, 2, 1. We are interested in the average length of hailstone sequences.

A serial program

A regular (serial) Python program for computing the answer might look as follows:

```
def f(n):
    curr = n
    tmp = 1
    while curr != 1:
        tmp = tmp + 1
        if curr % 2 == 1:
            curr = 3 * curr + 1
        else:
            curr = curr/2
    return tmp


def main( ):
    sum = 0
    for i in range(1, 101):
        sum = sum + f(i)
    avg = sum / 100.0
```

Detailed steps to download the code bundle are mentioned in the Preface of this book. Please have a look.

The code bundle for the book is also hosted on GitHub at https://github.com/PacktPublishing/Mastering-IPython-4. We also have other code bundles from our rich catalog of books and videos available at https://github.com/PacktPublishing/. Check them out!

A schematic of the processing would look like this:

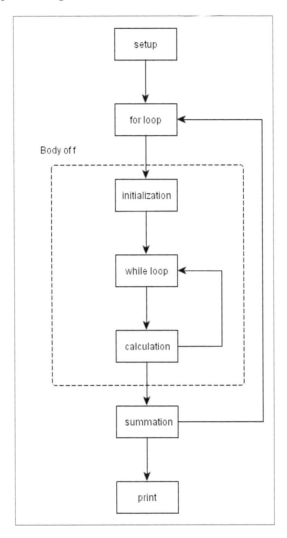

Without going into too much detail, it is easy to see that the running time of the preceding program can be expressed as:

- Setup (definition of f, initialization of sum, and so on)
- Loop body (the sum of the amount of time to compute 100 hailstone sequences one at a time)
- Teardown (calculate the average)

It is obvious that the running time of the program will be dominated by one of the loops. There is not much to be done about the `while` loop inside of `f`. Each iteration after the first depends on the result of a previous iteration. There is no way to, for example, do the tenth iteration without having already done the ninth, eighth, and so on.

The `for` loop inside of `main` has more potential for parallelization. In this case, every iteration is independent. That is:

- Each iteration computes its own value, `(f(i))`
- The computation of each `f(i)` does not depend on any other iteration
- The values can easily be combined (via summation)

This algorithm can be converted to a parallel equivalent with a few extra commands. As they stand, these functions are pseudo-code—equivalent IPython functions will be described in later chapters:

- `getProcs(num)`: Returns a list of `num` processors
- `proc.setFun(fun, arg)`: Assigns a function `fun` with an argument `arg` to the `proc` processor
- `procs.executeAll( )`: Executes `fun` on all processors in `proc` in parallel
- `proc.fetchValue( )`: Returns the value computed on the `proc` processor when the calculation is complete

A parallel equivalent

With these additions, a parallel equivalent might look as follows:

```
def f(n):
    curr = n
    tmp = 1
    while curr != 1:
        tmp = tmp + 1
        if curr % 2 == 1:
            curr = 3 * curr + 1
        else:
            curr = curr/2
    return tmp

def main( ):
    sum = 0
    procs = getProcs(100)
    i = 1
```

```
for proc in procs:
    proc.setFun(f, i)
    i = i + 1

procs.executeAll( )

for proc in procs:
    sum = sum + proc.fetchValue( )

avg = sum / 100.0
```

A schematic of the processing would look as follows:

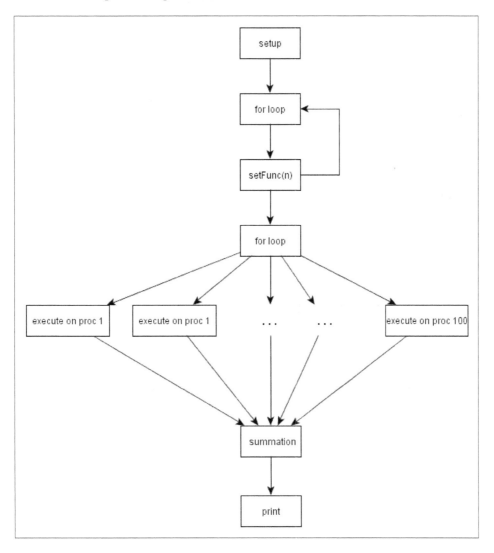

Discussion

While the parallel version is slightly longer (20 lines of code compared to 15), it is also faster, given enough processors. The intuitive reason is that the invocations of f are not queued up waiting for a single processor. With a single processor, the invocation of f(i) has to wait in line behind all the previous invocations of f(a) where $1 \leq a < i$, even though there is no dependency between them. The single processor is an unnecessary bottleneck. In this case, as no call to f depends on any other call, this algorithm is embarrassingly parallel.

When a series of functions calls, *(f1, f2, ..., fn)*, is queued up for an algorithm *A*, it is easy to see that the cycle time required to complete all *n* function calls is:

$$C(A,1) = \sum_{i=1}^{n} f_i$$

In the embarrassingly parallel case, the cycle time becomes (potentially) much smaller:

$$C(A,n) = \max(f_i)$$

This results in a speedup (ignoring setup and teardown) of:

$$S_C(A,n) = \left(\frac{\sum_{i=1}^{n} f_i}{\max(f_i)} \right)$$

In the case where all *fi* use the same number of cycles, this simplifies to the following:

$$S_C(A,n) = n$$

Several issues important to parallel programming have been glossed over in the preceding discussion. These issues are important enough to have all of *Chapter 3, Stepping Up to IPython for Parallel Computing*, devoted to them.

Summary

In this chapter, we looked at the basics of parallel computing and situated IPython in relation to its primary competitor, Fortran.

We started with the history of computing and saw how each advancement was driven by the need to solve more difficult problems and simulate more complex phenomena. Computers are simply the latest in the line of computational tools and have brought with them their own difficulties.

Fortran provided answers to problems of readability, portability, and efficiency within the computing environments that existed in early machines. These early machines prized runtime efficiency above everything else, and Fortran was geared toward this end.

Decades have passed since the earliest machines, and cycles have become cheaper. This has meant that other criteria have become important in mainstream commercial computing. In particular, the cost of creating and maintaining software has become an increasingly important consideration. This had led to increased emphasis on programmer productivity, testability, and maintainability. This chapter presented examples of how Python/IPython, while not originally designed for runtime efficiency, takes these new considerations into account.

The final step in the quest for efficiency — parallel programming — was introduced. Some of the terminology used in the field was presented, and some examples illustrated basic parallel concepts.

The following chapters will attempt to expand on the case for using IPython for projects in general, and for parallel projects in particular. While choosing a tool is often a personal (and not always rational) process, the author hopes that a fair presentation of the capabilities of IPython, in particular its strengths in parallel and scientific computing, will persuade developers and managers to adopt it for their next project.

2
Advanced Shell Topics

In this chapter, we are going to look at the tools the IPython Interactive Shell provides. With the split of the Jupyter and IPython projects, the command line provided by IPython will gain in importance.

This chapter covers the following topics:

- What is IPython?
- Installing IPython
- Starting out with the terminal
- IPython beyond Python
- Magic commands
- Cython
- Configuration
- Debugging
- A brief introduction to the IPython architecture
- Alternative development environments

What is IPython?

IPython is an open source platform for interactive and parallel computing. It started with the realization that the standard Python interpreter was too limited for sustained interactive use, especially in the areas of scientific and parallel computing.

Overcoming these limitations resulted in a three-part architecture:

- An enhanced, interactive shell
- Separation of the shell from the computational kernel
- A new architecture for parallel computing

This chapter will provide a brief overview of the architecture before introducing some basic shell commands. *Chapter 3, Stepping Up to IPython for Parallel Computing,* will cover the more advanced features. The parallel architecture will be covered in *Chapter 4, Messaging with ZeroMQ and MPI.* Before we proceed further, however, IPython needs to be installed.

Those readers who have experience in parallel and high-performance computing but are new to IPython will find the following sections useful in quickly getting up to speed. Those experienced with IPython may skim the next few sections or refer to *Chapter 11, Into the Future,* to know the history of the project, noting where things have changed, now that Notebook is no longer an integral part of development.

Installing IPython

The first step for installing IPython is to install Python. Instructions for the various platforms differ but the instructions for each of them can be found on the Python home page at http://www.python.org. IPython requires Python 2.7 or ≥ 3.3. This book will use 3.5. Both Python and IPython are open source software, so downloads and installations are free.

A standard Python installation includes the pip package manager. **pip** is a handy command-line tool that can be used to download and install various Python libraries. pip will be used throughout this book when libraries are required. Once Python is installed, IPython can be installed with the following command:

```
pip install ipython
```

IPython comes with a test suite called iptest. To run it, simply issue the following command:

```
iptest
```

A series of tests will be run. It is possible (and likely on Windows) that some libraries will be missing, causing the associated tests to fail. Simply use pip to install those libraries and rerun the test until everything passes.

It is also possible that all tests will pass without an important library being installed. This is the `readline` library (also known as PyReadline). IPython will work without it but will be missing some features that are useful for the IPython terminal, such as command completion and history navigation. To install `readline`, use `pip`:

```
pip install readline
pip install gnureadline
```

At this point, issuing the `ipython` command will start up an IPython interpreter:

```
ipython
```

All-in-one distributions

Part of the power of IPython comes from the large number of packages that can be installed for it. This power, however, comes with a price—installing and managing all those packages can be a chore. There exist binary distributions that will install Python, IPython, and a lot of widely used external packages. Popular installers include:

- **Anaconda by Continuum Analytics**: https://www.continuum.io/downloads
- **Canopy by Enthought**: https://store.enthought.com/downloads/

Both distributions support Windows, Linux, and Mac.

Even with an all-in-one distribution, there will still be new packages to install and old ones to update. When `pip` and easy-install are not enough, both Anaconda and Canopy have their own built-in package management systems.

Package management with conda

Anaconda provides a powerful command-line tool called **conda**. conda can be used for package management as well as environment management. Every program runs in an environment that includes the version of Python, IPython, and all included packages.

Every programmer develops with the latest versions of every library, but not every user has the same setup. This can lead to problems when bug reports come in. Testing by the developer will not reproduce the error, but the user will be able to provide screenshots and core dumps. Eventually, the problem will be traced to something in the user's environment. The user will be unwilling/unable to update their environment, so the developer will have to configure their own machine to machine the target environment. This is a tedious, time-consuming, and error-prone process, especially for widely deployed systems. Environment management is the sort of thing that no one thinks of until they realize that they need it, and having a tool to simplify it can save time and sanity.

Canopy Package Manager

Sometimes, managing over 14,000 packages requires a graphical tool. Canopy Package Manager provides a graphical interface to the extensive set of IPython libraries. Enthought provides additional packages based on the subscription level:

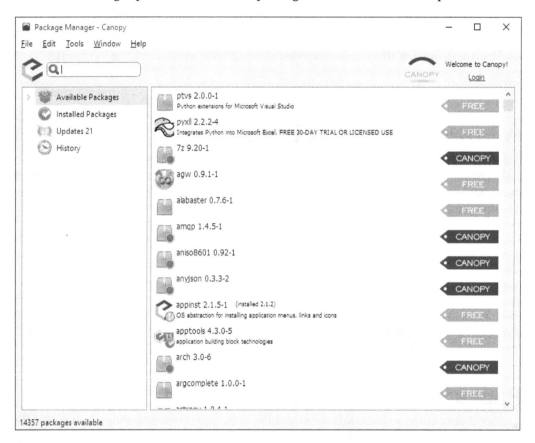

What happened to the Notebook?

Readers familiar with previous versions of IPython might notice that nothing has been said about the Notebook. That is because the Notebook has split off from the main IPython project. It is now a project on its own, named `Jupyter`, which can be found at `https://jupyter.org/`. As the IPython project grew, it was determined that it was trying to be too many things to too many people: a terminal, a Python kernel, a notebook, a parallel framework, and much more. The decision was made to split the project into two main parts, Jupyter and IPython, with IPython calving off into several subprojects.

As such, this book will focus on IPython and its interactive terminal. An overview of Jupyter will be provided in *Chapter 11, Into the Future*, but the primary focus will be on working with the terminal. This does not mean that graphical I/O will be neglected. The truth is far from it, in fact, as the terminal supports many quality graphics packages.

Starting out with the terminal

Typing `ipython` into your command line should present you with a window that resembles this:

```
Administrator: Command Prompt - ipython                                    —   □   ×

C:\WINDOWS\system32>ipython
Python 3.5.0 (v3.5.0:374f501f4567, Sep 13 2015, 02:27:37) [MSC v.1900 64 bit (AMD64)]
Type "copyright", "credits" or "license" for more information.

IPython 4.0.0 -- An enhanced Interactive Python.
?          -> Introduction and overview of IPython's features.
%quickref -> Quick reference.
help       -> Python's own help system.
object?    -> Details about 'object', use 'object??' for extra details.

In [1]:
```

This is the (somewhat underwhelming) IPython command line. Do not be deceived by its plain looks.

The primary language used with IPython is, not surprisingly, Python. As a convenience, the `help` command provides access to Python's help documents. The `help(<object>)` will display the *help* page for <object> (for example, `help(string)`), while `help( )` will open up an interactive `help` prompt.

For help with IPython itself, use the ? command. It displays a lot of text outlining functionality available through the terminal.

In addition, either prepending or appending ? to an object or command will display information about it. For example, to display information about the built-in Python type `list`:

```
In [9]: ?list
Type: type
String form: <type 'list'>
Namespace: Python builtin
Docstring:
```

```
list() -> new empty list
list(iterable) -> new list initialized from iterable's items
```

If one question mark is not enough, two will provide more information, including source code. For example, to see more information about a program from a later chapter, use this:

```
In [8]: import code2


In [9]: ??code2.TestHailStones
Init signature: code2.TestHailStones(self, methodName='runTest')
Source:
class TestHailStones(unittest.TestCase):
    """
    The main class for testing the hailstone sequence generator.
    """

    def test_f(self):
        """currently the only test in this suite."""
        ans = [0, 0, 1, 7, 2, 5, 8, 16, 3, 19, 6]
        for i in range(1, 11):
            print(i)
            self.assertEqual(f(i), ans[i])
File:           ~/Packt/chap09/code2.py
Type:           type
```

Of course, as an extension of the Python command line, IPython supports direct evaluation of simple expressions:

```
In [6]: 1 + 1
Out[6]: 2
```

The result is in the special _ variable:

```
In [7]: _ * 10
Out[7]: 20
```

Other Python terminal features are also supported, such as auto-indent, syntax highlighting, and so on and so forth. In fact, using IPython simply as a nicer Python command line is a viable option.

An important fact to remember when using IPython is that a great deal of what is going on is just standard Python. Even when using IPython-specific capabilities, a lot of the code, libraries, and general concepts are Python. The relationship, for the most part, is more like *jQuery::JavaScript* than *C++::C*.

IPython beyond Python

No one would use IPython if it were not more powerful than the standard terminal. Much of IPython's power comes from two features:

- Shell integration
- Magic commands

Shell integration

Any command starting with ! is passed directly to the operating system to be executed, and the result is returned. By default, the output is then printed out to the terminal. If desired, the result of the system command can be assigned to a variable. The result is treated as a multiline string, and the variable is a list containing one string element per line of output. Here is an example:

```
In [22]: myDir = !dir


In [23]: myDir
Out[23]:
[' Volume in drive C has no label.',
 ' Volume Serial Number is 1E95-5694',
 '',
 ' Directory of C:\\Program Files\\Python 3.5',
 '',
 '10/04/2015  08:43 AM    <DIR>          .',
 '10/04/2015  08:43 AM    <DIR>          ..',]
```

While this functionality is not entirely absent in straight Python (the OS and subprocess libraries provide similar abilities), the IPython syntax is much cleaner. Additional functionality such as input and output caching, directory history, and automatic parentheses is also included.

History

The previous examples had lines that were prefixed by elements such as In [23] and Out [15]. In and Out are arrays of strings in which each element is either an input command or the resulting output. They can be referred to using the array notation, or "magic" commands can accept the subscript alone.

Magic commands

IPython also accepts commands that control IPython itself. These are called "magic" commands and start with % or %%. A complete list of magic commands can be found by typing %lsmagic in the terminal.

Magics that start with a single % sign are called line magics. They accept the rest of the current line for arguments. Magics that start with %% are called cell magics. They accept not only the rest of the current line but also the following lines.

There are too many magic commands to go over in detail, but there are some related families to be aware of:

- **OS equivalents**: %cd, %env, and %pwd
- **Working with code**: %run, %edit, %save, %load, %load_ext, and %%capture
- **Logging**: %logstart, %logstop, %logon, %logoff, and %logstate
- **Debugging**: %debug, %pdb, %run, and %tb
- **Documentation**: %pdef, %pdoc, %pfile, %pprint, %psource, %pycat, and %%writefile
- **Profiling**: %prun, %time, %run, and %timeit
- **Working with other languages**: %%script, %%html, %%javascript, %%latex, %%perl, and %%ruby

With magic commands, IPython becomes a more full-featured development environment. A development session might include the following steps:

1. Set up the OS-level environment with the %cd, %env, and ! commands.
2. Set up the Python environment with %load and %load_ext.
3. Create a program using %edit.
4. Run the program using %run.
5. Log the input/output with %logstart, %logstop, %logon, and %logoff.
6. Debug with %pdb.
7. Create documentation with %pdoc and %pdef.

This is not a tenable workflow for a large project, but for exploratory coding of smaller modules, magic commands provide a lightweight support structure.

Creating custom magic commands

IPython supports the creation of custom magic commands through function decorators. Luckily, you do not have to know how decorators work in order to use them. An example will explain this.

First, grab the required decorator from the appropriate library:

```
In [1]: from IPython.core.magic import (register_line_magic)
```

Then, prepend the decorator to a standard IPython function definition:

```
In [2]: @register_line_magic
   ...: def getBootDevice(line):
   ...:         sysinfo = !systeminfo
   ...:         for ln in sysinfo:
   ...:                 if ln.startswith("Boot Device"):
   ...:                         return(ln.split()[2])
   ...:
```

Your new magic is ready to go:

```
In [3]: %getBootDevice
Out[3]: '\\Device\\HarddiskVolume1'
```

Some observations are in order:

- Note that the function is, for the most part, standard Python. Also note the use of the !systeminfo shell command. You can freely mix both standard Python and IPython in IPython.
- The name of the function will be the name of the line magic.
- The line parameter contains the rest of the line (in case any parameters are passed).
- A parameter is required, although it need not be used.
- The Out associated with calling this line magic is the return value of the magic.
- Any print statements executed as part of the magic are displayed on the terminal but are not part of Out (or _).

Cython

You are not limited to writing custom magic commands in Python. Several languages are supported, including R and Octave. We will look at one in particular, Cython.

Cython is a language that can be used to write C extensions for Python. The goal for Cython is to be a superset of Python, with support for optional static type declarations. The driving force behind Cython is efficiency. As a compiled language, there are performance gains to be had from running C code. The downside is that Python is much more productive in terms of programmer hours. Cython can translate Python code into compiled C code, achieving more efficient execution at runtime while retaining the programmer friendliness of Python.

The idea of turning Python into C is not new to Cython. The default, most widely used interpreter (CPython) for Python is written in C. In some sense then, running Python code means running C code, just through an interpreter. There are other Python interpreter implementations as well, including those in Java (Jython) and C# (IronPython).

CPython has a foreign function interface to C. That is, it is possible to write C language functions that interface with CPython in such a way that data can be exchanged and functions invoked from one to the other. The primary use is for calling C code from Python. There are two primary drawbacks:

- Writing code that works with the CPython foreign function interface is difficult in its own right
- Doing so requires knowledge of Python, C, and CPython

Cython aims to remedy this problem by doing all the work of turning Python into C and interfacing with CPython internally to Cython. The programmer writes Cython code and leaves the rest to the Cython compiler. Cython is very close to Python. The primary difference is the ability to specify C types for variables using the `cdef` keyword. Cython then handles type checking and conversion between Python values and C values, scoping issues, marshalling and unmarshalling of Python objects into C structures, and other cross-language issues.

Cython is enabled in IPython by loading an extension. In order to use the Cython extension, do this:

```
In [1]: %load_ext Cython
```

At this point, the `cython` cell magic can be invoked:

```
In [2]: %%cython
   ...: def sum(int a, int b):
   ...:     cdef int s = a+b
   ...:     return s
```

And the Cython function can now be called just as if it were a standard Python function:

```
In [3]: sum(1, 1)
Out[3]: 2
```

While this may seem like a lot of work for something that could have been written more easily in just Python in the first place, it is the price to be paid for efficiency. If, instead of simply summing two numbers, a function is expensive to execute and is called multiple times (perhaps in a tight loop), it can be worth it to use Cython for a reduction in runtime.

There are other languages that have merited the same treatment, GNU Octave and R being among them, which will be covered in later chapters.

Configuring IPython

IPython runs with certain settings by default. These setting are built into Python and are not generally user-visible. In order to modify them, they must be modified in config files. This can be accomplished at the command line, as follows:

```
ipython profile create <profilename>
```

This will create a blank file named `ipython_config.py` in `~/.ipython/profile/default`, along with a few directories. IPython is configured, not by a plaintext file in the `.conf` or `.ini` format, but by a Python program in its own right. The first line is generally the following:

```
c = getconfig( )
```

This calls a special function that is only visible in the configuration file. The rest of the program consists of assignment statements to various objects contained within c. For example, consider this line:

```
c.TerminalIPythonApp.display_banner = True
```

It will determine whether IPython will display a banner upon starting or not. While there are too many configuration options for us to go through them all, the latest list can be found at `http://ipython.readthedocs.org/en/latest/config/options/terminal.html`

Upon creation, `ipython_config.py` will contain a large number of lines of Python code, setting potential configuration values. All lines will be commented out. This can serve as a handy reminder of what configuration options exist, although it is unclear whether every option will always be present.

A few options deserve to be noted:

```
InteractiveShellApp.extensions : List
```

```
Default: []
```

```
A list of dotted module names of IPython extensions to load on
IPython startup.
```

```
InteractiveShellApp.exec_lines : List
```

```
Default: []
```

```
Lines of Python code to run at IPython startup.
```

```
TerminalInteractiveShell.editor : Unicode
```

```
Default: 'vi' (on Unix boxes)
```

```
Set the editor used by IPython.
```

```
Application.log_level : 0|10|20|30|40|50|'DEBUG'|'INFO'|'WARN'|'ERROR'|'C
RITICAL'
```

```
Default: 30
```

```
Set the log level by value or name.
```

Debugging

Python's ipdb debugger is the default for IPython. It is similar to the standard pdb for Python but has extensions to make IPython easier to work with.

There are several different ways to access the debugger, both post-mortem and at program startup.

Post-mortem debugging

After an exception has occurred, the `%debug` magic will start a post-mortem debugging session. This will launch the debugger at the point in the program at which the exception was raised.

The `%pdb` magic will automatically launch the debugger upon the next exception, similar to manually calling `%debug`. IPython can be started with the `--pdb` switch for the same behavior.

Outside of IPython, post-mortem debugging can be invoked by including the following lines in your program:

```
import sys
from IPython.core import ultratb
sys.excepthook = ultratb.FormattedTB(mode='Verbose',
color_scheme='Linux', call_pdb=1)
```

Debugging at startup

The `%run` magic has a switch that can be used to start up a program under the ipdb debugger:

```
In [9]: %run -d <filename>
```

This starts the program with a breakpoint at line 1. To run to a specified line before stopping, use -b:

```
In [9]: %run -d -b<line number> <filename>
```

Debugger commands

When the debugger is started, the prompt will change to `ipdb>`. Whether used post-mortem or upon program start, the `ipdb` commands are the same. Issuing the `?` command will list the available commands, like this:

```
========================
l   list   ll   longlist

ipdb> ?

Documented commands (type help <topic>):
========================================
EOF    c          d         h         next    pp        retval   u          whatis
a      cl         debug     help      p       psource   run      unalias    where
alias  clear      disable   ignore    pdef    q         rv       undisplay
args   commands   display   interact  pdoc    quit      s        unt
b      condition  down      j         pfile   r         source   until
break  cont       enable    jump      pinfo   restart   step     up
bt     continue   exit      n         pinfo2  return    tbreak   w

Miscellaneous help topics:
==========================
exec   pdb

Undocumented commands:
======================
l   list   ll   longlist

ipdb>
```

Covering all debugging commands is outside the scope of this book, but some are worth noting.

A full complement of commands is available for navigation:

- `u`/`d` for moving up/down in the call stack.
- `s` to step into the next statement. This will step into any functions.
- `n` to continue execution until the next line in the current function is reached or it returns. This will execute any functions along the way, without stopping to debug them.
- `r` continues execution until the current function returns.
- `c` continues execution until the next breakpoint (or exception).
- `j <line>` jumps to line number `<line>` and executes it. Any lines between the current line and `<line>` are skipped over. The `j` works both forward and reverse.

And handling breakpoints:

- `b` for setting a breakpoint. The `b <line>` will set a breakpoint at line `number` `<line>`. Each breakpoint is assigned a unique reference number that other breakpoint commands use.

- `tbreak`. This is like `break`, but the breakpoint is temporary and is cleared after the first time it is encountered.

- `cl <bpNumber>` clears a breakpoint, by reference number.

- `ignore <bpNumber> <count>` is for ignoring a particular breakpoint for a certain number (`<count>`) of times.

- `disable <bpNumber>` for disabling a breakpoint. Unlike clearing, the breakpoint remains and can be re-enabled.

- `enable <bpNumber>` re-enables a breakpoint.

Examining values:

- `a` to view the arguments to the current function

- `whatis <arg>` prints the type of `<arg>`

- `p <expression>` prints the value of `<expression>`

Read-Eval-Print Loop (REPL) and IPython architecture

Most interpreted languages follow the same underlying event model—**Read-Eval-Print Loop (REPL)**—and IPython are no exception. In REPL, interaction with the user is broken down into three steps:

1. The system reads the input from the user and parses it into an internal format.
2. The system evaluates the parsed input.
3. The result of this evaluation is printed to the user.

In a "standard" interpreter, all phases of REPL are executed within the same thread. An important feature of IPython is that the "eval" phase has been separated out into its own process. This process is called a **kernel**, and it communicates with the other components via messaging. This allows for great flexibility; terminals and kernels can run on different machines, one kernel can support multiple terminals, and development of different terminals and kernels for specialized uses is possible. It also makes for a clean parallel architecture, as will be demonstrated in *Chapter 4, Messaging with ZeroMQ and MPI*.

The IPython project provides an informative diagram of the architecture at `http://ipython.readthedocs.org/en/latest/development/how_ipython_works.html`:

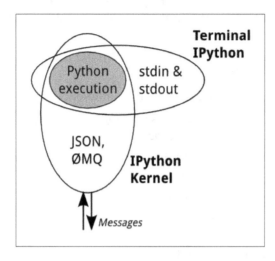

Currently, the following user interface components are compatible with the IPython kernel:

- `console`
- `qtconsole`
- `notebook`

At the command line, issue this command:

`ipython <component>`

This will start the user interface component, an IPython kernel, and connect them via messaging. For example, suppose you issue this command:

`ipython notebook`

It will start up a Jupyter Notebook, as the Jupyter project includes a user interface component compatible with the IPython kernel.

Alternative development environments

There is a slew of alternative user interfaces for developers looking for a graphical interface to some (or all) of the IPython development environment. Most mainstream development has moved to integrated, graphical IDEs and there is no reason for the IPython developer to be left behind.

Graphical IDEs provide several useful features:

- A graphical editor, with syntax highlighting, code completion, PyLint integration, and more.

- An interactive object inspector. Just place the cursor before any object and press *Ctrl + I*. The documentation for that object/class will be displayed.

- The IPython console is still present, but many useful commands have associated buttons and keyboard shortcuts.

- Debugger integration. A multi-window display allows code to be viewed in one window, an object inspector in another, and interactive expression evaluation in yet another.

Spyder

Spyder stands for **Scientific PYthon Development EnviRonment**. It is supported on Windows, OS X, and Linux. It can be installed on its own or as a part of a package. The Windows all-in-one distributions, Anaconda, WinPython, and Python(x,y) include Spyder by default. Anaconda on OS X also includes Spyder. On Linux, Spyder is included in various distributions. Check your manual for details.

Here is an example screenshot of Spyder in action:

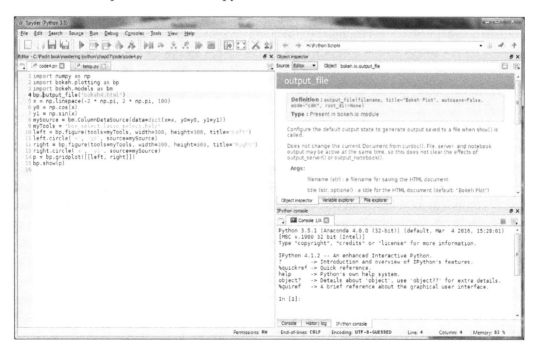

Canopy

Canopy is Enthought's graphical environment for IPython. The base version is free, while additional features (including a graphical debugger) require a license. Here is a screenshot of Canopy in action:

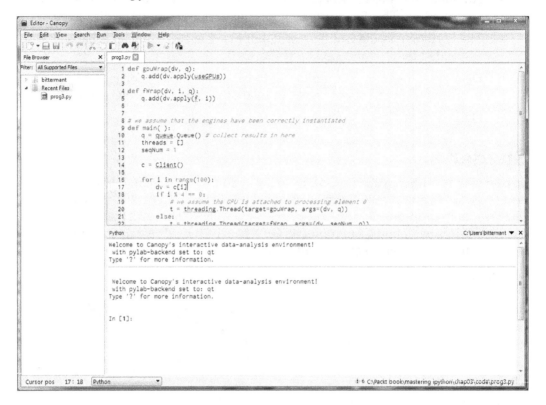

PyDev

PyDev is an open source/free plugin for the Eclipse development environment. It is interesting in the sense that it is, by default, a Python development system but will use IPython if available. As an eclipse plugin, PyDev provides access to lots of useful eclipse features, including possibly the most powerful debugger out there.

The Eclipse environment provides plugins for just about any functionality a developer could want. If your team will be developing a multi-lingual system, or you are transitioning from more mainstream development, Eclipse provides a flexible, powerful environment.

Others

There are plenty of other Python development environments (PyCharm, NetBeans, PythonToolkit, Python Tools for Visual Studio, SPE, and so on). Developers are notoriously loyal to their development tools, and IDEs are no exception. It is possible that an experienced Python developer has already chosen an IDE not mentioned previously. This does not mean that their preferred IDE will not work with IPython.

The landscape is continuously changing, so it is difficult to say anything with certainty that would apply to all the various IDEs. However, given the nature of IPython as a replacement shell for Python (with some important additions), it is likely that most Python IDEs can be configured so as to use an IPython shell/ interpreter in place of standard Python. Furthermore, it is likely such a solution would not be as full-featured as one created expressly for IPython, but morale and productivity also play a role in picking an IDE.

Summary

In this chapter, we covered many of the basics of using IPython for development. IPython can be installed by hand, but there are also several all-in-one distributions available. These distributions automatically install many popular packages and provide advanced package management capability.

IPython offers functionality beyond a Python command line, however. In this chapter, we introduced configuration and magic commands. Configuration is accomplished by writing an IPython program to control various aspects of the environment through manipulating the configuration object.

Magic commands fall into many categories: OS equivalents, working with code, logging, debugging, documentation, profiling, and working with other languages, among others. Add to this the ability to create custom magic commands (in IPython or another language) and the IPython terminal becomes a much more powerful alternative to the standard Python terminal.

Also included is the debugger — ipdb. It is very similar to the Python pdb debugger, so it should seem familiar to Python developers.

All this is supported by the IPython architecture. The foundation is a Read-Eval-Print Loop in which the *Eval* section has been separated out into its own process. This decoupling allows different user interface components and kernels to communicate with each other, making for a flexible system.

This flexibility enables many different IDEs to interoperate with IPython. A few popular IDEs were covered.

This chapter introduced some of the features of the IPython shell that make it such a powerful development environment. In the next chapter, we will look under the hood at the IPython parallel architecture.

3
Stepping Up to IPython for Parallel Computing

In this chapter, we are going to look at the tools that IPython provides for parallel computing.

This chapter covers the following topics:

- Multi-tasking
- Threading
- Multi-processing
- IPython's parallel architecture
- Getting started with ipyparallel
- IPython parallel magic commands
- Types of parallelism
- SIMD and GPUs
- SPMD and MapReduce
- MIMD and MPMD
- Task farming and load balancing
- Data parallelism
- Application steering

Serial processes

When first learning to program, many students find it difficult to think in terms of doing "one thing at a time". The advent of parallel machines relaxed this restriction. Unfortunately, doing several things at the same time is even more difficult than doing one thing at a time. In this section, we describe how a process is structured and some different scheduling mechanisms: batch systems, multitasking, and time slicing.

Program counters and address spaces

A program can be viewed as a series of instructions acting on data. When it is executed, the processor must keep track of which instruction(s) is to be executed during the current clock cycle, and what data the instruction refers to. The mechanism used by the processor to keep track of instructions is called a program counter. The idea of an address space is similar, but applicable to data. The move from serial to parallel architectures can be described in terms of the increasing complexity of these mechanisms.

Batch systems

It is a truism that a single processor can only execute one instruction at a time. For many tasks this is perfectly adequate. The basic REPL paradigm implicitly assumes this model. A schematic diagram is provided as follows:

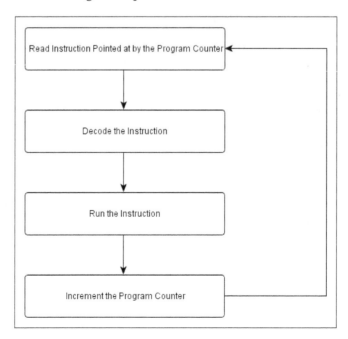

This can be extremely efficient in that the program counter can reside in a register while the program is stored in main memory. When the current program is finished and a new program is ready to run, the new program is loaded into memory and the program counter is set to the first instruction of the new program.

The idea of a single program counter matched with an address space is the basis of the idea of a *process*. A batch system is one in which a single process can be run at a time, from beginning to end, before another process can start.

A pure batch architecture can run into difficulties in three areas, as follows:

- Error recovery
- Blocking
- Responsiveness

If a program errors out (say, by entering an infinite loop), it can be difficult for a batch system to recover. Some sort of outside intervention, whether manual or automatic, is required in these cases.

If a program blocks forever (say, by waiting for input that never comes), the system has the same problem as if there were an error.

Responsiveness is related to blocking but manifests itself primarily in terms of user experience. For example, in the author's environment, starting Emacs appears to bring the machine to a halt for several seconds. The machine has not actually stopped working, although it appears that way. It is just that, with only a single processor, the process controlling the command line is blocked while the CPU executes code related to starting the editor.

All these difficulties point to a need for some mechanism that could stop the current process so that some other process could use the main processor.

Multitasking and preemption

Multitasking is a way in which an operating system can support concurrently executing processes. Concurrency, while not true parallelism, allows several different processes to be in progress at the same time, even though only one process is actually running at any given time. The underlying idea is that any given process can be stopped and started without having to run through to its end. The process by which processes are stopped and started is known as a context switch.

A context switch can be a complicated process, but the basic outline involves the following:

- The processor stops executing the current process (that is, it stops incrementing the program counter and executing instructions)
- The state of the current process (its context - including the program counter, all registers, and all data) is stored somewhere
- Data from the new process is copied into memory
- A new value is written to the programming counter

A context switch is a similar process to the one that occurs when a program is done running on a batch system. The biggest difference is that, after a context switch, a process's state is stored so that it could be loaded back into memory and its execution restarted. When a process stops executing and its state is written to storage it is said to be "switched out". The new program is said to be "switched in".

An operating system that can initiate context switches is said to be a multitasking operating system. Virtually all modern operating systems (outside of the batch systems found in HPC centers) support multitasking.

The primary benefits of multitasking are as follows:

- **Responsiveness**: The processor can continue to do work on one process while another is blocking
- **Resiliency**: An error in a single process cannot take down the entire system

The primary drawback is that context switches are inefficient. The system is not doing anything the user would regard as productive while the switch is going on.

Given the ability to multitask, the next obvious question is: when should context switching happen? There are two primary approaches:

- Cooperative multitasking
- Preemptive multitasking

In cooperative multitasking, context switches only occur when a process "voluntarily" cedes time to another. This could happen for many reasons, including being in a blocking state, program termination, and so on. This approach was used in early time-sharing systems and persisted into early OSes meant for personal computers. It has the weakness of being very susceptible to errors resulting from hung processes that will not cede time.

In preemptive multitasking, the operating system initiates context switches. In this case the process has no choice – it will be switched in or out based on whatever criteria the OS uses. The OS can use a multitude of criteria: process priority, aging, I/O status, real-time guarantees, and so on. An interesting and popular choice is time slicing.

Time slicing

In time slicing, the OS performs a context switch on a regular schedule. Each process is allocated an amount of time (a time slice, or quantum) during which it can run. When the quantum is over, the OS switches the current process out and another switches in. Time slicing is a form of preemptive multitasking.

This provides some interesting options for controlling the performance of the system as a whole. A long quantum makes for an efficient system by minimizing the number of context switches. A shorter quantum can make the system more responsive by quickly switching out hung and blocking processes.

With time slicing (and multitasking in general), the process model becomes more complicated:

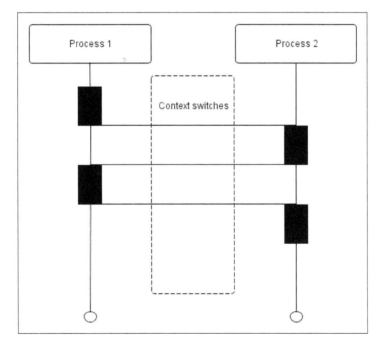

Threading

Experience with multitasking systems showed that a smaller unit of control was required than the process itself. Two inter-requirements presented themselves:

- The need for a single process to perform multiple activities
- The need for these activities to share data with each other

The process model, where each process has its own address space and program counter and an expensive context switch is required to change the instruction stream, was a poor fit for these requirements. In particular, the feature of the context switch, in which the process's memory was swapped out directly contradicted the need for data sharing.

The solution was the idea of threads. A thread is like a process in that it is a sequence of instructions with an associated process counter. The difference is that several threads can share the same address space. In general, threads are components of processes that share the entire process address space, but can be scheduled separately. Switching from one thread to another is easier, as the entire state does not need to be sent to storage, just the program counter and registers. The entirety of the process's data can (and should) remain where it is.

If one considers a process as an "area" of memory, then a thread would be a smaller area enclosed completely within it, with some private space, but access to the rest of the process's memory. The following diagram is illustrative:

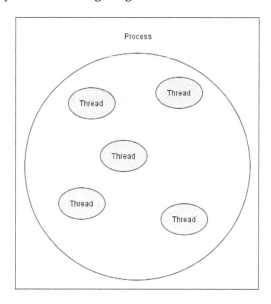

Threading in Python

There is no need to go to IPython-specific libraries for threading support. Python has a built-in library that will perform all the important threading operations. This library is called "threading".

Another useful library is "queue". The queue library implements multi-producer, multi-consumer, thread-safe queues. It is very useful when a set of threads all need to be able to write to a common data area. In our example, each call to f creates an integer corresponding to a hailstone run length. This value is then added to a queue. Because we are summing all the values, it does not matter in which order they are added.

The use of a queue (or other synchronized data structure) for communication between threads is a side-effect of the fact that all threads started by a single process share the same address space. In this case, every thread can write to the queue because it is the shared address space, and comes into scope through the standard parameter-passing mechanism. Were these threads separate processes, they would not be able to share a data structure in this manner.

Example

Let us take another look at the example of calculating hailstones from *Chapter 1, Using IPython for HPC*:

```
import queue
import threading

def f(n, q):
    curr = n
    tmp = 1
    while curr != 1:
        tmp = tmp + 1
        if curr % 2 == 1:
            curr = 3 * curr + 1
        else:
            curr = curr/2
    q.put(tmp)

def main( ):
    sum = 0
    q = queue.Queue()
    threads = []

    for i in range(100):
```

```
        t = threading.Thread(target=f, args=(i+1, q))
        threads.append(t)

    for thread in threads:
        thread.start()

    for thread in threads:
        threads[i].join()

    while (not q.empty()):
        sum = sum + q.get()

    avg = sum / 100.0
    print("avg = ", avg)
```

Limitations of threading

Some test runs of the code yield a surprising result: the threaded code actually runs more slowly. While not the initial goal, this result should not be entirely surprising.

The algorithm that calculates the hailstone sequence is CPU-bound, that is, it spends most of its time using the CPU and little time blocked or waiting (for example, for I/O). As such, although any two calls of f with different arguments do not depend on each other, there is still a shared resource – the CPU. All threads share the same CPU, so this in effect turns our threaded program back into a serial one.

Why is it worse? There is a price to be paid for threading that the serial algorithm did not. There are several steps that the threaded program has to take that the serial algorithm does not, and each step takes time:

- Creation of the thread objects
- Assignment of the function to be executed and the arguments to each thread
- Signaling each thread to start
- Waiting for each thread to finish
- Time for the queue to enqueue and dequeue each result
- Disposal of all the thread objects

As this example shows, using multiple threads yields better results when most of threads can be counted on to be in some sort of blocked or waiting state at any given time. The more threads that are CPU-bound, the more similar to a serial program things become. In that case, the overhead of threading can degrade performance to even lower levels than the serial version.

Global Interpreter Lock

Much has been said about **Global Interpreter Lock** (**GIL**) in Python and how it affects multithreaded applications. Some description of how Python handles threads is required before an explanation of what GIL is would make sense.

What happens in an interpreter?

An interpreter is simply a program that takes code as input and performs actions based on that code. As a program, an interpreter has all the usual internals of a program: variables, data structures, functions, included libraries, and so on.

The code being run by the interpreter can have access to some subset of its internal state. As such, the interpreter needs to control this access so that the programs the interpreter runs do not break the interpreter itself. This includes problems that can be caused when the interpreter is running programs in parallel.

Many of the things a program wants to do are straightforward to support in an interpreter (for example, declaring variables, if statements, and looping). Threading is more complicated to support, however, because the language designer has two options:

- Green threading (the interpreter implements threads)
- Native threads (the interpreter uses the operating system's thread implementation)

Green threading provides the language designer the most control over how threads are implemented. This control can be used to ensure that threaded programs do not break the interpreter by controlling the behavior of the threads. The downside is that green threading makes the interpreter more complex and (potentially) slower.

Native threads are provided by the operating system. This brings simplicity and efficiency at the cost of decreased control.

Python has elected to use native threads. This brings up the question: given that multiple threads can (potentially) access the interpreter simultaneously, can they execute in such a way as to break the interpreter (that is, is the interpreter thread-safe)?

CPython

The most popular Python interpreter is CPython. CPython is, not surprisingly, written in C. C requires manual memory management that can be especially tricky in a multithreaded environment. As a result, CPython (and some of the libraries it depends on) is not thread-safe. Because CPython is not thread-safe, only one Python thread is able to run in the interpreter simultaneously. In effect, the other threads are "locked out" of the interpreter. Hence the term "Global Interpreter Lock".

GIL is not an inherent property of Python (or IPython), but rather the way a particular interpreter is implemented. For example, Jython and IronPython are Python interpreters that do not have GIL.

Multi-core machines

This would ordinarily not be an issue. On a single-processor machine only one thread can execute at a time in any case, so only allowing one thread in the interpreter is not a bottleneck. The complication comes with multi-core machines. A multi-core architecture site in-between the single and multi-processor architectures. A single-processor architecture has one processor and one address space. A multi-processor architecture has multiple processors and multiple address spaces. A multi-core machine has multiple processors, but a single address space.

At first glance it would appear that multi-core machines are exactly what threads need. Threads could run simultaneously while still accessing a common address space. This would combine the best of the single and multi-processor architectures. The problem lies in the interpreter. Even with multiple cores there can still be only one, and therefore only one thread can run at a time, leaving the other cores unused.

Kill GIL

Given the prevalence of multi-core architectures, this limitation is glaring and has caused much confusion and consternation. Developers have attempted to remove GIL several times over the years, but all such efforts have been rejected. There are many reasons for the rejections, but the most important are as follows:

- **Simplicity**: All fixes have made CPython more complicated and harder to maintain
- **Speed**: The constructs necessary to ensure thread safety in the absence of GIL are expensive in terms of processor time
- **Back-compatibility**: Any changes must continue to support all current CPython features
- **Extensions**: All external libraries used by CPython must be protected, or alternatives developed

Given this list of requirements, it is not likely that GIL in CPython will be removed soon.

Using multiple processors

Given the limitations of threading for CPU-bound code, perhaps a solution can be found using multiple processors. The problem with CPU-bound algorithms and threading was that there was an implicitly-shared resource: the CPU. With multiple processors this limitation can be eased – each function call can have its own CPU, up to the physical number of CPUs. Each CPU would work independently and in parallel rather than being a bottleneck. We will examine the tools that IPython provides for working with multiple processors in the following sections.

The IPython parallel architecture

The `IPython.parallel` package has moved to the `ipyparallel` project. While not a major change, this has introduced a dependency on the ZeroMQ messaging library.

Overview

The ipyparallel architecture is a natural extension of the serial IPython architecture. The decoupling of the client from the interpreter lends itself to an architecture in which multiple interpreters and clients can run in parallel.

Components

The IPython architecture consists of four components:

- The IPython Engine
- The IPython Controller/Client
- The IPython Hub
- The IPython Scheduler

The IPython Engine

An IPython Engine is a Python instance that accepts Python commands and objects over a network connection. The ability to run engines on different processors is what makes distributed computing in IPython possible.

The IPython Controller

The IPython Controller provides an interface for working with a set of engines. It consists of a hub and a set of schedulers. The Controller provides the single point of contact for users who wish to interact with the engines.

The IPython Hub

The IPython Hub keeps track of engine connections, schedulers, clients, task requests, and results. The Hub has two primary roles:

- Facilitate queries of the cluster's state
- Handle the information required to establish connections to client and engines

The IPython Scheduler

All actions performed by an engine go through a scheduler. The engines block while running code, and the schedulers hide that from the user.

The following diagram is a courtesy of "The IPython Development Team":

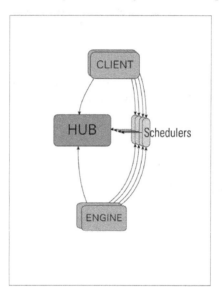

Getting started with ipyparallel

We will start with a simple parallel "Hello world" program using `ipcluster`.

ipcluster

To use IPython for parallel computing, you will need a controller and one or more engines. The easiest way to get them is to start them on your localhost using the `ipcluster` command:

```
ipcluster start -n 4
```

It will start a controller and four engines.

This can be somewhat fraught with subtle errors, however, as the engines do not necessarily have the same environment as the command line that started them. You may have more luck starting the entire thing from inside an IPython session, using the ! escape for system commands, shown as follows:

```
In [5]: !ipcluster start -n 4 &

In [6]: 2015-10-26 15:52:53.738 [IPClusterStart] Using existing profile
dir: '/nfs/02/wit0096/.ipython/profile_default'

2015-10-26 15:52:53.828 [IPClusterStart] Removing pid file: /nfs/02/
wit0096/.ipython/profile_default/pid/ipcluster.pid

2015-10-26 15:52:53.828 [IPClusterStart] Starting ipcluster with
[daemon=False]

2015-10-26 15:52:53.830 [IPClusterStart] Creating pid file: /nfs/02/
wit0096/.ipython/profile_default/pid/ipcluster.pid

2015-10-26 15:52:53.926 [IPClusterStart] Starting Controller with
LocalControllerLauncher

2015-10-26 15:52:54.830 [IPClusterStart] Starting 4 Engines with
LocalEngineSetLauncher

2015-10-26 15:53:25.155 [IPClusterStart] Engines appear to have started
successfully
```

We will cover a method for synchronizing environments between distributed engines in a later section.

Hello world

A simple interactive session that uses a cluster of four engines to compute the value of the "Hello world" string:

```
In [1]: !ipcluster start -n 4 &


In [2]: 2015-10-27 14:11:30.276 [IPClusterStart] Starting ipcluster with
[daemon=False]

2015-10-27 14:11:30.276 [IPClusterStart] Creating pid file: /nfs/02/
wit0096/.ipython/profile_default/pid/ipcluster.pid

2015-10-27 14:11:30.277 [IPClusterStart] Starting Controller with
LocalControllerLauncher

2015-10-27 14:11:31.280 [IPClusterStart] Starting 4 Engines with
LocalEngineSetLauncher
```

```
2015-10-27 14:12:01.599 [IPClusterStart] Engines appear to have started
successfully
```

```
In [2]: def hello( ):
   ...:      return "Hello world"
   ...:
```

```
In [3]: from ipyparallel import Client
```

```
In [4]: c = Client( )
```

```
In [5]: dv = c[:]
```

```
In [6]: dv.apply_sync(hello)
Out[6]: ['Hello world', 'Hello world', 'Hello world', 'Hello world']
```

This contains enough features to warrant a closer look.

Line 1:

```
In [1]: !ipcluster start -n 4 &
```

```
In [2]: 2015-10-27 14:11:30.276 [IPClusterStart] Starting ipcluster with
[daemon=False]
2015-10-27 14:11:30.276 [IPClusterStart] Creating pid file: /nfs/02/
wit0096/.ipython/profile_default/pid/ipcluster.pid
2015-10-27 14:11:30.277 [IPClusterStart] Starting Controller with
LocalControllerLauncher
2015-10-27 14:11:31.280 [IPClusterStart] Starting 4 Engines with
LocalEngineSetLauncher
2015-10-27 14:12:01.599 [IPClusterStart] Engines appear to have started
successfully
```

This starts the four engines that will be running our function. We use an IPython shell escape here, and they are started in the background so control returns to the IPython shell. Starting the engines does not block the terminal, but we wait until the system reports success.

Line 2:

```
In [2]: def hello( ):
   ...:      return "Hello world"
```

The return value of this function is the value returned to the terminal after the engine runs the function.

Line 3:

```
In [3]: from ipyparallel import Client
```

The `parallel` library has been moved from `IPython.parallel` to `ipyparallel`.

Line 4:

```
In [4]: c = Client( )
```

The `Client` object will allow us to get access to the `DirectView` objects that we can use to interact with the engines.

Line 5:

```
In [5]: dv = c[:]
```

This is the `DirectView` object. It is created by indexing a `Client`. `DirectView` contains functions that can be used to have the various engines do work. In this case, our `DirectView` refers to all of the engines. Any function called upon dv will affect all the engines.

Asking about dv will yield the following helpful information:

```
In [12]: ?dv
Type:        DirectView
String form: <DirectView [0, 1, 2, 3]>
Length:      4
File:        ...
Docstring:
Direct Multiplexer View of one or more engines.
```

These are created via indexed access to a client:

```
>>> dv_1 = client[1]
>>> dv_all = client[:]
>>> dv_even = client[::2]
>>> dv_some = client[1:3]
```

The `DirectView` class is the primary means through which the user can interact with the engines. A `DirectView` object can refer to all, or a subset, of the engines, depending on how it was created. The engines it refers to are called the *target* of the object.

Line 6:

```
In [6]: dv.apply_sync(hello)
Out[6]: ['Hello world', 'Hello world', 'Hello world', 'Hello world']
```

Here is where the actual parallel work is done. The `apply_sync` function sets off several steps behind the scenes:

1. dv submits the `hello` function to the controller.
2. The controller places the `hello` function in each engine's queue for execution.
3. The `apply_sync` call then blocks, waiting for all the engines to finish execution.

The output is just the return value of each engine, collected in a list.

Using map_sync

If you have a program that already uses Python's map function, there is a straightforward way to modify the code so that it runs in parallel – `map_sync` function of `DirectView`.

Consider a function to compute hailstone sequences:

```
def f(n):
    curr = n
    tmp = 1
    while curr != 1:
        tmp = tmp + 1
        if curr % 2 == 1:
            curr = 3 * curr + 1
        else:
            curr = curr/2
    return tmp
```

With the same setup as before, `map_sync` will make the parallel calls:

```
In [35]: !ipcluster start -n 4&


In [36]: c = Client()
```

```
In [37]: dv = c[:]
```

```
In [38]: dv.map_sync(f, range(1, 5))
Out[38]: [1, 2, 8, 3]
```

Asynchronous calls

Both `apply_sync` and `map_sync` end with `_sync`. This is a hint that something synchronous is happening. In particular, the terminal halts at the `apply_sync` or `map_sync` call and will not continue until every engine has completed (that is, synchronous calls are *blocking*). It is possible to perform the same calculation(s) without waiting for the result – that is, asynchronously.

```
In [58]: async_res = dv.map(f, range(1, 11))
```

When `map` and `apply` are called asynchronously, the terminal does not wait for the call to be completed, but continues on (that is, asynchronous calls are *nonblocking*). This raises the question of how the results can be obtained.

Asynchronous methods accomplish this by returning an `AsyncMapResult` object. The simplest thing to do is to simply turn it into a list:

```
In [73]: list(async_res)
Out[73]: [1, 2, 8, 3, 6, 9, 17, 4, 20, 7]
```

`AsyncMapResult` also supports the `enumerate` method:

```
In [84]: for a, b in enumerate(async_res):
    print(a, b)
   ....:
0 1
1 2
2 8
3 3
4 6
5 9
6 17
7 4
8 20
9 7
```

Whether gathering the results as a list or enumerating them, the command that actually retrieves the results (list or enumerate) will block until the calculations are complete.

You are guaranteed to get the same results regardless of synchronization:

```
In [85]: sync_res = dv.map_sync(f, range(1, 11))


In [86]: async_res = dv.map(f, range(1, 11))


In [87]: sync_res == list(async_res)
Out[87]: True
```

Synchronizing imports

As mentioned earlier, newly-started engines need not have the same environment as the instance from which they were started. The DirectView class provides a context manager, sync_imports, for performing simultaneous imports.

Given dv, our DirectView object from earlier, we could import numpy on all engines as follows:

```
In [13]: with dv.sync_imports():
   ....:         import numpy
   ....:
importing numpy on engine(s)
```

Parallel magic commands

IPython provides several magics for interactive use in parallel situations.

%px

The %px magic executes a single Python command on the engines specified by the targets attribute of the DirectView object.

Here we will tell all four engines to create 3x3 arrays and fill them with random numbers in *[0, 1]*:

```
In [25]: %px arrays = numpy.random.rand(3, 3)
```

Note that nothing is returned in this case. Each engine, however, has its own copy of the `arrays` object, and we can perform operations on it:

```
In [27]: %px numpy.linalg.eigvals(arrays)
Out[0:7]: array([ 1.49907907,  0.28987838,  0.49496096])
Out[1:7]: array([ 1.43756182,  0.27747814,  0.45153931])
Out[2:7]: array([ 1.51325036+0.j, -0.06614375+0.30396195j, -0.06614375-
0.30396195j])
Out[3:7]: array([ 1.71117020+0.j, -0.13081468+0.42304986j, -0.13081468-
0.42304986j])
```

Magics can also be run remotely. In order to start the `%pylab` magic on multiple engines:

```
In [44]: %px %pylab inline
[stdout:0] Populating the interactive namespace from numpy and matplotlib
[stdout:1] Populating the interactive namespace from numpy and matplotlib
[stdout:2] Populating the interactive namespace from numpy and matplotlib
[stdout:3] Populating the interactive namespace from numpy and matplotlib
```

%%px

This cell magic allows for arguments to control execution.

For example, `--targets` controls which engines the command will run on. Compare the following sets of commands.

Command 1:

```
In [46]: %px print("hello")
[stdout:0] hello
[stdout:1] hello
[stdout:2] hello
[stdout:3] hello
```

Command 2:

```
In [51]: %%px --targets 0::2
print("hello")
[stdout:0] hello
[stdout:2] hello
```

%px also accepts the following:

- --[no]block for specifying blocking behavior
- --group-outputs, which changes how output is presented

%pxresult

DirectView supports a block field. When block is True, any command issued using the DirectView object will block. On False, it will not. When a command is not blocking, no output is presented. This output is not gone, however. %pxresult contains it. For example:

```
In [17]: dv.block = False

In [18]: %px print("hello")
Out[18]: <AsyncResult: finished>

In [19]: %pxresult
[stdout:0] hello
[stdout:1] hello
[stdout:2] hello
[stdout:3] hello
```

%pxconfig

Default targets and blocking behavior are set by the block and targets attributes of the active DirectView object. They can be changed directly from there, or by using the %pxconfig magic. For example:

```
In [21]: %pxconfig --block
```

The preceding code will set further %px magics to block.

%autopx

This switches to a mode where every command is executed on the engines until %autopx is executed again. For example:

```
In [13]: %autopx
%autopx enabled
```

```
In [14]: max_evals=[]

In [15]: for i in range(200):
    a=numpy.random.rand(5, 5)
    eig=numpy.linalg.eigvals(a)
    max_evals.append(eig[0].real)
    ....:

In [16]: print("avg max eigenvalue is", sum(max_evals)/len(max_evals))
[stdout:0] avg max eigenvalue is 2.50716697002
[stdout:1] avg max eigenvalue is 2.50225575352
[stdout:2] avg max eigenvalue is 2.49584794775
[stdout:3] avg max eigenvalue is 2.52453590807
```

Note that `max_evals` is not shared between the engines. Each engine has its own copy.

Types of parallelism

In 1966 Michael Flynn proposed a taxonomy of parallel programming models:

- **SISD**: Single Instruction stream, Single Data stream
- **SIMD**: Single Instruction stream, Multiple Data stream
- **MISD**: Multiple Instruction stream, Single Data Stream
- **MIMD**: Multiple Instruction stream, Multiple Data stream

This has not proven to be a completely satisfactory system. For example, it is possible for the same program to run in different categories during the same session, and the same hardware can be configured to operate in categories. In addition, experience with parallel systems has pointed out the need for additional models, including:

- **Single Program, Multiple Data streams (SPMD)**
- **Multiple Programs, Single Data streams (MPMD)**
- Task farming
- Data parallelism

In this chapter, we will look at the various categories and IPython's support for each.

The SISD model will not be covered here. The SISD model is the standard programming model for single processor machines and is covered in many other books.

SIMD

The Single Instruction stream, Multiple Data stream model specifies a single instruction stream that is applied in lockstep to multiple data elements. In this architecture, multiple processing elements apply the same instruction to multiple pieces of data simultaneously.

Schematically (*attr: Colin M. L. Burnett,* `https://en.wikipedia.org/wiki/File:SIMD.svg`):

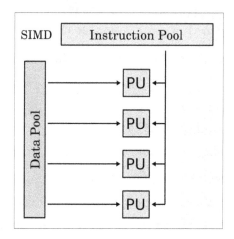

The earliest SIMD machines were vector processors in supercomputers. They were particularly applicable to matrix multiplication, important in many different scientific computations. It is often the case that a "standard" algorithm can be refactored into a form that will run efficiently in the SIMD paradigm. The process of refactoring a program in this manner is known as *vectorization*.

An important contemporary application of the SIMD architecture can be found in GPUs. Many important operations in graphics processing can be naturally vectorized.

It is possible to write GPU-specific code inside a Python program using various modules (for example, PyCUDA, PyOpenCL). We will use NumbaPro, as it allows the developer to stay primarily within Python. It is up to NumbaPro to take hints from the coder as to what parts to generate CUDA code for and how to handle the details of working with the GPU.

Consider the following program:

```
import numpy
from numbapro import vectorize

@vectorize(["float32(float32, float32)"], target="gpu")
def vectorAdd(a, b):
    return a + b

def main( ):
    N = 64

    A = numpy.random.rand(N).astype(numpy.float32)
    B = numpy.random.rand(N).astype(numpy.float32)
    C = numpy.zeros(N, dtype=numpy.float32)

    C = vectorAdd(A, B)
    print(C)

if __name__ == "__main__":
    main()
```

There is no need to go through this line-by-line, but some pieces bear closer inspection.

Line 4:

The @vectorize decorator instructs the interpreter to construct a *NumPy ufunc* – a universal function that will execute in parallel on its arguments. It does so by performing its core function element-wise on its inputs. In this case, the core function is adding the two elements.

@vectorize takes two arguments. The first describes the types of things it will be handling. "float32(float32, float32)" means that the function will return a float32 value and accept as arguments two float32 values. The second argument specifies where the function should run. By default, it is "cpu", but we would like this demo to run on the GPU.

Closely related to @vectorize is @guvectorize. @guvectorize creates a NumPy generalized universal function, which works on arrays instead of scalars. If we had wanted to multiply arrays instead of simply adding vectors, the decorator may have looked more like the following:

```
@guvectorize(['void(float64[:,:], float64[:,:], float64[:,:])'],
'(m,n),(n,p)->(m,p)')
```

Lines 11-13:

It is important that the types stored in the Python variables match the types that NumbaPro is expecting. Python might be forgiving of type mismatches, but a graphics card is not.

SPMD

Although often conflated with SIMD, the Single Program Multiple Data stream paradigm is more flexible. SIMD requires that all processing units execute the same instruction at the same time on different data streams. SPMD only requires that the processing units be executing the same program. There is no requirement that every unit be executing exactly the same instruction in that program at every point in time.

The parallel commands we have seen so far – `apply` and `map` – and the magics – `%px` and related – are all designed to work with an SPMD architecture. The difference between running on a single machine and on several is in how the engines are set up.

ipcluster and mpiexec/mpirun

If your system has **Message Passing Interface (MPI)** (see: `http://www.mpi-forum.org/`) installed, and the `mpiexec` and `mpirun` command are configured correctly, it is relatively painless to configure `ipcluster` to use them.

We will start by creating a new profile just for use with MPI:

```
-bash-4.1$ ipython profile create --parallel --profile=mpi
```

Next, edit your `IPYTHONDIR/profile_mpi/ipcluster_config.py` file.

Look for a line that sets a value for the `c.IPClusterEngines.engine_launcher_class` field. Uncomment it, and ensure that it reads as follows:

```
c.IPClusterEngines.engine_launcher_class = 'MPIEngineSetLauncher'
```

Now you can launch engines using MPI with the following command:

```
-bash-4.1$  ipcluster start -n 4 --profile=mpi
```

At this point you will have broken all the code that had previously worked. Using `ipcluster` like this will launch engines that will attempt to communicate over SSH tunnels. For security reasons, they will not communicate over these tunnels without further setup. There are ways to fix this, but the easiest fix is to find the section of the `ipcluster_config.py` file that contains the lines that configure the `LocalControllerLauncher`, and add the following:

```
    c.LocalControllerLauncher.controller_args = ["--ip='*'"]
```

This will set the local controller so that it will accept connections from any IP address. This is not particularly secure if you are on a publicly accessible network. As a practical matter, the network in most supercomputers is walled off from the outside, so the only threat would have to come from another user on the same cluster. If you are on a cluster in which other users are attempting to break into your process, you should consider using a different cluster.

ipcluster and PBS

Supercomputers are primarily batch machines. As such, each program (job) must be submitted to a central scheduler that determines when and where it will run. As part of this submission process, a control script must be created and submitted to the scheduler. This control script contains information about the program that is to be executed. For example, the scheduler may require information pertaining to:

- Job name
- Input and output files
- The number of nodes required to run the job
- Logging level
- Special resources requested (for example, a graphics card)
- How to set up the environment for this job

A popular scheduler is **Portable Batch System** (**PBS**). The scripts that are submitted to PBS are called PBS scripts, and they are submitted using the qsub utility. Of course, different systems will use different schedulers, and each will have its own way of doing things, but PBS is popular and well-supported in IPython, so we will discuss it in this book.

Writing a good PBS script is a bit of an art, but we will only need the basics. Things are a little more complicated, as we will have to start the engines and the controller separately, rather than use the ipcluster command.

Starting the engines

Here is a PBS template that will start some number of engines:

```
#PBS -N ipython
#PBS -j oe
#PBS -l walltime=00:10:00
#PBS -l nodes={n//4}:ppn=4
#PBS -q {queue}
```

```
cd $PBS_O_WORKDIR
export PATH=$HOME/usr/local/bin
export PYTHONPATH=$HOME/usr/local/lib/python3.5/site-packages
/usr/local/bin/mpiexec -n {n} ipengine --profile-dir={profile_dir}
```

Note the use of template variables: {n}, {n//4}, {queue}, and {profile_dir}.
These will allow us to pass in values. The variables correspond to the following:

- {n}: The number of nodes desired.
- {n//4}: We will use four engines per node. This can be varied based on job characteristics.
- {queue}: The job queue to run on. Many batch systems have different queues based on various job characteristics – memory requirements, expected run time, and so on.
- {profile_dir}: The profile to use.

Starting the controller

The controller template is a little simpler:

```
#PBS -N ipython
#PBS -j oe
#PBS -l walltime=00:10:00
#PBS -l nodes=1:ppn=4
#PBS -q {queue}

cd $PBS_O_WORKDIR
export PATH=$HOME/usr/local/bin
export PYTHONPATH=$HOME/usr/local/lib/python3.5/site-packages
ipcontroller --profile-dir={profile_dir}
```

Using the scripts

Save the scripts with useful names such as pbs.engine.template and pbs.controller.template. They can then be loaded into ipcluster_config.py by adding the following lines:

```
c.PBSEngineSetLauncher.batch_template_file = "pbs.engine.template"
c.PBSControllerLauncher.batch_template_file = "pbs.controller.template"
```

Also in `ipcluster_config.py`, we can set n (and any other template value) as follows:

```
c.PBSLauncher.queue = 'lowmem'
c.IPClusterEngines.n = 16
```

This will have the same problem of listening on ports that using `mpiexec`/`mpirun` had, so `ipcluster_config.py` will also need the following:

```
c.HubFactory.ip = '*'
```

At this point the cluster can be started with the following:

```
ipcluster start --profile=pbs -n 12
```

Other schedulers can be scripted in a similar manner, including Sun Grid Engine and Amazon EC2 (using **StarCluster**).

MapReduce

The idea underlying MapReduce is a specialization of the SPMD paradigm. In its simplest form, a MapReduce architecture contains:

- A mapping node
- Several computation nodes
- A reducing node

In addition to the processing nodes, three algorithms are required:

- A way to map the data to the computation nodes
- A function to apply at all the computation nodes
- A function to reduce the results at the computation nodes to a final result

Graphically it looks like the following:

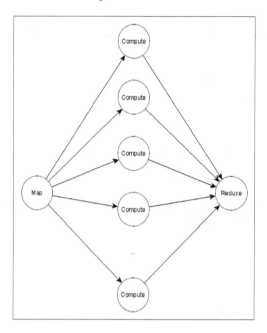

In practice, the algorithms used to distribute the data to the computation nodes, and those used to bring the data from the computation nodes to the reduce node, are very complex. IPython cannot compete with the likes of Apache Hadoop for large data sets.

The idea of MapReduce is worthwhile for even small programs, and IPython does have a quick-and-dirty way to support it. The map and map_sync calls (in the DirectView class) were introduced earlier. They work in tandem with the AsyncMapResult class to copy data to a set of engines, and gather the results of functions running on those engines into a single data structure.

Scatter and gather

A simple way to avoid sending all the data to each engine is to use the scatter and gather methods. The scatter method depends on the fact that Python namespaces are just dicts, which allows remote namespaces to be viewed as local dictionaries. This means that adding an entry to the currently active engine set implicitly sends that data to every engine in the set. For example:

```
In [51]: dv['a']=['foo','bar']

In [52]: dv['a']
Out[52]: [ ['foo', 'bar'], ['foo', 'bar'], ['foo', 'bar'], ['foo',
'bar'] ]
```

Scatter allows the developer to send a subset of data from the interactive session to the engines, and gather brings the data back. For example:

```
In [58]: dv.scatter('inputs',range(16))
Out[58]: [None,None,None,None]

In [59]: dv['inputs']
Out[59]: [ [0, 1, 2, 3], [4, 5, 6, 7], [8, 9, 10, 11], [12, 13, 14,
15] ]

In [60]: dv.gather('inputs')
Out[60]: [0, 1, 2, 3, 4, 5, 6, 7, 8, 9, 10, 11, 12, 13, 14, 15]
```

Of course, once the data is sent to the individual engines, an apply call (or similar mechanism) would need to be executed so that each engine could operate on the data it received.

A more sophisticated method

Scatter and gather will send more-or-less evenly split subsets of the data to every engine, but there is no reason to limit oneself to such a simple model. The `Client` contains references to all the engines, and you can create a `DirectView` object by indexing (as illustrated previously). Although the examples tended to grab all of the available engines as follows, this is not a requirement:

```
In [36]: c = Client()

In [37]: dv = c[:]
```

Code in the following format would send each engine only the subset of data that it needed to perform its part of the task:

```
c = Client()
numEngines = 4
dv = c[:]
asyncResults = []

for i in range(numWorkers):
    data = bigData.subset(i)
    dv.targets = i % numEngines
    asyncResults.append(dv.apply(func, data))

for r in asyncResults:
    results.append(r.get())
```

Given a function `func` to process the data, and a `subset` function to determine what data to send to each engine, this will put the results of all the parallel calls into the results list.

While not as powerful or sophisticated as Hadoop, these mechanisms provide a lightweight alternative suitable for exploratory analysis on smaller data sets.

MIMD

The Multiple Instruction Multiple Data stream paradigm describes a situation where multiple processors can be executing different instructions on different data streams. It can be viewed as a slightly more general form of SIMD, where each processing unit does not have to be in sync with all the other processing units. In practice, the term usually refers to the (even more general) MPMD paradigm, which will be discussed later.

MPMD

The Multiple Program Multiple Data stream paradigm is the most general form of parallel computing. In this paradigm, the individual processing units are essentially independent programs that may or may not communicate with each other. This can be especially handy in heterogeneous environments, where different portions of the system may require various specialized resources.

Given a program using slight modifications of earlier examples, we would want to ensure that the `useGPUs` function was executed only on nodes with an attached GPU:

```
import numpy
from numbapro import vectorize

@vectorize(["float32(float32, float32)"], target="gpu")
def vectorAdd(a, b):
    return a + b

def useGPUs( ):
    N = 64

    A = numpy.random.rand(N).astype(numpy.float32)
    B = numpy.random.rand(N).astype(numpy.float32)
    C = numpy.zeros(N, dtype=numpy.float32)

    C = vectorAdd(A, B)
    print(C)
```

```
def f(n, q):
    curr = n
    tmp = 1
    while curr != 1:
        tmp = tmp + 1
        if curr % 2 == 1:
            curr = 3 * curr + 1
        else:
            curr = curr/2
    q.put(tmp)
```

The function f should be limited to non-GPU nodes so as to reserve that limited resource for code that requires it. We can combine some of the ideas from the threading example to assign tasks correctly and not have to wait for each to complete, as follows:

```
def gpuWrap(dv, q):
    q.add(dv.apply(useGPUs))

def fWrap(dv, i, q):
    q.add(dv.apply(f, i))


# we assume that the engines have been correctly instantiated
def main( ):
    q = Queue.Queue() # collect results in here
    threads = []
    seqNum = 1

    c = Client()

    for i in range(100):
        dv = c[i]
        if i % 4 == 0:
            # we assume the GPU is attached to processing element 0
            t = threading.Thread(target=gpuWrap, args=(dv, q))
        else:
            t = threading.Thread(target=fWrap, args=(dv, seqNum, q))
            seqNum = seqNum + 1

        threads.append(t)

    for thread in threads:
        thread.start()
```

```
    for thread in threads:
        threads[i].join()

    # at this point q should be full of AsyncResult objects that can be
    used to
    # get the results of the individual processes as they complete
```

This is a fairly complex example, yet still somewhat underpowered. On the positive side, it ensures that only processes that need a GPU get one, and that no process that does not need one, gets one. An important drawback, however, is that there is no concept of processor load. Every fourth task is assigned to each processor, regardless of whether that processor is already busy. Assigning tasks in this manner is non-trivial – it requires some way to monitor the load on individual processing elements at the same time as keeping track of waiting tasks and handling task startup/shutdown. While this could certainly be built using the tools we have seen so far, it would be a complicated and error-prone construction.

The general problem of task scheduling is hard and this book will not address it. As it is, our example does not need the full power of a general-purpose task scheduler – a special case will suffice. The particular form of task scheduling required for our current example is known as task farming. Luckily, IPython implements this form of task farming through load balancing.

Task farming and load balancing

As the various processors will not all be executing the same code at the same time, or even necessarily the same program, it is possible for an MPMD system to have some processing units that are idle, while others have too much work. This can lead to unnecessary waiting on completion. A straightforward way to handle this is to allow the controller to balance the load – that is, to keep a pool of work that needs to be done, and assign that work to processing units as they become free.

IPython provides the `LoadBalancedView` to support this. For example:

```
In [4]: rc = Client()

In [5]: balView = rc.load_balanced_view()
```

At this point, `balview` can do most of the things that a normal `DirectView` instance can do. For example, using `map` to calculate asynchronously:

```
In [19]: ar = balView.map(lambda x:x**10, range(8))

In [20]: list(ar)
Out[20]: [0, 1, 1024, 59049, 1048576, 9765625, 60466176,
282475249]
```

Load balanced view also supports the `targets` field, so that not all engines must be load-balanced. For example:

```
In [54]: balView.targets = [1, 3]
```

This will ensure that only engines 1 and 3 are targets of future `apply` and `map` requests, which will be load balanced. The use of the `targets` field makes for a very straightforward way of distributing different functions to different sets of processors – simply complete the following steps:

1. Choose a target set and function.
2. Use `map` or `apply` asynchronously, keeping the `AsyncResult` in a local variable.
3. Go to 1 until done.
4. Use the local variable to obtain all the results as they arrive.

The `@parallel` function decorator will aid in this process by allowing standard Python function to be easily converted to parallel execution.

The @parallel function decorator

`LoadBalancedView` provides a decorator to simplify running the same function on multiple processors: the `@parallel` decorator. It should work as follows:

```
In [38]: @balView.parallel()
   ....: def f(n):
   ....:     curr = n
   ....:     tmp = 1
   ....:     while curr != 1:
   ....:         tmp = tmp + 1
   ....:         if curr % 2 == 1:
   ....:             curr = 3 * curr + 1
   ....:         else:
   ....:             curr = curr / 2
   ....:     return tmp

In [40]: ar = f.map(range(16))

In [41]: list(ar)
```

However, at present there appears to be a bug in its implementation, as "Exception: Unhandled message type: apply_request" is returned instead. Such is the danger of working with a product that is under development.

Data parallelism

So far we have talked primarily about the way tasks are distributed, and have left the data in the background. It can be instructive to look at the way data is obtained and made available to the tasks, also. After all, if a task is starved for data it cannot produce any results.

No data dependence

This is the situation where each task either needs no data, or can independently generate it (perhaps through sensor readings or a random number generator). This can often happen when running Monte Carlo simulations, where the only input to each simulation is a random number.

Monte Carlo simulation

It is often the case in a simulation, that exact values for parameters are not known. When this is the case, the Monte Carlo method entails running the simulation multiple times, with each run using a valid but randomly chosen value for each parameter. The results of the runs can then be combined statistically to provide an estimate of the desired result.

In this example, each instance of the simulation may as well generate its own random number, so the only data exchanges are as follows:

- At the beginning of the run, some minimal amount of configuration data will be sent (for example, number of steps or tolerance)

- At the end of the run, when results are collected

Consider the following Monte Carlo calculation of Pi:

```
def monteCarloPI(n):
    s = 0
    for i in xrange(n):
        x = random()
        y = random()
        if x*x + y*y <= 1:
            s+=1
    return 4.*s/n

def parCalcPI(view, n):
    p = len(view.targets)

    ar = view.apply(monteCarloPI, n)
    return sum(ar)/p
```

Given the standard setup and a value for the number of samples to take:

```
rc = Client()
balView = rc.load_balanced_view()
samples = 100000
```

A call to:

```
parCalcPI(view, samples)
```

This should produce a reasonable approximation of Pi.

If the random number generator requires a seed, a handy trick is to use the process ID of the engine. For example:

```
import os
processID = os.getpid()
```

This will provide the process ID. Given a set of engines, issuing the following command from the controller will yield the list of PIDs:

```
In [8]: dv.apply_sync(os.getpid)
Out[8]: [30838, 30841, 30842, 30840]
```

External data dependence

A second way to use independent data sources is to have the data in different files. The solution is to pass the file name into each task as it starts, in a manner similar to the previous section. The advantage of using files is that, while a small amount of data is actually transferred (the file name as a string), a large amount of data is being implicitly transferred (the entire contents of each file). Consider the following (not terribly efficient) function that counts the number of words in a file:

```
def countWords(filename):
    int numWords = 0
    f = open(filename, "r")
    for line in f:
        words = line.split( )
        numWords += len(words)
    return numWords
```

The following code should count the words in several files in parallel:

```
c = Client()
numEngines = 4
dv = c[:]
asyncResults = []
```

```
for i in range(numFiles):
    filename = "infile" + i + ".txt"
    dv.targets = i % numEngines]
    asyncResults.append(dv.apply(countWords, fileName))

for r in asyncResults:
    results.append(r.get())
```

Readers will recognize this as similar to the scatter-gather method described earlier, the primary difference being that the data used by the individual engines is not primarily what was sent in the original call, but instead data that was stored in separate files.

The primary drawback to this form of data parallelism has to do with the underlying architecture of the physical machine. As a rough guide, most HPC machines will have local storage and remote storage. Local storage consists of RAM and a small hard drive. Remote storage consists of banks of hard drives and lots of tape. When a process starts on a node, the remote storage from that node is effectively blank. This means that any files used by that node have to be read from remote storage into local storage. Local and remote storage are connected by a network that is shared by all nodes regardless of who owns the processes running on them.

If, as in our toy example, a large number of nodes simultaneously try to open files in remote storage for reading, the network connecting local and remote storage will be overwhelmed by the need to transfer these files from remote storage to the individual nodes that need access. This is not, in itself, a fatal error. It will, however, kill performance, and is the sort of thing that will merit an angry e-mail from the system administrator.

In order to avoid such problems, it is necessary to control both what task accesses which file, but also where the files are physically located. This problem is beyond the scope of this book – if the reader is interested, **Hadoop Distributed File System (HDFS)** provides an interesting approach.

The preceding approaches all share a common feature – the data flows exclusively between the controller and the engines. Flows that are more sophisticated will be addressed in a later chapter.

Application steering

Application steering is the interactive manipulation of a program with the purpose of affecting its behavior. It allows the user to monitor and control their application during execution. The tools that IPython provides to enable some basic forms of application steering have been laid out in this chapter. This section will limit itself to describing some simple applications.

Debugging

The simplest and oldest form of application steering is using a debugger. Using a debugger provides the ultimate in control over an application – the entire state can be accessed and modified, and execution can proceed in arbitrarily small increments. While using a debugger is well-understood, it has the drawback of requiring an extremely high degree of user interaction. This may seem counterintuitive: after all, if some interactivity is good, should not more be better? But consider running 1500 simultaneous tasks, and trying to debug them all at the same time. If nothing else, this would require a larger monitor than most developers have.

First to the post

When running algorithms that involve a lot of searching (for example, optimization or machine learning) it is often the case that:

- The only real difference between tasks is the part of the search space they are exploring
- Once a solution is found by one task, the rest could be terminated

When this is the case, the easiest thing to do is to monitor the progress of the individual tasks until one completes. The simplest way is to use the `ready( )` function of `AsyncResult` and `progress` field. `ready( )` returns true if all calls have completed, while `progress` contains the number of calls that have completed. Using these, we can write a loop that pools an `AsyncResult` to determine if any of the calls have completed, and returns true if at least one has the following:

```
def areAnyDoneYet(ar):
    while not (ar.ready( )):
    if ar.progress > 0:
        return true
    time.sleep(1)
```

At this point the user could take any action required on the `DirectView` used to create the `AsyncResult`, including killing all the engines.

Graceful shutdown

Of course, there is no requirement that each engine be forcefully shut down. They may have resources open that should be returned (for example, open files). In this case, it would be better to have some way to notify each engine that it should terminate itself. To do this, we can take advantage of IPython's use of dictionaries for namespaces to set a variable to a value on all the engines.

The following code would loop through all the engines, setting a variable named `stop` to `True`. It is the responsibility of each task to check the `stop` variable on a regular basis, and take the appropriate action when it is `True`:

```
c = Client()
numEngines = 4

# we assume the number of engines and the number of tasks is equal
for i in range(numEngines):
    e = c[i]
    e['stop'] = True
```

There is, of course, no need for the individual tasks to stop themselves. Obtaining an initial result may just mean that the next phase of processing is to begin, and setting such a variable allows each engine to start on the next phase. While this is a simple and effective way for processes to communicate with each other, it is inefficient. More sophisticated ways will be addressed in the next chapter(s).

Summary

This chapter took a brief tour through some parallel programming patterns and introduced the basics of IPython's parallel capabilities. IPython's parallel architecture was described and the functionality of its components outlined. Examples were provided to show how IPython's ipyparallel library is able to support many different types of parallel structures. Overall, IPython provides a powerful, flexible, modern interface to parallel machines.

In the next chapter we will take a deeper look at IPython's support for communication between parallel processes, both natively and through the third-party mechanisms provided by ZeroMQ and MPI.

4
Messaging with ZeroMQ and MPI

This chapter covers messaging and its use in parallel programming. Unlike threading, a system that utilizes multiple processes does not have a single memory area that the entire system can access. This means that if different subprocesses are to communicate, they must pass data back and forth in the form of messages. In this chapter, we will introduce and discuss two popular message passing mechanisms: ZeroMQ and MPI.

The following topics will be covered:

- The storage hierarchy address spaces, and data locality
- Concepts of ZeroMQ
- Messaging patterns in ZeroMQ
- Concepts of MPI
- Messaging patterns in MPI
- MPI and process control

The storage hierarchy

It is easy to ignore where data is stored in serial applications. This was not always so. A lot of work has gone into abstracting away the details of various layers of the storage hierarchy from the programmer. The following graphic illustrates a typical storage hierarchy:

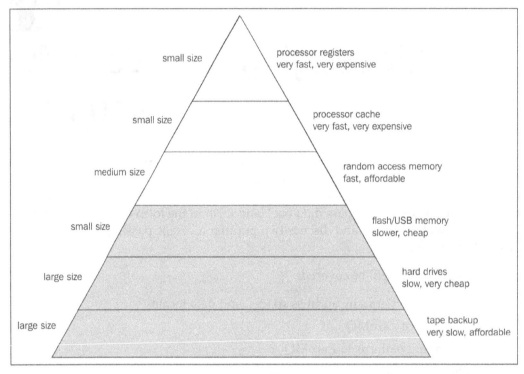

Modified from
https://en.wikipedia.org/wiki/Memory_hierarchy#/media/
File:ComputerMemoryHierarchy.svg

The hierarchy shows differences on three axes: persistence, size, and cost. The clear levels are volatile; their contents decay when power is no longer applied. The shaded levels are persistent; they retain data even when not powered.

As one travels down the hierarchy, storage capacity grows. There is variation within each level, but the basic trend is clear. This is also true over time; for example, the amount of RAM available has grown to the point where it is larger than hard drives from an earlier period, but hard drives have also grown in size to maintain the differential.

Although not a strictly technical factor, moving down the hierarchy also reduces the monetary cost per bit.

The trade-off is clear; more space means slower but cheaper storage.

Compounding this problem is the fact that the processor can only access data at the very top of the pyramid. The goal then is to have as much data as possible in the faster (but smaller) levels of the storage hierarchy so that the processor does not have to sit idle waiting for it to be transferred to a place where it can be acted upon.

The solution to this problem lies in virtual memory systems. It is the responsibility of a virtual memory system to move data from one level of the hierarchy to another so that the data that the process is likely to need is near the top, in fast memory, when it needs it. These systems are very complex, and their design is outside of the focus of this book, but they do introduce the idea of data locality.

Address spaces

For the purposes of this discussion, an address space refers to a set of unique identifiers that can be used to denote a unit of data storage.

For example, the preceding hierarchy has several address spaces:

Storage type	Address space type
Registers	Names (for example, R1 and ACR)
Cache	Numeric
RAM	Numeric
Flash/USB	Block structure
Hard drives	Logical block addressing/Cylinder-head-sector
Tape	Volume/track

An important feature of a virtual memory system is that it translates requests for data from all levels from a single format to the native format (or formats) of each level. In doing so, it makes the system appear as if it had a single address space:

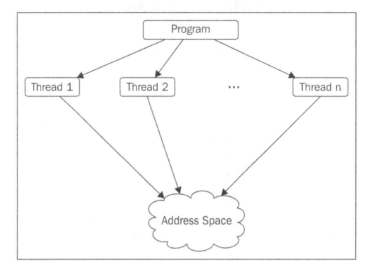

This is admittedly a vastly simplified version of what actually goes on — there are systems at every level to help this process work — but it brings to the surface an important point that is often ignored because virtual memory systems work so smoothly without developer intervention. The point is that dealing with where data is actually stored is non-trivial.

Data locality

The concept underlying data locality is that the physical location of data matters. Many of the issues that a virtual memory system handles in a serial system come back to haunt the parallel developer. In particular, any system for handling distributed data must address three important questions:

- Where is the data?
- How can I send it somewhere else?
- What format is it in?

We will consider two methods of handling distributed data: ZeroMQ and MPI.

ZeroMQ

ZeroMQ grew out of what would seem to be the obvious initial answer to the question of communicating distributed processes: why not just use sockets? The answer was that the implementation of sockets, while good for a wide area network, did not fit the needs of parallel development. After a certain point, it becomes too difficult to scale sockets as the level of detail can obscure higher-level concerns, such as publish-subscribe patterns and reliable messaging. ZeroMQ layers some helpful functionality on top of the socket interface, while keeping an eye on efficiency and ease of use.

ZeroMQ is not an all-in-one messaging solution. Instead, it can be used to build a variety of different messaging patterns based on what the particular problem calls for. ZeroMQ attempts to keep the familiar socket interface while adding just enough extra functionality to handle the specific needs of parallel computing. It aims, not to solve your problem, but to give you the tools you need to solve your problem. The website describes its birth as:

> *"We took a normal TCP socket, injected it with a mix of radioactive isotopes stolen from a secret Soviet atomic research project, bombarded it with 1950-era cosmic rays, and put it into the hands of a drug-addled comic book author with a badly-disguised fetish for bulging muscles clad in spandex. Yes, ZeroMQ sockets are the world-saving superheroes of the networking world."*

A sample ZeroMQ program

Let's start with a simple `"Hello World"` client-and-server pair. Many thanks to the folks at `http://zguide.zeromq.org/`, from which this server and client were adapted.

The server

The following is a simple server that waits for a request on port `5678` and replies with a random number:

```
import time
import zmq
import random

context = zmq.Context()
socket = context.socket(zmq.REP)
socket.bind("tcp://*:5678")

while True:
    #  Wait for next request from client
```

```
message = socket.recv()
print("Received request: %s" % message)

#  So everything does not happen too fast to see
time.sleep(2)

#  Send reply back to client
socket.send(str(random.random())
```

- **Line 5**: ZeroMQ applications always start by creating a context and use it to create sockets. There should be only a single context for any process.

- **Line 6**: This creates a socket object contained in our new context. Every socket has a type. The type of a socket determines how it operates, which determines which sort of messaging pattern it should be used in. We will cover various messaging patterns in a later section. This socket is of type zmq.REP, which means it will wait to *REPly* to a request.

- **Line 7**: This line does four things:
    - ° First, it binds the socket to an endpoint so that it can start waiting for a request to come in.
    - ° Second, it specifies that the transport protocol for the request should be TCP.
    - ° Third, the * is a wildcard that accepts connections from any address.
    - ° Fourth, :5678 determines the port the socket will listen on. Any would-be requestor is required to have compatible settings in order to connect to this process.

- **Line 9**: This is a server, so it customarily runs forever. In reality, however, there are several stopping conditions:
    - ° The server itself is shut down
    - ° The server process is killed externally (for example, using a SIGKILL signal)
    - ° The server process is attacked from outside
    - ° The server process itself errors out

The ZeroMQ team has a definite stand on the final two causes of error (from http://zguide.zeromq.org/):

"ZeroMQ's error handling philosophy is a mix of fail-fast and resilience. Processes, we believe, should be as vulnerable as possible to internal errors, and as robust as possible against external attacks and errors."

To some extent then, ZeroMQ will attempt to recover from external errors. For example, it will try to handle network errors in an intelligent manner, even automatically retrying when that makes sense. While the framework cannot handle every error that could occur, it is likely that any error that does prevent successful completion of a call really requires the attention of the process that initiated the call. If it did nothing else, ZeroMQ would be worth using just for this feature.

If it cannot succeed for whatever reason, at a low level, this means that every ZeroMQ call will return a status code or fail an assertion. The Python wrapper for ZeroMQ will tend to throw exceptions for any sort of error event. The following table summarizes these exceptions:

Exception	Condition
ZMQError	Wraps a ZeroMQ error number
ZMQVersionError	This is raised when a feature is not provided by the linked version of `libzmq`
Again	Wrapper for ZeroMQ's EAGAIN error
ContextTerminated	Wrapper for ZeroMQ's ETERM error
NotDone	Timeout while waiting for a message
ZMQBindError	When a socket fails to bind to a port

The complete details can be found at `https://pyzmq.readthedocs.org/en/latest/api/index.html`. Every call to ZeroMQ should be wrapped in a `try-catch` block, and liberal use of assertions is encouraged. However, as important as error handling is in production, it can tend to clutter up otherwise clean code. All examples will be provided without it:

- **Line 14**: Receiving a request is a blocking statement. This process will wait indefinitely for a connection on the port specified previously. A limit can be specified so that the wait times out.

- **Line 21**: After the message is received and (some minimal) processing occurs, a response can be sent back to the process that initiated the connection. At a low level, ZeroMQ sends bytes, not Python characters. If both the client and the server are Python (and possibly the same version), sending a string in this manner should work without issue.

Cross-language and cross-platform applications may want to use this:

```
socket.send(b"World")
```

Instead of using the following line of code:

```
socket.send("World")
```

This is so that Python explicitly translates the characters into bytes before sending. A complete coverage of Unicode and the issues surrounding internationalization is beyond the scope of this book. A good introduction can be found in *Python 2.6 Text Processing: Beginners Guide* (https://www.packtpub.com/application-development/python-26-text-processing-beginners-guide).

The client

The following is the matching client. It sends a simple "Hello" message on port 5555 and receives a message containing a random number:

```python
import zmq


context = zmq.Context()


# Socket to talk to server
socket = context.socket(zmq.REQ)
socket.connect("tcp://localhost:5678")


socket.send("Load request")


# Get the reply
message = socket.recv()
print("Received reply %s [ %s ]" % (request, message))
```

- **Line 6**: For the client, we create a different type of socket: zmq.REQ (for REQuest). The REP and REQ sockets work in pairs to form the REQUEST/REPLY message pattern.

- **Line 7**: The example client is running on the same machine as the example server, so it connects to localhost at the appropriate port using the appropriate protocol.

- **Lines 9 and 12**: Note that the client sends first and then listens. This is in contrast to the server, which listens first and then sends. This order is important—listening when it should be sending, or the reverse, can cause an exception to be thrown.

Messaging patterns in ZeroMQ

Two or more processes can communicate in many different ways. ZeroMQ supports more than what can be covered here, but some popular options are as follows:

- Pairwise
- Client-Server
- Publish-Subscribe
- Push-Pull

ZeroMQ supports these through its use of socket types. We will look at each of these patterns in turn.

Pairwise

Pairwise ZeroMQ sockets allow one-to-one, bidirectional communication. They are otherwise similar to "normal" sockets. The designation of "client" or "server" is arbitrary—both use the PAIR designation:

Server

This is a variant of the previously covered random number server, using a PAIR socket:

```
import zmq
import random


context = zmq.Context()
socket = context.socket(zmq.PAIR)
socket.connect("tcp://localhost:5678")


while True:
    msg = socket.recv()
    socket.send(str(random.random()))
```

Client

This is a variant of the preceding client, also using a PAIR socket:

```
import zmq

context = zmq.Context()
socket = context.socket(zmq.PAIR)
socket.bind("tcp://*:5678" % port)

while True:
    socket.send("What is the load?")
    msg = socket.recv()
    print(msg)
    time.sleep(1)
```

Discussion

There is a slight difference here from normal sockets in that either the server or client can bind, and either can connect. There should be one of each, however. The side that connects must specify which machine to send the request to, while the side that binds specifies where it will accept requests from.

Client/server

The client/server connection pattern relaxes some of the restrictions of the pairwise pattern. In particular, the client can connect to many servers. The server (or servers) uses the **REP** designation while the client uses **REQ**:

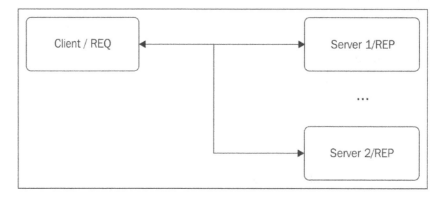

Server 1

This server uses a REP socket to wait for a request:

```
import zmq
import random

context = zmq.Context()
socket = context.socket(zmq.REP)
socket.bind("tcp://*:5678")

while True:
    msg = socket.recv()
    socket.send(str(random.random())
```

Server 2

A duplicate of the previous server, this will be started on another node:

```
import zmq

context = zmq.Context()
socket = context.socket(zmq.REP)
socket.bind("tcp://*:5679")

while True:
    msg = socket.recv()
    socket.send("peanut butter jelly time")
```

Client

This client uses a REQ socket to request the time from either of the servers in turn:

```
import zmq

context = zmq.Context()
socket = context.socket(zmq.REQ)
socket.connect("tcp://localhost:5678" % port)
socket.connect("tcp://localhost:5679" % port)

while True:
    socket.send("Report status")
    msg = socket.recv()
    print(msg)
    time.sleep(1)
```

Discussion

One would start `server 1`, `server 2`, and `client` as separate processes. In this case, the client would send one message to `server 1`, the next to `server 2`, the next to `server 1`, and so on. It is important that the servers bind to their ports and that the client connects.

It is also important that the client(s) and server(s) take turns *send-ing* and *recv-ing*. The client(s) should send first and then recv, while the server(s) should *recv* first and then send. Any deviation will result in an error.

Publish/subscribe

It is not always the case that a process that is sending messages cares what other processes, if any, receive them. On the receiving side, it is possible that a process will only care about a subset of messages that a process it is listening to is sending out. This is analogous to a traditional magazine—an issue is published each month, of which some number of subscribers read some (or all). Hence the name: the *Publish Subscribe* model.

Publishers are created with the **PUB** designation, while subscribers are **SUB**:

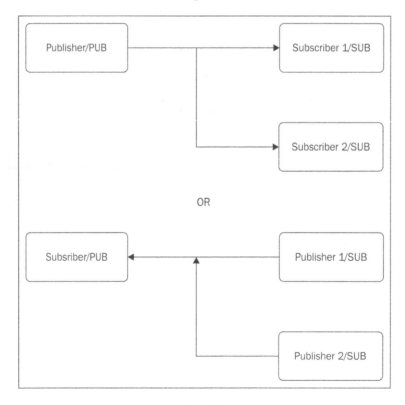

Publisher

This is the publisher. It uses a PUB socket to send the time and weather to an arbitrary number of subscribers:

```
import zmq
import random

context = zmq.Context()
socket = context.socket(zmq.PUB)
socket.bind("tcp://*:5678")

while True:
    topic = "load"
    socket.send(topic + " " + str(random.random()))

    topic = "weather"
    messagedata = "dark and stormy night"
    socket.send(topic + " " + messagedata)

    time.sleep(1)
```

Subscriber

This subscriber uses a SUB socket to listen to the preceding publishers. It is, however, only interested in the weather:

```
import zmq

context = zmq.Context()
socket = context.socket(zmq.SUB)
socket.connect("tcp://localhost:5678")
socket.setsockopt_string(zmq.SUBSCRIBE, "weather")

while True:
    wtr = socket.recv_string()
    print("the weather is: " + wtr)
```

Discussion

The subscriber in this case will process only those messages that start with "weather". Messages starting with "time" (or any other string) are quietly dropped by ZeroMQ before they reach the Subscriber. Other subscribers are still eligible to receive them, however.

This pattern is very flexible. There can be as many publishers and subscribers as desired. A publisher's messages can reach as many subscribers as exist and subscribers can receive messages from as many publishers as desired.

Publishers and subscribers are not in any meaningful dialogue. A publisher does not need to wait for a response before sending a new message, nor does a client need to respond to a message. Attempting to do either of these results in an error.

Push/Pull

The Push/Pull pattern is similar to the MapReduce pattern. In both, a single process distributes messages to a set of worker processes, which perform work, and then each sends a message to a sink process that gathers the messages.

The sockets used to send messages are created with the **PUSH** designation, while the sockets used to receive messages are **PULL**:

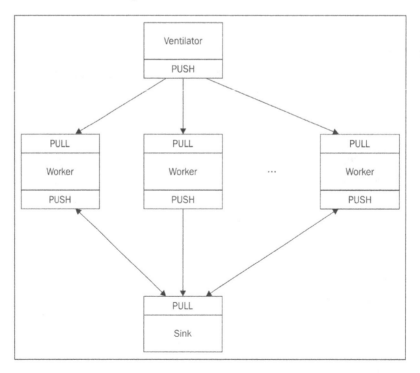

Ventilator

A PUSH socket is used to send messages to multiple workers:

```
import zmq
import random
import time


context = zmq.Context()


# socket to send messages on
sender = context.socket(zmq.PUSH)
sender.bind("tcp://localhost:5678")


while True:
    # messages come in batches of 16, for this example
    # perhaps there are 16 workers
    for i in range(16):
        seed = random.randint(1, 20000)
        sender.send_string(str(seed))

    # give 0MQ time to deliver and workers time to work
    time.sleep(10)
```

Worker

Each worker uses a PULL socket to receive messages from the ventilator and a PUSH socket to send the results to the sink:

```
import zmq
import random
import time


context = zmq.Context()


# from the ventilator
receiver = context.socket(zmq.PULL)
receiver.connect("tcp://localhost:5678")


# to the sink
sender = context.socket(zmq.PUSH)
```

```
sender.connect("tcp://localhost:5679")

while True:
    s = receiver.recv()

    #do some "work"
    time.sleep(int(s)*0.001)

    #send "results" to sink
    tm = str(time.time())
    sender.send_string(tm)
```

Sink

The sink uses a PULL socket to receive results from all workers:

```
import zmq

context = zmq.Context()

# socket to receive messages on
receiver = context.socket(zmq.PULL)
receiver.bind("tcp://localhost:5679")

while True:
    s = receiver.recv_string()
    # do work - maybe log time for each completed process
```

Discussion

Messages will be distributed to the workers evenly. That is, work is distributed using a round-robin algorithm. Messages are collected from the workers evenly. This is called fair queuing.

 Using PUSH and PULL for load balancing can yield unexpected results if one PULL socket starts significantly before the others and is sent all the currently pending messages. If this is an issue, using the ROUTER and DEALER sockets can fix the problem.

Workers may come and go. ZeroMQ will dynamically handle connects and disconnects. The source and sink, however, should always be up and in the same place.

Important ZeroMQ features

A complete discussion of the inner workings of ZeroMQ is beyond the scope of this book. Some details about what is going on under the hood may prove illuminating, however. The following paragraphs outline some important features.

I/O is handled asynchronously in the background. ZeroMQ applications need no locks, semaphores, or other wait states. That is not to say that no ZeroMQ call ever blocks—recv certainly does. It is just that such blocking is part of the semantics of the function, not a limitation imposed by ZeroMQ's implementation.

Message sending is done through queues when required. If a message must be queued, it is queued as close to the receiver as possible. Queues that fill up can either block or throw away messages depending on the message pattern in use.

ZeroMQ will automatically connect and disconnect components as they come and go. This does not guarantee the correctness of the program using those components, but it does mean that ZeroMQ will not crash or behave erratically under these conditions.

Messages are delivered as they are sent. The size and format of the message are irrelevant.

ZeroMQ will attempt to handle network errors transparently. For example, it may automatically attempt to resend a message that was not received if a retry would make sense.

Issues using ZeroMQ

No tool is complete without a set of issues to deal with. ZeroMQ does a good job of cleaning up many of the low-level issues that come with messaging in a distributed system, but issues at other levels remain.

Startup and shutdown

The preceding examples all used infinite loops. While this is a valid choice for a system that is expected to run continuously, it is not a universal feature. It does, however, avoid some annoying behavior that can occur at startup and shutdown.

Consider the PUSH/PULL architecture outlined previously. The ventilator, workers, and sink can all be spread to different processors by the scheduler. At some point, the ventilator will begin execution, open its socket, and start sending messages. It does not know how many workers will be there in total. The ventilator will simply start sending messages out as fast as it can to whoever is listening. If, when the first message is ready to be sent, there are only two workers that have started (and connected), one of those workers will get the message. ZeroMQ will not block the ventilator from sending messages until every worker is ready to accept them. If there is some delay such that the other 14 workers do not start within the time period that is required for the ventilator to send out all 16 messages, then the first two workers will get eight messages each and the remaining 14 workers will get none.

The sink has a similar problem. In this case, the sink does not know whether any workers are still processing a message. There is no necessary connection at the ZeroMQ level between the number of messages sent out, the number of workers that are connected to either the ventilator or the sink, and the number of messages that the sink should expect.

The solution in both cases is to set up "extra" sockets on other ports for out-of-band communication. In the aforementioned situation, the ventilator should set up a REP socket and each worker should connect to the REP socket using a REQ socket. When a worker started up, but before it started receiving "actual" messages, it would send a message to the ventilator to let the ventilator know that the worker was up and ready to receive messages. The server would delay sending any "actual" messages until it has received these out-of-band messages from all the workers.

A similar setup would work for the sink. In this case, the ventilator and the sink should set up a separate PAIR socket to communicate with each other. Every time the ventilator sent out a message to a worker, it would also send out an out-of-band message to the sink, letting the sink know that it should receive one more message from a worker. This way the sink could make sure that the number of messages it received was the same as the number of messages the ventilator sent. A special "no more messages" message could be used when the ventilator is done so that the sink does not sit around forever waiting to see if another message is going to be sent.

Discovery

All the previous examples assumed that all the communication processes were running on the same machine. Certainly, the servers could accept messages from other machines, but all client connections were to localhost. This was done at least partially to make the examples easy to run—putting everything on localhost means not needing a parallel machine on your desk.

It also obviates another, more serious problem: how do the clients know where to connect to? Depending on the pattern, a process that wants to communicate needs to know on what machine and what port to send or listen.

A popular solution to this problem is to create an intermediary between the client and the server, called a broker or proxy. The broker sits in one well-known place that every server and client knows about (by having it hardcoded). This reduces the problem of finding where all the other processes are to simply connecting to a single endpoint.

Heavyweight solutions (for example, RabbitMQ and IBM Integration Bus) come with the broker built in. There are three reasons ZeroMQ avoids mandating the use of a broker:

*   Brokers tend to become more complicated over time
*   Brokers become bottlenecks for messages, as they all must pass through them
*   The broker becomes a single point of failure

A directory architecture could be used as an alternative. In this case, there would be a single process responsible for knowing where all the endpoints were. When a process needs to know where to send/receive a message, it will check with the directory to find the server/port/socket type, and then set up its own socket. In this case, the directory does not pass any messages through itself, instead simply receiving and answering queries about the communications setup. While this may sound simpler than a broker, it is not without its issues.

Whether the solution to discovery is a broker, a directory, or some other scheme, ZeroMQ provides enough flexibility to implement a solution.

MPI

The **Message Passing Interface (MPI)** is a language-independent message passing library standard. It has been implemented in several languages, including Fortran, C/C++, and Python. This book will use the Mpi4py implementation. *Chapter 3, Stepping Up to IPython for Parallel Computing*, outlined the process for starting IPython using MPI. It will be assumed that IPython has been started this way in the following examples.

Hello World

Here is the MPI `"Hello world"` program. It has every process reply with a simple string, along with the rank of the process:

```
from mpi4py import MPI
comm = MPI.COMM_WORLD
rank = comm.Get_rank()
print("hello world from process ", rank)
```

- **Line 2**: This obtains a communicator object. A communicator is a logical structure that defines which processes are allowed to send and receive messages. COMM_WORLD is the communicator that contains all the processes in this session.

- **Line 3**: The Get_rank( ) method returns the rank of this process. Each process inside a communicator is assigned an incremental rank starting from zero. Ranks are useful for specifying the source and destination of messages. A process may belong to several communicators at a time, so it may have different ranks depending on which communicator is being used.

- **Line 4**: Each process started will receive its own rank, so this should print out a different number for each process started. Normally, the child processes should not perform I/O, but this is a good example.

A sample run might look like this:

```
In [13]: !mpiexec -n 4 python hellompi.py
hello world from process 2
hello world from process 1
hello world from process 0
hello world from process 3
```

Rank and role

When using ZeroMQ, different processes played different parts in the communication pattern; for example, in a PUB/SUB pattern, one process would be the publisher and others would be subscribers. Because they were different processes, started independently, the code for the publisher and subscribers could be different.

When an MPI program runs, every process receives the same code. This would seem to remove the possibility that the various processes play different roles in a communication pattern.

That is not the case. Each process receives a unique rank from the COMM_WORLD communicator. The process can use its rank to determine what it should do. The basic idea is to put the code for all patterns into the process and then have the process use its rank to determine which subset of the code it should execute. In our PUB/SUB example, the process that received rank 0 might become the publisher and execute that code, while all other processes might execute the subscriber code.

Point-to-point communication

The simplest form of communication is point-to-point; one process will initiate communication by sending a message and the other will receive the message.

The following is an example:

```
import time
from mpi4py import MPI
comm = MPI.COMM_WORLD
rank = comm.Get_rank()

if rank == 1:
    messagedata = str(time.time())
    comm.send(messageData, dest=0)

if rank == 0:
    msg = comm.recv(source=1)
    print("The time was " + msg)
```

- **Lines 6 and 10**: This is where the code checks to see what it should do. The copy of the code that has ended up on the processor of rank 1 should send a message, while the code on processor 0 should receive it.
- **Line 8**: When a message is sent in MPI, the recipient(s) must be specified (broadcast is also supported). The recipient must have a different rank than the sender.
- **Line 11**: The recipient of a message can specify whom it must be from (accepting a message from any process is also supported).

Broadcasting

Broadcasting would seem to be inapplicable when using MPI: after all, every process has the same code, so what could one know that another did not? One example of asymmetry comes from the use of I/O. Consider a program that receives input from the user, and then acts upon that input in each process. It would be madness for each process to ask for user input independently. The rank 0 process should gather the input and then send it to all the other processes, for example:

```
from mpi4py import MPI


comm = MPI.COMM_WORLD
rank = comm.Get_rank()


if rank == 0:
    data = input("Please enter random number seed")
else:
    data = None


# mpi4py wants to send an object, so we will leave the
# input in that format
data = comm.bcast(data, root=0)
```

Reduce

With all the processes performing separate operations, it can be useful to combine their results. For example, when computing the Reimann integral of a function, it can be much more efficient to divide the work across several processes. The result is then the sum of the values calculated in each process, for example:

```
import numpy
import sys
from mpi4py import MPI


comm = MPI.COMM_WORLD
rank = comm.Get_rank()


# integrate from in [0, 4] using 8 rectangles
a = 0
b = 4
```

```python
n = 8

#the function to integrate
def f(x):
    return x*x*x

# use the left-most point in the range as the height
defcalcArea(lft, dx):
    ht = f(lft)
    returnht * dx

# use regular intervals
dx = (b-a)/n

# local_a is the leftmost point
local_a = rank * dx

#initializing variables
# when using capital-R Recv, mpi4py requires that we pass buffer-like
# objects, so why not use numpy?
integral = numpy.zeros(1)
total = numpy.zeros(1)

# perform local computation
integral[0] = calcArea(local_a, dx)

# communication
# root node receives results with a collective "reduce"
comm.Reduce(integral, total, op=MPI.SUM, root=0)

# root process prints results
if comm.rank == 0:
    print("With n =", n, "trapezoids, our estimate of the integral from",
a, "to", b, "is", total)
```

- **Line 23**: The use of the process's rank here ensures that each process works on a different "chunk" of the integral. The 0th process will work on the leftmost chunk, the first process the next, and so on.

- **Line 37**: This is where the reducing communication and computation happen. It can seem a bit odd at first, as there was no corresponding broadcast or scatter of data before the reduce. Because of the way MPI runs, the initial mpiexec that kicked off all the processes did an implicit broadcast by copying the program to all the processing elements.

The op can be any of several built-in operations, including MAX, MIN, SUM, and PROD. See the documentation for the MPI.Op class for details on the currently supported operations.

Discussion

Note that this program works only when there are eight processes (more generally, when *n* is the same as the number of processes). This sort of problem crops up frequently when splitting work across processing elements. There are three patterns to solve it.

Change the configuration

Change the number of processing elements. This is the easiest to code but may not be practical.

Divide the work

Have each process determine how many "work units" it should handle. In the preceding example, this would mean that each process calculates the area of some number (> *1*) of rectangles, adds those areas, and assigns the result to the integral variable.

The number of rectangles each process handles would depend on the total number of rectangles to be used and the total number of processes. The total number of rectangles is the variable n. The total number of processes is available from the comm object by calling the Get_size() method. The area calculations can then be placed in a loop, as follows:

```
numRectangles = n/comm.getSize()
mydx = dx/numRectangles
tmpArea = 0
for i in range(numRectangles):
    local_a = a * dx + i * mydx
```

```
tmpArea = tmpArea + calcArea(local_a, mydx)
integral[0] = tmpArea
```

The important idea is that each process needs the following:

- Enough information to figure out what part of the work it needs to do
- The ability to divide and recombine its individual tasks as part of the group
- Not to do any (unnecessary) overlapping work with other processes

Parcel out the work

This is a somewhat un-MPI-like mechanism, but it is the most flexible. In this case, the root process sets up a loop, which simply receives messages from each non-root process. The message serves a dual purpose: to communicate the answer from that process, and to let the root process know that the non-root process that sent the message is ready for more input. Although more flexible, it is also more complicated, which brings us to the topic of process control using MPI.

Process control

MPI supports spawning processes through a communicator. The spawned processes are associated with the communicator that spawned them (that is, they receive their own rank each, unique within that communicator). This allows the use of a broadcast/reduce message pattern to send data to/receive data from each spawned process.

The code structure for doing this is slightly different from the examples covered so far. In particular, the code for the "master" process is different from the code for the "worker" processes, and neither type of process checks its rank.

We will look at dividing the calculation of the integral of a function from 0 to the number of processors.

Master

The master is responsible for starting the workers using Spawn and sending out their data through a `bcast`:

```
from mpi4py import MPI
import sys

comm = MPI.COMM_SELF.Spawn(sys.executable, args=['workermpi.py'],
maxprocs=4)
```

```
# use 16 slices
comm.bcast([16, MPI.INT], root=MPI.ROOT)

# gather and sum results when done
comm.reduce(None, [area, MPI.DOUBLE], op=MPI.SUM, root=MPI.ROOT)

print(area)

comm.Disconnect()
```

Worker

Each worker has a bcast to receive data, and then it uses its rank to determine which portion of the problem to work on:

```
from mpi4py import MPI

def f(x):
    return x**3

comm = MPI.Comm.Get_parent()
size = comm.Get_size()
rank = comm.Get_rank()

comm.bcast([N, MPI.INT], root=0)

width = 1.0 / N
sum = 0
i = rank - 1
while i < rank:
    sum = sum + f(i) * width
    i = i + width

comm.reduce([sum, MPI.DOUBLE], None, op=MPI.SUM, root=0)

comm.Disconnect()
```

ZeroMQ and IPython

ZeroMQ is more than a messaging library for parallel environments: IPython has moved to using ZeroMQ as its internal messaging infrastructure. In this section, we will provide further details on the operation of IPython in terms of the ZeroMQ mechanisms underlying it.

To do this, we will introduce some additional socket types, describe how they interact to enable some of IPython's parallel components, and finish up with some use cases employing those components. While this section cannot hope to cover all the details of the IPython parallel architecture, it is hoped that these examples will provide the user with a basic understanding of the underlying mechanisms.

ZeroMQ socket types

ZeroMQ supports a large number of different socket types, 14 at last count (version 4.2.0). The preceding section provided an overview of some of the important types, but a discussion of the IPython architecture requires at least cursory knowledge of some advanced socket types:

- DEALER: This is similar to a REQ socket, but is asynchronous. Each message sent is sent among all connected peers in a round-robin fashion, and each message received is fair-queued from all connected peers. It is compatible with ROUTER, REP, and DEALER sockets.

- ROUTER: This is similar to a REP socket but is asynchronous. It keeps track of all connected peers. Every message sent by a router includes the identity of the message's source. This allows the socket to route messages based on their origination. Situations where a ROUTER has multiple REQ and REP sockets connected require that messages be sent to the correct endpoints.

IPython components

Chapter 3, Stepping Up to IPython for Parallel Computing, provided an overview of the major IPython architectural components. We will provide more details in this section, with an emphasis on how each component uses messaging to perform its tasks.

Client

The Client is the interface between the user and the IPython system. It accepts an input from the user, passes it along to the Hub and Schedulers, and accepts the output from the Schedulers.

Engine(s)

An IPython Engine is a Python instance that accepts Python commands and objects over a network connection. The ability to run engines on different processors is what makes distributed computing in IPython possible.

Controller

The goal of the Controller is to manage and monitor the connections and communications between the clients and the engines. It consists of 1-5 processes: the Hub and four Schedulers.

Hub

The Hub's primary responsibility is the well-being of the engines and the messages that flow between them. It allows engines to register as available, passes notifications around, and keeps track of which engines are alive through its Heartbeat Monitor process.

Scheduler

The Schedulers send messages back and forth from the clients and engines. This includes propagating `stdout`/`stderr` from the engines to the clients.

Connection diagram

The following diagram illustrates the connections between the components:

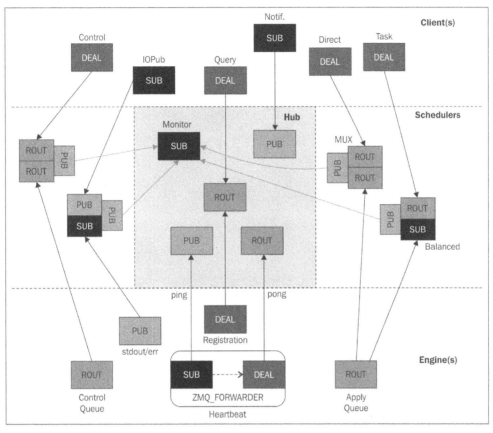

Messaging use cases

The various components of IPython communicate to perform a large number of tasks, many more than can be covered here. Examples of some simpler use cases will serve to illustrate the power and flexibility of the architecture.

Registration

An important step in any distributed system is making the initial connection between a new process and the infrastructure. Simpler is generally better, as it reduces the amount of configuration required. While a certain amount of configuration will always be necessary, too much can lead to a complicated, brittle system.

ZeroMQ goes for minimum configuration: clients and engines only need to know the IP address and port of the Hub's ROUTER socket in order to connect. Once this initial connection is established, any information needed to establish further connections is sent over. In addition, clients can use this connection to query the **Hub** for state information concerning the engines. This results in a simple connection architecture where the client and engine both use **DEAL** sockets and the hub uses a **ROUT**:

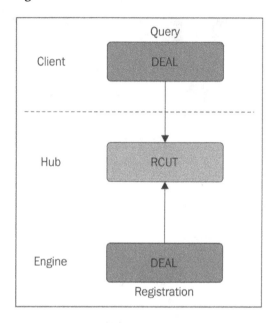

Heartbeat

The Hub is also responsible for checking which engines are still responding. It does this by periodically sending a message to each engine. The engine then responds with the same message, with a prefix denoting which engine responded. If an engine does not respond, the Hub will attempt to terminate it.

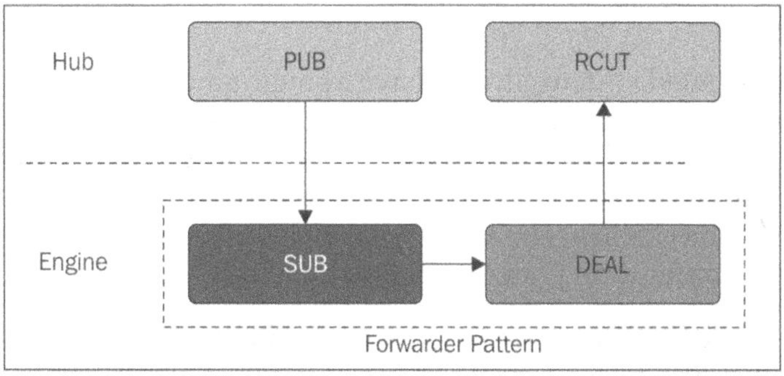

IOPub

stdout/stderr are captured and published via a **PUB** socket. Both the **Client** and the **Hub** receive a copy:

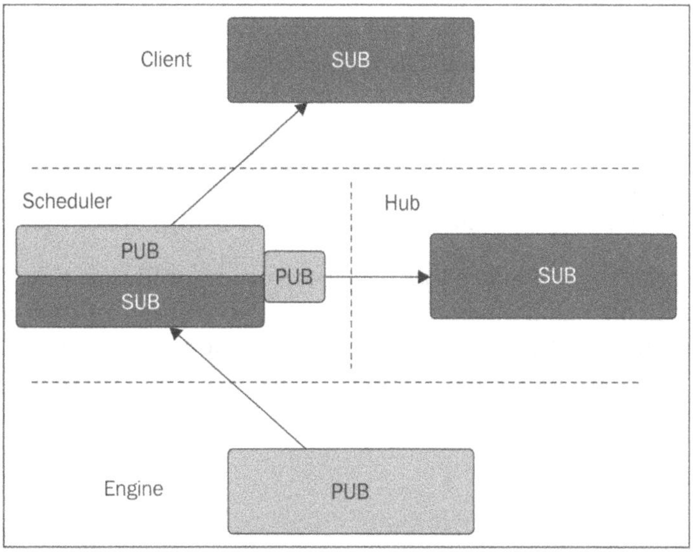

Summary

The fact that distributed systems do not have a single address space means that the usual mechanisms for sharing data between modules (parameters and global variables) are not available. Instead, data movement must be explicitly specified. While IPython provides for the use of a "global" dictionary (which implicitly uses a message passing mechanism similar to what is described in this chapter), more sophisticated communication patterns require more full-featured tools.

In this chapter, we looked at two of these tools: ZeroMQ and MPI. ZeroMQ is a lightweight, socket-like mechanism that has become the basis of IPython's internal architecture. It is easy to use, is efficient, supports many different messaging patterns, and provides support for user-defined patterns. MPI is the workhorse of most HPC applications. It has been in use for a long time and is efficient and thoroughly debugged. The ability to dynamically create processes is an important feature.

Either mechanism is capable of supporting even the most complex communication configuration. Which one should be used on any given project will depend on factors external to the messaging system itself, such as legacy code, software support, and so on.

A brief description of how IPython relies on ZeroMQ as its internal messaging framework was provided. This description provided important information on the internals of IPython as well as illustrated some interesting capabilities of ZeroMQ.

In the next chapter, we will take a look at some important libraries included in the IPython API. This will include more details on accessing results from parallel computations, creating and manipulating workers, and performance profiling.

5
Opening the Toolkit – The IPython API

This chapter covers some useful features of IPython that did not fit in elsewhere and some features that deserved deeper coverage.

The following topics will be covered:

- Performance profiling
- The `AsyncResult` class
- Results metadata
- The `Client` class
- The `View` class (including `DirectView` and `LoadBalancedView`)

 IPython libraries are very flexible in terms of parameters. Most parameters are optional, with sensible defaults. This chapter will not attempt to describe every parameter for every function, but will instead cover the more interesting features provided by these libraries. I have added respective links to the official documentations for further reference.

Performance profiling

Before optimizing a system, it is handy to know exactly which part is slow. IPython adds some specialized tools for this purpose, along with the tools that Python provides.

Using utils.timing

IPython provides a library called `IPython.utils.timing` to time code execution. The library can be useful as relatively lightweight calls to include in code. Here is an example:

```
In [64]: import IPython


In [65]: IPython.utils.timing.clocku()
Out[65]: 218.533777


In [67]: IPython.utils.timing.clocku()
Out[67]: 218.542776
```

This library distinguishes between two categories of time — user CPU time and system CPU time — as evidenced in the following functions:

Function	Description
clocku ( )	Returns the user CPU time in seconds since the start of the process
clocks ( )	Returns the system CPU time in seconds since the start of the process
clock ( )	Returns the total (user + system) CPU time in seconds since the start of the process
clock2 ( )	Returns a tuple of user/system times

Another helpful function is `timings_out`. It takes four arguments:

- `reps`: The number of times to repeat the function
- `func`: The function to call
- `*args`: A list of optional, ordered arguments
- `**kw`: A list of optional keyword/value pair arguments

Here is an example:

```
In [70]: IPython.utils.timing.timings_out(100, math.factorial, 10000)
Out[70]:
(0.44493199999999433,
 0.004449319999999943,
 28462596809170545189990641 … <many more digits> … )
```

The preceding command executed `math.factorial(10000)` one hundred times and returned a tuple consisting of:

- The elapsed CPU time in seconds
- The time per call in seconds
- The output

Using %%timeit

First, an example using plain old Python:

```
In [42]: %%timeit
    ....: sum([1.0/i**3 for i in range(1, 1000)])
    ....:
1000 loops, best of 3: 512 µs per loop
```

And then comes numpy:

```
In [51]: %%timeit
numpy.sum([1.0/numpy.arange(1, 1000)**3])
    ....:
1000 loops, best of 3: 208 µs per loop
```

Note that numpy is not always faster. First, we will see plain old Python:

```
In [52]: %%timeit -n10
s = 0
for i in range(1, 100):
    s = s + 1.0/math.factorial(i)
print(s)
    ....:
1.7182818284590455
1.7182818284590455
1.7182818284590455
1.7182818284590455
1.7182818284590455
1.7182818284590455
1.7182818284590455
1.7182818284590455
1.7182818284590455
```

```
1.7182818284590455
1.7182818284590455
1.7182818284590455
1.7182818284590455
1.7182818284590455
1.7182818284590455
1.7182818284590455
1.7182818284590455
1.7182818284590455
1.7182818284590455
1.7182818284590455
1.7182818284590455
1.7182818284590455
1.7182818284590455
1.7182818284590455
1.7182818284590455
1.7182818284590455
1.7182818284590455
1.7182818284590455
1.7182818284590455
10 loops, best of 3: 209 μs per loop
```

And now, using numpy:

```
In [36]: %%timeit -n10
facts = map(math.factorial, numpy.arange(1,100))
invs = map(lambda x: 1.0/x, facts)
s = numpy.sum(list(invs))
print(s)
   ....:
1.71828182846
1.71828182846
1.71828182846
1.71828182846
1.71828182846
1.71828182846
```

```
1.71828182846
1.71828182846
1.71828182846
1.71828182846
1.71828182846
1.71828182846
1.71828182846
1.71828182846
1.71828182846
1.71828182846
1.71828182846
1.71828182846
1.71828182846
1.71828182846
1.71828182846
1.71828182846
1.71828182846
1.71828182846
1.71828182846
1.71828182846
1.71828182846
1.71828182846
1.71828182846
10 loops, best of 3: 344 µs per loop
```

The %%timeit (and %timeit) accepts a number of options — use ?timeit for details.

Using %%prun

The %%prun magic uses Python's built-in cProfile module. It provides a great deal of more information about where time was spent. In particular, it can break down execution time by function. Here is an example:

```
In [58]: %%prun
s = 0
for i in range(1, 1500):
    s = s + 1/math.factorial(i)
```

```
print(s)
   ....:
1.7182818284590455
         1503 function calls in 0.131 seconds

   Ordered by: internal time

   ncalls  tottime  percall  cumtime  percall filename:lineno(function)
     1499    0.129    0.000    0.129    0.000 {built-in method factorial}
        1    0.002    0.002    0.131    0.131 <string>:2(<module>)
        1    0.000    0.000    0.131    0.131 {built-in method exec}
        1    0.000    0.000    0.000    0.000 {built-in method print}
        1    0.000    0.000    0.000    0.000 {method 'disable' of '_
lsprof.Profiler' objects}
```

It is easy to see from this output that a great deal of time was spent in the factorial function (as expected).

The %% (and %prun) also accepts a number of options — use ?prun for details.

The AsyncResult class

In our previous discussion on IPython in parallel computing (refer to *Chapter 3, Stepping Up to IPython for Parallel Computing*), it was demonstrated how using the map and apply functions can enable parallel computation with a minimal setup by the programmer. These methods return objects of the AsyncResult class (or a subclass). At that time, only a small subset of the class's functionality was required, so a more thorough exploration was delayed. In this section, we will provide a more complete description of the capabilities of an AsyncResult object.

The AsyncResult class provides a superset of the multiprocessing.pool. AsyncResult interface. We will start by looking at the multiprocessing.pool version before examining the new features.

multiprocessing.pool.Pool

This class allows you to create a pool of processes. The constructor takes several optional arguments, including the ones given here:

Argument	Effect
processes	This is the number of worker processes to use. If it is None, then the number returned by os.cpu_count() is used.
initializer	If not None, then each worker process will call initializer(*initargs) when it starts.
maxtasksperchild	Each worker will complete at most maxtasksperchild before being replaced by a new worker. This allows any unused resources owned by a worker to be freed (the default is None, which means that worker processes will live as long as the pool).

Pool provides several useful methods for starting processes and obtaining their results. They fall into two broad categories: blocking and nonblocking.

Blocking methods

Function	Arguments	Effect
apply	func, args, and kwargs	Call func with the args arguments and kwds keyword arguments.
map	func and iterable	This is a parallel equivalent of the built-in map( ) function. It blocks until all results are ready.
imap	func and iterable	This is similar to map but iterates over iterable, one element at a time, and sends them each to a worker process.
imap_unordered	func and iterable	This is similar to imap, but the results are in an arbitrary order.

The map and imap work in a similar manner from the outside, but the differences are worth discussing. The primary difference is that map turns the entire iterable into a list, breaks the list into chunks, then sends the chunks to the workers. On the other hand, imap iterates over iterable, sending one element at a time to the workers. This makes map faster but imap easier on memory, especially when the list produced by iterable is large.

Another effect is that map will block until all results are back, while imap will return results as they are ready, blocking only when they are not. This brings up the difference between imap and imap_unordered—imap will return results in order, blocking if the result for element *i* is not complete, even if the result for element *i+1* is ready. The imap_unordered will return results as they are ready.

Nonblocking methods

Function	Arguments	Effect
apply_async	func, args, and kwargs	This is like apply( ) but returns an ApplyResult
map_async	func and iterable	This is like map ( ) but returns a MapResult

Obtaining results

Each of the results classes have methods that can be used to pull back results. The timeout argument is optional:

Class	Function	Arguments	Effect
ApplyResult	get	timeout	Returns the result
MapResult	get	timeout	Inherited from ApplyResult
IMapIterator	next	timeout	Is iterable
IMapUnorderedIterator	next	timeout	Is iterable

An example program using various methods

The following program illustrates the apply and map styles of function invocation, both synchronously and asynchronously:

```
from multiprocessing import Pool

def f(n):
    curr = n
    tmp = 1
    while curr != 1:
        tmp = tmp + 1
        if curr % 2 == 1:
            curr = 3 * curr + 1
        else:
            curr = curr/2
```

```
        return tmp

  if __name__ == '__main__':
      pool = Pool(processes=4)

      x = pool.apply(f, (1109,))
      print(type(x))
      print(x)

      x = pool.apply_async(f, (1109, ))
      print(type(x))
      print(x.get())

      x = pool.map(f, range(1100, 1110))
      print(type(x))
      print(x)

      x = pool.map_async(f, range(1100, 1110))
      print(type(x))
      print(x.get( ))

      x = pool.imap(f, range(1100, 1110))
      print(type(x))
      for i in x:
          print(i)

      x = pool.imap_unordered(f, range(1100, 1110))
      print(type(x))
      for i in x:
          print(i)
```

It yields the following output:

```
In [41]: %run mp.py
<class 'int'>
19
<class 'multiprocessing.pool.ApplyResult'>
19
<class 'list'>
[94, 94, 45, 45, 19, 94, 138, 138, 19, 19]
<class 'multiprocessing.pool.MapResult'>
[94, 94, 45, 45, 19, 94, 138, 138, 19, 19]
<class 'multiprocessing.pool.IMapIterator'>
```

```
94
94
45
45
19
94
138
138
19
19
<class 'multiprocessing.pool.IMapUnorderedIterator'>
94
94
45
45
94
19
19
138
19
138
```

Note how the imap_unordered method returns results in a different order than the ordered function, regardless of blocking. Different runs have yielded different orders for the same call.

mp.pool.AsyncResult

The mp.pool.AsyncResult class in ipyparallel includes some additional functionality.

Getting results

Function	Arguments	Effect
get	timeout	This blocks and returns the result when it arrives.
get_dict	timeout	This returns a dictionary keyed by engine_id (rather than a list). The get_dict is a wrapper around the get method, so it will block until all results are in.

An example program using various methods

Given a cluster with four engines:

```
from ipyparallel import Client
import os

c = Client( )
dv = c[:]

def f(n):
    from time import sleep
    import random
    curr = n
    tmp = 0
    while curr != 1:
        sleep(random.random( )/1000)
        tmp = tmp + 1
        if curr % 2 == 1:
            curr = 3 * curr + 1
        else:
            curr = curr/2
    return tmp

x = dv.apply(f, 1109)
print(type(x))
results = x.get_dict( )
print("results = ", results)

x = dv.apply_async(f, 63728127)
print(type(x))
print("done yet? ", x.ready( ))
results = x.get( )
print("done now? ", x.ready())
print("results = ", results)

x = dv.map(f, range(1, 10))
print(type(x))
results = x.get_dict( )
print("results in dict = ", results)

x = dv.map(f, range(1, 10))
print(type(x))
results = x.get( )
print("results in list = ", results)

x = dv.map_async(f, range(1100, 1110))
```

```
print(type(x))
results = x.get( )
print("results = ", results)

lbv = c.load_balanced_view( )

x = lbv.map(f, range(1100, 1110))
print(type(x))
results = x.get( )
print("results = ", results)
```

Preceding code yields the following output:

```
In [48]: %run asyncresult2.py
<class 'ipyparallel.client.asyncresult.AsyncResult'>
results =  {0: 18, 1: 18, 2: 18, 3: 18}
<class 'ipyparallel.client.asyncresult.AsyncResult'>
done yet?  False
done now?  True
results =  [949, 949, 949, 949]
<class 'ipyparallel.client.asyncresult.AsyncMapResult'>
results in dict =  {0: 0, 1: 1, 2: 7, 3: 2}
<class 'ipyparallel.client.asyncresult.AsyncMapResult'>
results in list =  [0, 1, 7, 2, 5, 8, 16, 3, 19]
<class 'ipyparallel.client.asyncresult.AsyncMapResult'>
results =  [93, 93, 44, 44, 18, 93, 137, 137, 18, 18]
<class 'ipyparallel.client.asyncresult.AsyncMapResult'>
results =  [93, 93, 44, 44, 18, 93, 137, 137, 18, 18]
```

Note that the same call to map will produce a different number of results depending on whether get or get_dict is called. In particular, get will return all results, while get_dict will return only one result per engine.

AsyncResultSet metadata

Every AsyncResult object has metadata associated with it, contained in its metadata attribute. Given a sample run, a complete listing appears as follows:

```
In [104]: ar = dv.map(f, range(1, 11))

In [105]: ar.get()
Out[105]: [0, 1, 7, 2, 5, 8, 16, 3, 19, 6]
```

```
In [106]: ar.metadata
Out[106]:
[{'after': [],
  'completed': datetime.datetime(2015, 12, 28, 11, 50, 19, 413719),
  'data': {},
  'engine_id': 0,
  'engine_uuid': '845c8de9-dc79-4cd0-94cd-2819855f1111',
  'error': None,
  'execute_input': None,
  'execute_result': None,
  'follow': [],
  'msg_id': '1a8044e3-08a0-4e97-b609-bef89bc452bd',
  'outputs': [],
  'outputs_ready': True,
  'received': datetime.datetime(2015, 12, 28, 11, 50, 23, 852909),
  'started': datetime.datetime(2015, 12, 28, 11, 50, 19, 413062),
  'status': 'ok',
  'stderr': '',
  'stdout': '',
  'submitted': datetime.datetime(2015, 12, 28, 11, 50, 19, 410646)},
 {'after': [],
  'completed': datetime.datetime(2015, 12, 28, 11, 50, 19, 415310),
  'data': {},
  'engine_id': 1,
  'engine_uuid': 'f28f7d85-210e-4686-bbb8-65f8ba7f24e9',
  'error': None,
  'execute_input': None,
  'execute_result': None,
  'follow': [],
  'msg_id': 'd344228f-f2c6-4bbf-a60f-6e956ca27609',
  'outputs': [],
  'outputs_ready': True,
  'received': datetime.datetime(2015, 12, 28, 11, 50, 23, 853522),
  'started': datetime.datetime(2015, 12, 28, 11, 50, 19, 414684),
  'status': 'ok',
  'stderr': '',
  'stdout': '',
  'submitted': datetime.datetime(2015, 12, 28, 11, 50, 19, 412487)},
```

```
{'after': [],
 'completed': datetime.datetime(2015, 12, 28, 11, 50, 19, 416880),
 'data': {},
 'engine_id': 2,
 'engine_uuid': '26875a75-94e9-487f-919a-2dca38138ae0',
 'error': None,
 'execute_input': None,
 'execute_result': None,
 'follow': [],
 'msg_id': '755ffff2-ce9c-492c-966d-d52b19318482',
 'outputs': [],
 'outputs_ready': True,
 'received': datetime.datetime(2015, 12, 28, 11, 50, 23, 854108),
 'started': datetime.datetime(2015, 12, 28, 11, 50, 19, 416270),
 'status': 'ok',
 'stderr': '',
 'stdout': '',
 'submitted': datetime.datetime(2015, 12, 28, 11, 50, 19, 414236)},
{'after': [],
 'completed': datetime.datetime(2015, 12, 28, 11, 50, 19, 418690),
 'data': {},
 'engine_id': 3,
 'engine_uuid': '89c5dda3-3e39-4502-99e3-0cca2b740764',
 'error': None,
 'execute_input': None,
 'execute_result': None,
 'follow': [],
 'msg_id': 'fbd6df9d-e69c-474e-a738-3096fd92c120',
 'outputs': [],
 'outputs_ready': True,
 'received': datetime.datetime(2015, 12, 28, 11, 50, 23, 854686),
 'started': datetime.datetime(2015, 12, 28, 11, 50, 19, 418075),
 'status': 'ok',
 'stderr': '',
 'stdout': '',
 'submitted': datetime.datetime(2015, 12, 28, 11, 50, 19, 416005)}]
```

In this example, there were four engines, so `metadata` is a list of four elements, one per engine. Each element is a dictionary that contains metadata about the execution on that engine.

Metadata keys

Some of the metadata keys deserve a description:

Key	Meaning
submitted	When the job left the client
started	When the engine started executing the job
completed	When the engine completed the job
received	When the client received the result
engine_id	The engine's ID (an int, 0 through n)
pyout	The Python output
pyerr	A Python exception (if one occurred)
status	A string: "ok" or "error"

Other metadata

IPython provides other useful information about `AsyncResults`. For example, given our earlier `AsyncResult`, are:

```
In [107]: ar.elapsed
Out[107]: 4.44404


In [108]: ar.progress
Out[108]: 4


In [109]: ar.serial_time
Out[109]: 0.0025080000000000002


In [110]: ar.wall_time
Out[110]: 4.44404
```

The table outlines the following properties:

Property	Meaning
elapsed	Seconds since job submission
progress	Number of jobs that have completed so far
serial_time	The sum of all times used in computation
wall_time	The elapsed time between the submission of the first job and the reception of the output of the last job

These properties allow for the calculation of some interesting metrics:

Metric	Calculation
progress	ar.progress/len(ar)
speedup	ar.serial_time/ar.wall_time
average compute time	ar.serial_time/len(ar)

The Client class

Although the primary purpose of the Client class is to provide a means to obtain access to one or more View objects, it also has some utility attributes and methods.

Attributes

The following attributes are noteworthy:

Attribute	Meaning
results	A dict of results, keyed by msg_id
outstanding	A set of msg_ids that have been submitted but for which no results have been received

For example:

```
In [112]: c.results
Out[112]:
defaultdict(dict,
            {'0543fa4b-43d6-4280-9424-45c574b75e90': [19, 6],
             '0cde1111-35a9-4fe7-90af-920d4a83a9c9': [16, 3],
             '15c29a7c-b7b9-4738-9d3c-6350dc8953bc': [7],
             '187e9830-8962-438f-a2a6-c0986330c7ff': [7],
```

```
        '1a8044e3-08a0-4e97-b609-bef89bc452bd': [0, 1, 7],

        '2267f2e1-3dd9-4514-804c-6c8cb9c97521': ipyparallel.error.
RemoteError('TypeError', "'int' object is not subscriptable"),

        'e9aac8f6-8625-467e-aa28-a04f20c13274': ipyparallel.error.
RemoteError('TypeError', "'int' object is not subscriptable"),

        'ead4287d-39e0-4f25-86c4-4cad85a3b504': [0, 1, 7],

        'eb7cdb74-721e-4858-81b8-7af69dd2abfd': [2, 5, 8],

        'fbd6df9d-e69c-474e-a738-3096fd92c120': [19, 6]})


In [114]: c.outstanding
Out[114]: set()
```

Methods

The following methods are noteworthy. The functionality provided concerns process control—checking status and killing processes:

Method	Arguments	Effect
abort	jobs (one of): (list of) msg_id AsyncResult target	This removes a job (or jobs) from the execution list of the target. If no jobs are specified, it will remove all outstanding jobs.
get_result	indices_or_msg_ids (one of): (list of) job index (list of) msg_ids	This gets the result of a job by msg_id or history index. The result is an AsyncResult object. This is useful when a job is blocked, as the client will not have access to the information.
queue_status	targets (one of): (list of) int (list of) str	This returns the status of the listed engine queues. It defaults to all queues.
shutdown	targets (one of): list of ints "all" hub: bool	This terminates engine processes. If hub is True, it also terminates the Hub.

For example:

```
In [116]: c.queue_status()
Out[116]:
```

```
{0: {'completed': 9, 'queue': 0, 'tasks': 0},
 1: {'completed': 9, 'queue': 0, 'tasks': 0},
 'unassigned': 0,
 3: {'completed': 9, 'queue': 0, 'tasks': 0},
 2: {'completed': 9, 'queue': 0, 'tasks': 0}}
```

The View class

The `ipyparallel` module declares a `View` class to provide views of engines. The `View` class itself is not meant for use. It should probably be treated as an abstract base class for most purposes. However, it does have two useful subclasses: `DirectView` and `LoadBalancedView`. We will cover the functionality provided by `View` in this section, and the differences introduced by `DirectView` and `LoadBalancedView` in their own sections.

View attributes

`View` provides some useful attributes:

Attribute	Meaning
history	A list of message IDs.
outstanding	The set of message IDs of jobs that are not complete.
results	A dict of `message_id` and result pairs.
targets	The IDs of engines in the current active set. Functions that are applied, mapped, and so on will be executed on these engines.
block	bool, if True, `apply` and `map` will work synchronously. Otherwise, they will work asynchronously. This defaults to False.

Calling Python functions

Many of these functions have been described in other sections. They are repeated here for reference.

Synchronous calls

All synchronous calls block until completion and return (a list of) the appropriate type:

Function	Arguments	Effect
apply_sync	f, *args, and **kwargs	This calls f(*args, **kwargs) on the engines.
map_sync	f, *sequences, and **kwargs	This is a parallel version of Python's built-in map. It applies f to every item of *sequences.

Asynchronous calls

All asynchronous calls return an AsyncResult:

Function	Arguments	Effect
apply_async	f, *args, and **kwargs	This calls f(*args, **kwargs) on the engines.
map_async	f, *sequences, and **kwargs	This is a parallel version of Python's built-in map. It applies f to every item of *sequences.
imap	f, *sequences, and **kwargs	This is a parallel version of itertools.imap. It computes f using arguments from each of the *sequences.

Configurable calls

These calls work as either the synchronous or asynchronous versions described previously, depending on whether the Client that the View is created from has blocking = True or blocking = False:

Function	Arguments	Effect
apply	f, *args, and **kwargs	This calls f(*args, **kwargs) on the engines.
map	f, *sequences, and **kwargs	This is a parallel version of Python's built-in map. It applies f to every item of *.
run	filename	This runs the code in filename on the current target (or targets).
execute	code	This runs code (a string) on the current target (or targets).

Job control

Each View also contains functions for controlling the job in its queue. These are similar to the functions provided in `Client`, but apply only to the engines in the View:

Method	Arguments	Effect
abort	jobs (one of): (list of) str None targets	The (list of) str is a list of msg_id to be aborted. If None, all jobs are aborted. This occurs on all engines listed in targets.
get_result	indices_or_msg_ids (one of): (list of) job index (list of) msg_ids	This gets the result of a job by msg_id or history index. The result is an AsyncResult object. This is useful when a job is blocked, as the client will not have access to the information.
queue_status	targets (one of): (list of) int (list of) str	This returns the status of the listed engine queues. It defaults to all queues.
shutdown	targets (one of): list of ints "all" hub: bool	This terminates engine processes. If hub is True, it also terminates the Hub.

DirectView

A `DirectView` object works as a multiplexer—it has a set of engines (`targets`) and it does the same thing to all of its engines. The basic concept is that a `DirectView` can be treated as if it were a single engine, except that it will execute on multiple engines in parallel.

The effect of this on function execution is straightforward:

- For `apply*` functions, f, `*args`, and `**kwargs` are sent to every engine in the target set.
- For `map*` functions, f, one item from `*sequences`, and `**kwargs` are sent to each engine in the target set. Each engine gets a different item from `*sequences`. If there are more elements in `*sequences` than there are engines, some engines will execute multiple times, with a different item each time.

Data movement

An important feature provided by a `DirectView` is the ability to move data from engine to engine or an engine to the Hub. These mechanisms operate independently of the ZeroMQ and MPI mechanisms discussed earlier.

Dictionary-style data access

The simplest way to handle the `move` data is to treat the entire namespace of all the engines as a simple `dict` contained in the `DirectView` object. This allows for data movement through assignment and subscripting. Given our standard `DirectView` object `dv`, an example will make things clear:

```
In [25]: dv["hello"] = "world"


In [26]: dv["hello"]
Out[26]: ['world', 'world', 'world', 'world']
```

Line 25:

This line sets up a name, `hello`, in each engine and binds it to the `"world"` value.

Line 26:

The value of `hello` can be accessed through the `DirectView` object through subscripting.

Note that as there are four engines, there are four copies of the value—one for each engine. The copying of the value was done automagically by IPython. The exact underlying mechanism is implementation dependent (and a particular mechanism should not be relied upon by an application), but it is probably ZeroMQ. At the application level, objects will be pickled before being sent, so take care to ensure that all data handled in this manner is pickle-able.

Scatter and gather

`DirectView` also supports `scatter` and `gather` operations. A `scatter` operation takes a name and a list of values, splits the list into *n* chunks (where *n* is the number of engines), and assigns the name on each engine to be the sublist corresponding to that engine. Again, an example will clarify this:

```
In [23]: dv.scatter("hello", [1, 3, 9, 27, 81])
Out[23]: <AsyncResult: finished>


In [24]: dv["hello"]
Out[24]: [[1, 3], [9], [27], [81]]
```

The list will be divided into sublists of as equal a size as possible. If an engine would ordinarily receive a single-element list and the optional `flatten` parameter is set, then that engine will receive the single element in the list rather than the entire list. Yet again, here is an example:

```
In [27]: dv.scatter("hello", [1, 3, 9, 27, 81], flatten=True)
Out[27]: <AsyncResult: finished>

In [28]: dv["hello"]
Out[28]: [[1, 3], 9, 27, 81]
```

The corresponding `gather` function will bring all the values back into the `DirectView`:

```
In [34]: dv.scatter("hello", [1, 3, 9, 27, 81])
Out[34]: <AsyncResult: finished>

In [35]: ar = dv.gather("hello")

In [36]: ar
Out[36]: <AsyncMapResult: finished>

In [37]: ar.get()
Out[37]: [1, 3, 9, 27, 81]
```

Push and pull

The `push` and `pull` functions provide straightforward mechanisms for fine-grained control of data movement. The `push` function accepts a dictionary and a (optional) list of targets as arguments and updates the targets' namespaces with that dictionary. The `pull` function accepts a name and a list of targets and returns a list containing the value of the name on those targets. For example:

```
In [43]: dv.push({"hello":"world"})
Out[43]: <AsyncResult: _push>

In [44]: dv["hello"]
Out[44]: ['world', 'world', 'world', 'world']

In [45]: dv.push({"hello":"dolly"}, [2,3])
Out[45]: <AsyncResult: finished>
```

```
In [46]: dv["hello"]
Out[46]: ['world', 'world', 'dolly', 'dolly']


In [48]: ar = dv.pull("hello", [1,2])


In [49]: ar
Out[49]: <AsyncResult: finished>


In [50]: ar.get()
Out[50]: ['world', 'dolly']
```

Imports

Consider the following straightforward computation of a hailstone sequence, with a random sleep thrown in:

```
import time
import random

def f(n):
    curr = n
    tmp = 0
    time.sleep(random.random())
    while curr != 1:
        tmp = tmp + 1
        if curr % 2 == 1:
            curr = 3 * curr + 1
        else:
            curr = curr/2
    return tmp
```

Calling `f` from the IPython command line works as expected:

```
In [15]: f(28)
Out[15]: 18
```

Running it in parallel also looks smooth:

```
In [7]: !ipcluster start -n 4 &


In [8]: 2015-12-29 11:35:37.593 [IPClusterStart] Removing pid file:
2015-12-29 11:35:37.593 [IPClusterStart] Starting ipcluster with
[daemon=False]
```

```
2015-12-29 11:35:37.619 [IPClusterStart] Starting Controller with
LocalControllerLauncher
2015-12-29 11:35:38.624 [IPClusterStart] Starting 4 Engines with
LocalEngineSetLauncher
2015-12-29 11:36:08.952 [IPClusterStart] Engines appear to have started
successfully



In [8]: from ipyparallel import Client


In [10]: c = Client()


In [11]: dv = c[:]


In [12]: %run hail2.py


In [13]: ar = dv.map(f, range(1, 11))


In [14]: ar
Out[14]: <AsyncMapResult: finished>
```

The problem first becomes apparent when attempting to access the results:

```
In [17]: ar[0]
[0:apply]:
-------------------------------------------------------------
----------NameError
     Traceback (most recent call last)<string> in <module>()
<remotefunction.py> in <lambda>(f, *sequences)
    229              if self._mapping:
    230                  if sys.version_info[0] >= 3:
--> 231                      f = lambda f, *sequences: list(map(f,
*sequences))
    232                  else:
    233                      f = map
<hail2.py> in f(n)
      5      curr = n
      6      tmp = 0
----> 7      time.sleep(random.random())
```

```
8        while curr != 1:
9            tmp = tmp + 1
NameError: name 'time' is not defined
```

One could (and should) always check the metadata to determine whether an error has occurred:

```
In [21]: ar.metadata[0].status
Out[21]: 'error'
```

```
In [22]: ar.metadata[0].error
Out[22]: ipyparallel.error.RemoteError('NameError', "name 'time' is not
defined")
```

However, the real question is: why did the error happen? The answer is that when IPython starts an engine, it does not copy the environment of the Hub to the engine. Running the program in the interactive session imports the libraries into the interactive session only. Calling the function on an engine does not import the library into the engine.

The solution is to simultaneously import modules locally and globally using the sync_imports context manager. This will force the import to happen on all active engines in the DirectView. The following lines will fix the problem:

```
In [23]: with dv.sync_imports( ):
   ....:       import time
   ....:
importing time on engine(s)
```

```
In [24]: with dv.sync_imports( ):
   ....:       import random
   ....:
importing random on engine(s)
```

```
In [25]: ar = dv.map(f, range(1, 11))
```

```
In [26]: ar
Out[26]: <AsyncMapResult: finished>
```

```
In [27]: ar.get()
Out[27]: [0, 1, 7, 2, 5, 8, 16, 3, 19, 6]
```

Discussion

An alternative way to achieve the same results without using `sync_imports` is to move the `import` statements into the function body. Both approaches have their advantages and drawbacks:

	sync_import	Function body
Advantages	There is centralized control of the environment. It clarifies what modules are being imported.	It is easier to determine what libraries are actually in use. This Eases refactoring.
Drawbacks	This moves `import` away from where it is used. It imports a module to every engine, even if only some use it.	This violates the PEP08 Style Guide. It is less efficient on repeated function calls.

At the bottom, the conflict between the two approaches is between centralization and localization. This conflict crops up whenever a system is complex enough to require configuration. There is no single solution that will be right for every project. The best that can be done is to settle for an approach and use it consistently while also keeping in mind any problems that the approach brings with it.

LoadBalancedView

A `LoadBalancedView` uses a scheduler to execute jobs one at a time, but without blocking. The basic concept is that a `LoadBalancedView` can be treated as if it were a single engine, except that instead of waiting for the engine to finish before submitting the next job, one can simply submit another immediately. The scheduler is responsible for determining when and where each job will run.

The effect of this on function execution is straightforward:

- For `apply*` functions, the scheduler provides an engine and `f`, `*args`, and `**kwargs` are executed on that engine.
- For `map*` functions, `*sequences` is iterated over. Moreover, `f`, the next item from `*sequences`, and `**kwargs` are sent to the engine provided by the scheduler.

Data movement

The data movement functionality of DirectView depends on knowing the engine on which each process is running. A LoadBalancedView allows the scheduler to assign each process to an engine, so this information is not available. As such, the data movement functionality of DirectView is not available in a LoadBalancedView.

Data movement in a LoadBalancedView requires external mechanisms, such as ZeroMQ or MPI. These mechanisms provide alternative ways of determining process location (for example, MPI's rank indicator) or a means of specifying a connection endpoint (such as ZeroMQ's use of port numbers).

Using MPI and ZeroMQ for data movement is a big enough topic to warrant a chapter on its own. See *Chapter 4*, *Messaging with ZeroMQ and MPI*, for more details.

Imports

The situation with imports is the same in a LoadBalancedView and a DirectView.

Summary

In this chapter, we saw a variety of useful features provided by IPython. While no single feature is of game-changing importance, each provides the right tool for its job.

IPython's timing utilities, whether through the utils.timing or the timeit and prun magics, provide a quick and easy way to measure application performance.

The AsyncResult class provides more than a variety of different methods of obtaining results from asynchronous jobs. Metadata about the results is also available, allowing the developer to access important information such as when a job was started and its error status.

Given this data about jobs, the Client class provides access to job-control functionality. In particular, queues can be accessed and jobs and engines can be stopped based on their status.

A Client object can be used to obtain a View object (either a DirectView or a LoadBalancedView). Both Views are the primary mechanisms by which jobs are started on engines.

`DirectView` works as a multiplexer. It has a set of engines (targets) and it does the same thing to all of its engines. This allows the developer to treat a set of engines as if they were a single entity. An important capability of a `DirectView` is its ability to make things "the same" on all of its target engines. In particular, `DirectView` provides mechanisms for data movement (a global dictionary, scatter-gather, and push-pull) and for managing the environment (the `sync_imports` context manager).

A `LoadBalancedView` also allows multiple engines to be treated as a single engine. In this case, however, the conceptual model is that of a single, nonblocking engine rather than a set of engines. The controller can feed multiple jobs to the `LoadBalancedView` without blocking. For its part, the `LoadBalancedView` depends on a scheduler to actually execute the jobs. This does not change the environmental management situation with respect to a `DirectView`, but it does necessitate an external data movement tool, such as MPI or ZeroMQ.

While this chapter briefly outlined some of the more useful features of IPython's libraries, IPython cannot do everything itself. In the next chapter, we will take a look at how additional languages can be combined with Python to further expand the range of available tools.

6
Works Well with Others – IPython and Third-Party Tools

No tool, even one as powerful and flexible as IPython, can be everything to everybody. This chapter takes a look at some specialized tools that integrate well with IPython and provide useful, if specialized, functionality. Of particular interest are tools that can be used for data analysis and machine learning.

The choice of which language to use on a project is impacted by many factors; familiarity, fitness to the task, supporting libraries, curiosity, managerial fiat, and many other considerations come into play. Each project has its own reasons, and general advice on which tool is "better" is very limited in applicability.

As such, this chapter will attempt to steer away from questions of the form, "Why would I use X instead of Y?" and instead stick to the more practical "How do other tools that I am interested in using work with IPython?" A few popular and interesting examples have been selected as important representatives of a growing set of tools that integrate well with IPython.

The following tools will be examined:

- The R language (used in statistics)
- Octave (for numerical processing)
- Hy (a functional language)

 Each of these tools is worthy of a book (or several) in its own right. This chapter will concentrate on getting the tool to integrate with IPython and note some situations in which this integration might be useful. The author apologizes in advance if the coding style used is not up to the highest standards in the various languages.

R

The R language (or just R) is a programming language that is widely used by statisticians and data analysts. It is similar to Python in that it is interpreted and supports a command line. It overlaps with NumPy in that it supports advanced mathematical objects such as arrays and matrix operations. It also provides built-in graphics functionality for visualization. The R language is free software under the FSF's GNU GPL. More information is available at `https://www.r-project.org`.

The rpy2 module/extension

The entry point for using R in IPython is the `rpy2` module/extension. When used as an extension, `rpy2` allows the use of the `%R` and `%%R` magics. When used as a module, `rpy2` can be imported and used as a "normal" module in Python/IPython programs. The magics are appropriate when R code is meant to be used in conjunction with standard Python, while the modules are useful when writing Python code that will invoke some R functionality. We will outline the installation procedure for `rpy2` and then discuss both approaches.

Using `rpy2` requires that an instance of R be installed on your system. `rpy2` works by starting up an instance of R that is shared by each magic invocation, so you must have permissions to start an instance of R. The directions for installing R vary from platform to platform, and some package managers (for example, Conda) can also install it.

Installing rpy2

The standard steps for installing any IPython module apply: use either `pip` or `easy_install`, as applicable. Here is an example:

```
pip install rpy2
```

This will install the required source files in the appropriate directory for extensions.

Using Rmagic

Once `rpy2` is installed, the following command can be issued at the IPython command line:

```
In [3]: %load_ext rpy2.ipython
```

At this point, the `%R`, `%%R`, `%Rpush`, and `%Rpull` magics become available for use.

The %R magic

The `%R` magic provides the ability to specify R one-liners:

```
In [10]: %R mat = matrix(c(1, 2, 3, 4, 5, 6), nrow=2, byrow=TRUE)
Out[10]:
array([[ 1.,   2.,   3.],
       [ 4.,   5.,   6.]])
```

The `%R` magic returns the value of the calculation performed, so it can be saved to a variable. Here, we transpose a matrix:

```
In [36]: x = %R t(matrix(c(1, 2, 3, 4, 5, 6, 7, 8, 9), nrow=3,
byrow=TRUE))


In [37]: x
Out[37]:
array([[ 1.,   4.,   7.],
       [ 2.,   5.,   8.],
       [ 3.,   6.,   9.]])
```

If multiple R statements are required, they can be separated by semicolons. Here, we multiply a matrix by its transposition:

```
In [4]: x = %R mat = matrix(c(1, 2, 3, 4, 5, 6, 7, 8, 9), nrow=3,
byrow=TRUE); mat %*% t(mat)


In [5]: x
Out[5]:
array([[  14.,    32.,    50.],
       [  32.,    77.,   122.],
       [  50.,   122.,   194.]])
```

And we find eigenvalues and eigenvectors. Note the automatic conversion of the results into appropriate Python classes:

```
In [9]: x = %R mat = matrix(c(1, 2, 3, 4, 5, 6, 7, 8, 9), nrow=3,
byrow=TRUE); eigen(mat)


In [10]: x
Out[10]:
<ListVector - Python:0x2b015f8e1348 / R:0x18c2e88>
```

```
[FloatVector, Matrix]
  values: <class 'rpy2.robjects.vectors.FloatVector'>
  <FloatVector - Python:0x2b015f8e1508 / R:0x332b058>
[16.116844, -1.116844, -0.000000]
  vectors: <class 'rpy2.robjects.vectors.Matrix'>
  <Matrix - Python:0x2b015a2304c8 / R:0x3329780>
[-0.231971, -0.525322, -0.818673, ..., 0.408248, -0.816497, 0.408248]
```

Take care while formatting your R. This code is very similar-looking:

```
In [45]: x = %R mat = matrix(c(1, 2, 3, 4, 5, 6, 7, 8,
9), nrow=3, byrow=TRUE); mat %*% t(mat);
```

But it yields an empty value:

```
In [46]: x
```

The %%R magic

The %%R magic allows for multiline R programs. This can be handy when writing a more involved program. In this example, we use the built-in mtcars data frame and run a t-test to determine whether four-cylinder cars get statistically different mileage from eight-cylinder cars:

```
In [30]: %%R
    ....: fourCyl <- mtcars[mtcars$cyl == 4,]
    ....: eightCyl <- mtcars[mtcars$cyl == 8,]
    ....: t.test(fourCyl$mpg, eightCyl$mpg)
    ....:


        Welch Two Sample t-test


data:  fourCyl$mpg and eightCyl$mpg
t = 7.5967, df = 14.967, p-value = 1.641e-06
alternative hypothesis: true difference in means is not equal to 0
95 percent confidence interval:
  8.318518 14.808755
sample estimates:
mean of x mean of y
 26.66364  15.10000
```

This code is interesting enough to look more closely at:

- **Line 1**: This magic starts the multiline R interpreter. Unlike the %R magic, it does not return anything to IPython by default. The values of variables can be pushed to/from R using commands that will be covered later in this section.

- **Lines 2-3**: These lines slice the mtcars dataset/array. A subscript notation is used, where the subscript is a test. In English, line 2 translates to "return all the lines in mtcars for which the cyl column has the value 4" (similarly for line 3 and eight cylinders). The comma is required.

 There is a subtle difference in R between = and <-, but it need not concern us here. For our purposes, replacing the equal to sign with the arrow would make no difference.

- **Line 4**: This performs a t-test comparing the mpg columns of the four- and eight-cylinder cars we separated out in the previous lines. To make a long story short, given the cars included in the dataset, four-cylinder cars almost certainly make better gas mileage than eight-cylinder cars.

Pulling and pushing

Given our previous example, it might be interesting to know which cars had four cylinders (perhaps they were not representative of four-cylinder cars in general and our test would be less informative than we thought). Despite the fact that the %%R magic does not return a value and the magic is over, that data has not gone away. It was stored in the fourCyl variable, which lives on in the shared R instance and can be pulled into IPython using the %Rpull magic:

```
In [40]: %Rpull fourCyl


In [41]: fourCyl
Out[41]:
```

	mpg	cyl	disp	hp	drat	wt	qsec	vs	am	gear
carb										
Datsun 710 1	22.8	4	108.0	93	3.85	2.320	18.61	1	1	4
Merc 240D 2	24.4	4	146.7	62	3.69	3.190	20.00	1	0	4
Merc 230 2	22.8	4	140.8	95	3.92	3.150	22.90	1	0	4

Fiat 128	32.4	4	78.7	66	4.08	2.200	19.47	1	1	4
1										
Honda Civic	30.4	4	75.7	52	4.93	1.615	18.52	1	1	4
2										
Toyota Corolla	33.9	4	71.1	65	4.22	1.835	19.90	1	1	4
1										
Toyota Corona	21.5	4	120.1	97	3.70	2.465	20.01	1	0	3
1										
Fiat X1-9	27.3	4	79.0	66	4.08	1.935	18.90	1	1	4
1										
Porsche 914-2	26.0	4	120.3	91	4.43	2.140	16.70	0	1	5
2										
Lotus Europa	30.4	4	95.1	113	3.77	1.513	16.90	1	1	5
2										
Volvo 142E	21.4	4	121.0	109	4.11	2.780	18.60	1	1	4
2										

The `%Rpush` magic works in a similar fashion, except that it supports moving values from IPython to R:

```
In [42]: testMat = [1, 2, 3, 4, 5, 6, 7, 8, 9]


In [43]: %Rpush testMat


In [44]: x = %R mat = matrix(testMat, nrow=3, byrow=TRUE); eigen(mat)


In [45]: x
Out[45]:
<ListVector - Python:0x2b015f8df3c8 / R:0x1262078>
[FloatVector, Matrix]
  values: <class 'rpy2.robjects.vectors.FloatVector'>
  <FloatVector - Python:0x2b01636c2ac8 / R:0x2866588>
[16.116844, -1.116844, -0.000000]
  vectors: <class 'rpy2.robjects.vectors.Matrix'>
  <Matrix - Python:0x2b01636c2f88 / R:0x3801d28>
[-0.231971, -0.525322, -0.818673, ..., 0.408248, -0.816497, 0.408248]
```

Note that in both cases, the name of the variable is the same in IPython and R.

Graphics

In order to make plotting work using Rmagics, it is necessary to start IPython in a mode that supports graphics. A simple way is to start it in a `qtconsole`:

```
ipython qtconsole
```

This will pop up a graphical interface. In this example, we simply call the `plot` function to bring up a simple scatter plot of each car's weight against its mileage:

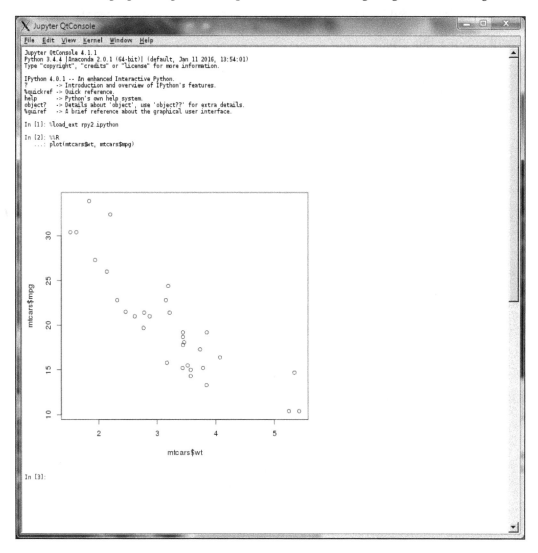

It looks as if heavier cars get worse mileage. We can always check by fitting a curve or two. Consider the following code:

```
%%R
plot(mtcars$wt, mtcars$mpg, xlab="Weight", ylab="MPG", main="Weight vs.
Mileage")
abline(lm(mtcars$mpg~mtcars$wt))
fit <- lm(mtcars$mpg~poly(mtcars$wt, 2, raw=TRUE))
lines(sort(mtcars$wt), fitted(fit)[order(mtcars$wt)], col="red")
```

It will produce this graph:

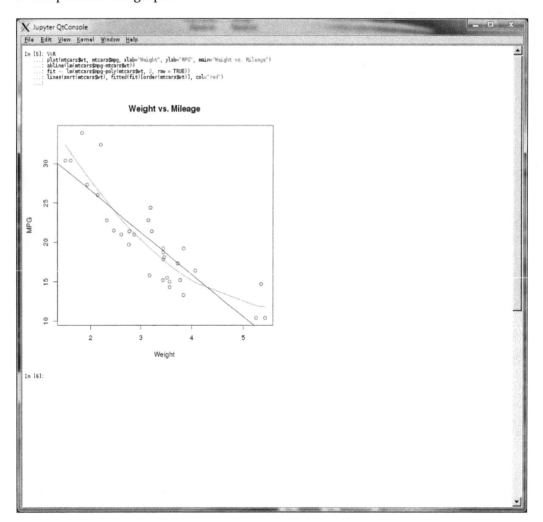

This fits a straight line and a quadratic equation to the data.

Using rpy2.robjects

rpy2 can be imported as a standard module and used from IPython's command line. There are various ways of doing this, and the option exists for the developer to build their own by building on top of rpy2.interface. The rpy2.objects module is a popular choice for general development.

The basics

When you import the rpy2.robjects module, a singleton object, r, is loaded. This is the entry point to an R process. Here is an example:

```
In [5]: import rpy2.robjects as robjects


In [6]: robjects.r
Out[6]: <rpy2.robjects.R at 0x2ad3d0960a90>
```

Elements from an R session are available as attributes of the robjects.r object:

```
In [7]: robjects.r.mtcars
Out[7]:
<DataFrame - Python:0x2ad3d0dfd6c8 / R:0x262cef0>
[Float..., Float..., Float..., ..., Float..., Float..., Float...]
  mpg: <class 'rpy2.robjects.vectors.FloatVector'>
  <FloatVector - Python:0x2ad3d0dfdb08 / R:0x2daf890>
[21.000000, 21.000000, 22.800000, ..., 19.700000, 15.000000, 21.400000]
  cyl: <class 'rpy2.robjects.vectors.FloatVector'>
  <FloatVector - Python:0x2ad3d0e03488 / R:0x345aba0>
[6.000000, 6.000000, 4.000000, ..., 6.000000, 8.000000, 4.000000]
  disp: <class 'rpy2.robjects.vectors.FloatVector'>
  <FloatVector - Python:0x2ad3d0e03988 / R:0x33ed340>
[160.000000, 160.000000, 108.000000, ..., 145.000000, 301.000000,
121.000000]
  ...
  mpg: <class 'rpy2.robjects.vectors.FloatVector'>
  <FloatVector - Python:0x2ad3d0e03fc8 / R:0x38dfd40>
[1.000000, 1.000000, 1.000000, ..., 1.000000, 1.000000, 1.000000]
  cyl: <class 'rpy2.robjects.vectors.FloatVector'>
```

```
<FloatVector - Python:0x2ad3d0e06508 / R:0x2847ca0>
[4.000000, 4.000000, 4.000000, ..., 5.000000, 5.000000, 4.000000]
  disp: <class 'rpy2.robjects.vectors.FloatVector'>
  <FloatVector - Python:0x2ad3d0e06a08 / R:0x3bc0b60>
[4.000000, 4.000000, 1.000000, ..., 6.000000, 8.000000, 2.000000]
```

For the most part, everything that can be done with an Rmagic can be done with `robjects.r`:

```
In [18]: %%R
   ....: letters
   ....:
 [1] "a" "b" "c" "d" "e" "f" "g" "h" "i" "j" "k" "l" "m" "n" "o" "p" "q"
"r" "s"
[20] "t" "u" "v" "w" "x" "y" "z"
```

```
In [19]: robjects.r.letters
Out[19]:
<StrVector - Python:0x2ad3d8887f48 / R:0x4735690>
['a', 'b', 'c', ..., 'x', 'y', 'z']
```

However, the correspondence is not exact, as this attempt to access the wt column of the mtcars data frame will demonstrate:

```
In [8]: robjects.r.mtcars$mpg
  File "<ipython-input-8-d46a62a01451>", line 1
    robjects.r.mtcars$mpg
                     ^
SyntaxError: invalid syntax
```

A numeric index is required:

```
In [17]: robjects.r.mtcars[5]
Out[17]:
<FloatVector - Python:0x2ad3d887efc8 / R:0x31b0650>
[2.620000, 2.875000, 2.320000, ..., 2.770000, 3.570000, 2.780000]
```

Interoperability issues

The complete details of element extraction are beyond the scope of this book. This is a case where the different semantics of R and Python make for less-than-seamless interoperability.

Interpreting a string as R

The r object can be fed a standard string, which it will interpret and execute as R:

```
In [24]: robjects.r("mat = matrix(c(1, 2, 3, 4, 5, 6, 7, 8, 9), nrow=3,
byrow=TRUE)")
Out[24]:
array([[ 1.,   2.,   3.],
       [ 4.,   5.,   6.],
       [ 7.,   8.,   9.]])
```

It will return the value in mostly the same way as the %R magic does:

```
In [26]: x = robjects.r("mat = matrix(c(1, 2, 3, 4, 5, 6, 7, 8, 9),
nrow=3, byrow=TRUE); eigen(mat)")


In [27]: x
Out[27]:
<ListVector - Python:0x2ad3db323148 / R:0x387e270>
[FloatVector, Matrix]
  values: <class 'rpy2.robjects.vectors.FloatVector'>
  <FloatVector - Python:0x2ad3db3231c8 / R:0x3284b38>
[16.116844, -1.116844, -0.000000]
  vectors: <class 'rpy2.robjects.vectors.Matrix'>
  <Matrix - Python:0x2ad3db323608 / R:0x27cf050>
[-0.231971, -0.525322, -0.818673, ..., 0.408248, -0.816497, 0.408248]


In [28]: print(x)
$values
[1]   1.611684e+01 -1.116844e+00 -1.303678e-15


$vectors
           [,1]         [,2]        [,3]
[1,] -0.2319707 -0.78583024   0.4082483
```

```
[2,] -0.5253221 -0.08675134 -0.8164966
[3,] -0.8186735  0.61232756  0.4082483
```

The `rpy2.robjects.RObject` class supports the `r_repr( )` method, which returns a string representation of the object, suitable for use by R. Here is an example:

```
In [4]: a = robjects.Vector([1, 2, 3, 4, 5])


In [5]: b = robjects.Vector([2, 3, 5, 7, 11])


In [6]: robjects.r("plot(%s, %s)" % (a.r_repr( ), b.r_repr( )))
Out[6]: rpy2.rinterface.NULL
```

It produces the following plot:

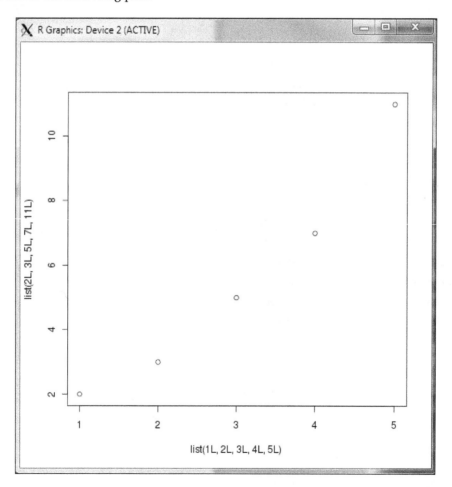

Octave

Octave is a language designed for numerical computing, available under the GNU General Public License. Its home page, at `https://www.gnu.org/software/octave/`, says:

> *"GNU Octave is a high-level interpreted language, primarily intended for numerical computations. It provides capabilities for the numerical solution of linear and nonlinear problems, and for performing other numerical experiments. It also provides extensive graphics capabilities for data visualization and manipulation. Octave is normally used through its interactive command line interface, but it can also be used to write non-interactive programs. The Octave language is quite similar to Matlab so that most programs are easily portable."*

Readers who have attended to the section on using R will find setting up and invoking R and Octave to be very similar. Similar examples are used to ease comparison.

The oct2py module/extension

The entry point for the use of Octave in IPython is the `oct2py` module/extension. When used as an extension, `oct2py` allows the use of the `%octave` and `%%octave` magics. When used as a module, it can be imported and used as a "normal" module in Python/IPython programs. We will outline the installation procedure for `oct2py`, and then discuss both approaches.

Installing oct2py

The standard steps for installing any IPython module apply: use either `pip` or `easy_install`, as applicable. For example:

```
pip install oct2py
```

This will install the required source files in the appropriate directory for extensions.

Using Octave magic

Once `oct2py` is installed, the following command can be issued at the IPython command line:

```
In [3]: %load_ext oct2py.ipython
```

At this, point the `%octave`, `%%octave`, `%octave_push`, and `%octave_pull` magics become available for use.

The %octave magic

The `%octave` magic provides the ability to specify Octave one-liners:

```
In [5]: %octave mat = [1 2 3; 4 5 6]
mat =


   1   2   3
   4   5   6
```

The `%octave` magic returns the value of its calculation, so it can be assigned to a variable. Here, we transpose a matrix:

```
In [6]: x = %octave [1 2 3; 4 5 6; 7 8 9]'
ans =


   1   4   7
   2   5   8
   3   6   9


In [7]: x
Out[7]:
array([[ 1.,   4.,   7.],
       [ 2.,   5.,   8.],
       [ 3.,   6.,   9.]])
```

If multiple Octave statements are needed, they can be separated by semicolons. Here, we multiply a matrix by its transposition:

```
In [2]: x = %octave mat = [1 2 3; 4 5 6; 7 8 9]; mat * mat'
ans =


    14     32     50
    32     77    122
    50    122    194


In [3]: x
Out[3]:
array([[  14.,    32.,    50.],
       [  32.,    77.,   122.],
       [  50.,   122.,   194.]])
```

We find the eigenvalues and eigenvectors:

```
In [13]: %octave mat = [1 2 3; 4 5 6; 7 8 9]; [vect, vals] = eig(mat)
vect =

  -0.231971  -0.785830   0.408248
  -0.525322  -0.086751  -0.816497
  -0.818673   0.612328   0.408248


vals =


Diagonal Matrix

   1.6117e+01            0            0
            0  -1.1168e+00            0
            0            0  -1.3037e-15
```

Tricky issues

Note that the syntax/semantics can be tricky here. The definition of the `eig` function in the Octave language specifies the following behavior:

- `lambda = eig(A)` returns the eigenvalues of A in the vector lambda.
- `[V, lambda] = eig(A)` also returns the eigenvectors in V, but `lambda` is now a matrix whose diagonals contain the eigenvalues. This relationship holds true (within round-off errors): `A =V*lambda*inv(V)`.

The `[a, b]` notation and multiple return values do not carry over cleanly into IPython.

So, this sort of works as expected (one might as well expect x to be a two-element vector):

```
In [14]: x = %octave mat = [1 2 3; 4 5 6; 7 8 9]; eig(mat)
ans =


   1.6117e+01
  -1.1168e+00
  -1.3037e-15


In [15]: x
```

```
Out[15]:
array([[  1.61168440e+01],
       [ -1.11684397e+00],
       [ -1.30367773e-15]])
```

But these do not:

```
In [16]: (x, y) = %octave mat = [1 2 3; 4 5 6; 7 8 9]; eig(mat)
  File "<ipython-input-16-dabd763ad744>", line 1
    (x, y) = %octave mat = [1 2 3; 4 5 6; 7 8 9]; eig(mat)
             ^
SyntaxError: invalid syntax


In [17]: [x, y] = %octave mat = [1 2 3; 4 5 6; 7 8 9]; eig(mat)
  File "<ipython-input-17-03cdb576522c>", line 1
    [x, y] = %octave mat = [1 2 3; 4 5 6; 7 8 9]; eig(mat)
             ^
SyntaxError: invalid syntax


In [18]: (x, y) = %octave mat = [1 2 3; 4 5 6; 7 8 9]; [vect, vals] =
eig(mat)
  File "<ipython-input-18-33006e3e67a7>", line 1
    (x, y) = %octave mat = [1 2 3; 4 5 6; 7 8 9]; [vect, vals] = eig(mat)
             ^
SyntaxError: invalid syntax
```

Even valid syntax yields unexpected results:

```
In [19]: x = %octave mat = [1 2 3; 4 5 6; 7 8 9]; [vect, vals] = eig(mat)
vect =

  -0.231971  -0.785830   0.408248
  -0.525322  -0.086751  -0.816497
  -0.818673   0.612328   0.408248


vals =

Diagonal Matrix

   1.6117e+01            0            0
```

```
        0   -1.1168e+00              0
        0              0  -1.3037e-15
```

```
In [20]: x
```

Unlike R, putting a semicolon at the end of the statement does not break the return value, although it will prevent Octave from printing the answer:

```
In [21]: x = %octave mat = [1 2 3; 4 5 6; 7 8 9]; eig(mat);
```

```
In [22]: x
Out[22]:
array([[  1.61168440e+01],
       [ -1.11684397e+00],
       [ -1.30367773e-15]])
```

The answer has not disappeared—it can be retrieved using the `%octave_pull` magic, discussed in the next section.

The %%octave magic

The `%%octave` magic allows for multiline Octave programs. This can be handy when writing a more involved program. In this example, we solve a system of linear equations:

$4x + y - 2z = 0$

$2x - 3y + 3z = 9$

$-6x - 2y + 1 = 0$

```
In [28]: %%octave
    ....: a = [4 1 -2; 2 -3 3; -6 -2 1]
    ....: b = [0 9 0]'
    ....: inv(a) * b
    ....:
a =

    4    1   -2
    2   -3    3
```

```
   -6   -2    1

b =

    0
    9
    0

ans =

    0.75000
   -2.00000
    0.50000
```

Note that the `%%octave` magic, like the `%%R` magic, does not return anything to IPython by default.

Pushing and pulling

Despite the fact that the `%%octave` magic does not return a value, the values that it calculates do not go away. They can be retrieved using the `%octave_pull` magic, like this:

```
In [31]: %octave_pull a

In [32]: a
Out[32]:
array([[ 4.,   1.,  -2.],
       [ 2.,  -3.,   3.],
       [-6.,  -2.,   1.]])
```

The same goes for `%octave_push`, except that it is from IPython to Octave:

```
In [27]: b = [16, -8, 0]

In [28]: %octave_push b

In [29]: %%octave
   ....: b = cast(b, 'double')
   ....: a = [7 5 -3; 3 -5 2; 5 3 -7]
   ....: b = b'
```

```
....: c = inv(a) * b;
....:
b =

   16    -8     0

a =

    7     5    -3
    3    -5     2
    5     3    -7

b =

   16
   -8
    0

In [30]: %octave_pull c

In [31]: c
Out[31]:
array([[ 1.],
       [ 3.],
       [ 2.]])
```

Note the required cast in the preceding Octave code. Leaving out the cast results in a stack trace and an error message: **binary operator '*' not implemented for 'matrix' by 'int64 matrix' operations**. Pushing to Octave is not as seamless as pulling from it.

Graphics

In order to make plotting work using Octave magics, it is necessary to start IPython in a mode that supports graphics. A simple way is to start it in a qtconsole:

```
ipython qtconsole
```

In this example, we plot a simple sine wave:

```
%%octave

x = linspace(0, 7, 100)

y = sin(x)

plot(x, y)
```

This yields the following graph:

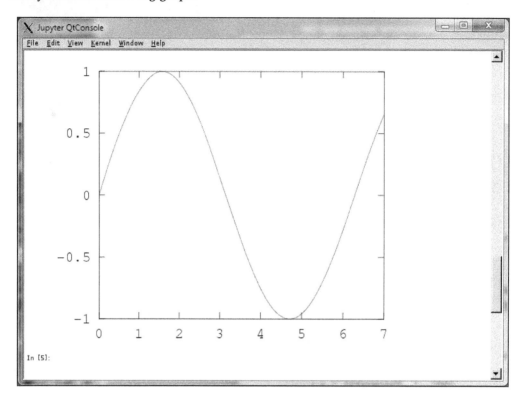

Of course, no example of Octave plotting is complete without the built-in sombrero plot:

```
%%octave
sombrero( )
```

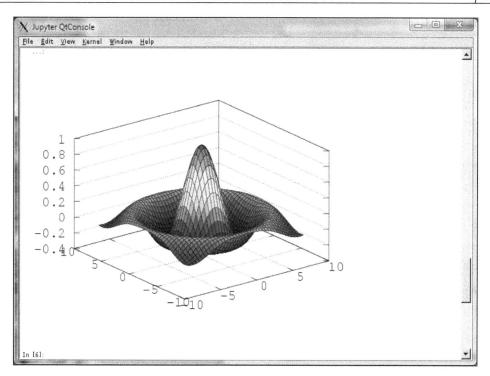

Using the Octave module

Octave functionality can also be accessed by using normal Python-style calls. This can be accomplished by importing from the `oct2py` library:

```
In [2]: from oct2py import octave
```

At this point, all of Octave's built-in functions are available:

```
In [4]: octave.ones(3)
Out[4]:
array([[ 1.,   1.,   1.],
       [ 1.,   1.,   1.],
       [ 1.,   1.,   1.]])


In [5]: octave.rand( )
Out[5]: 0.045109287947966467
```

This includes their help information:

```
In [6]: help(octave.rand)


Help on function rand in module oct2py.core:


rand(*args, **kwargs)
    'rand' is a function from the file /usr/local/octave/3.6.4/lib/
octave/3.6.4/oct/x86_64-unknown-linux-gnu/rand.oct


    -- Loadable Function:   rand (N)


<more help info omitted for space>
```

Pushing and pulling

Pushing and pulling variables and values is also supported:

```
In [7]: octave.push('smallPrimes', octave.primes(100))


In [8]: octave.pull('smallPrimes')
Out[8]:
array([[  2.,    3.,    5.,    7.,   11.,   13.,   17.,   19.,   23.,   29.,   31.,
         37.,   41.,   43.,   47.,   53.,   59.,   61.,   67.,   71.,   73.,   79.,
         83.,   89.,   97.]])
```

The details of how the IPython and Octave type systems work together are beyond the scope of this section, but there is an excellent list of conversions at the **Oct2Py** site:

```
https://blink1073.github.io/oct2py/source/conversions.html
```

More complicated data structures are provided by Oct2py's `Struct` library, which supports dictionary and attribute style access.

Running Octave code

One of the handiest features of `oct2py` is the ability to run Octave code stored in external text files (M-files). Given the following Octave script stored in `/nfs/02/wit0096/Packt/chap06/myIntegrate.m`:

```
function retval = myIntegrate( )
```

```
  retval = quad("myFunc", 0, pi)
  disp("hello")
endfunction


function y = myFunc(x)
  y = sin(x) * sqrt(abs(cos(x)))
endfunction
```

We can use these IPython commands to run it:

```
In [1]: from oct2py import octave


In [2]: octave.addpath("/nfs/02/wit0096/Packt/chap06/")


In [3]: octave.myIntegrate( )
Out[3]: 1.3333333333333326
```

This yields an easy integration of a complicated function.

Hy

Sometimes, nothing less than a functional programming language will do. This is especially true in machine learning and artificial intelligence, where Lisp and Scheme have a long tradition. Hy is a dialect of Lisp that translates expressions into Python's abstract syntax tree format.

An abstract syntax tree is a high-level representation of a program's structure, independent of the source code. The Python parser turns all Python programs into abstract syntax trees, after which the interpreter performs further operations on the tree on the path to creating executable bytecode. Because the Hy frontend accepts Hy code as input and produces as output an abstract syntax tree compatible with Python's interpreter, Hy code runs in the same interpreter as your Python code.

In practical terms, Hy programs can call any Python libraries and Python code can invoke Hy code.

It is available under the MIT (Expat) license from its home page at `http://docs.hylang.org/en/latest/`:

> *"Hy is a wonderful dialect of Lisp that's embedded in Python.*
>
> *Since Hy transforms its Lisp code into the Python Abstract Syntax Tree, you have the whole beautiful world of Python at your fingertips, in Lisp form!"*

Readers who have attended to the section on using R and Octave will find setting up and invoking Hy to be very similar.

The hymagic module/extension

The entry point for the use of Hy in IPython is the hymagic module/extension. When used as an extension, hymagic allows for the use of the `%hylang` and `%%hylang` magics. When used as a module, it can be imported and used as a "normal" module in Python/IPython programs. We will outline the installation procedure for hymagic and then discuss both approaches.

Installing hymagic

The standard steps for installing any IPython module apply: use either `pip` or `easy_install`, as applicable. For example:

```
pip install hymagic
```

This will install the required source files in the appropriate directory for extensions.

Using hymagic

Once `oct2py` is installed, the following command can be issued at the IPython command line:

```
In [3]: %load_ext hymagic
```

At this point, the `%hylang` and `%%hylang` magics become available for use.

The %hylang magic

The `%hylang` magic provides the ability to specify Hy one-liners. It is worth noting that the `%hylang` magic does not have a return value. So, assigning it to a variable, while not an error, does not provide the variable with a value.

The %%hylang magic

The `%%hylang` magic allows for multiline Hy programs.

A quick introduction to Hy

Although Hy ultimately runs on top of Python, it is a dialect of Lisp. This makes it a very different language from the others that we have covered in this book. This quick introduction will help you with the basics of the language.

Lisp dialects are turning up all over in some interesting areas. Clojure in particular is gaining in popularity. For further reading, check out:

- *Mastering Clojure Data Analysis* by Eric Rochester (https://www.packtpub.com/big-data-and-business-intelligence/mastering-clojure-data-analysis)
- *Clojure High Performance Programming* by Shantanu Kumar (https://www.packtpub.com/application-development/clojure-high-performance-programming)
- *Clojure for Machine Learning* by Akhil Wali (https://www.packtpub.com/big-data-and-business-intelligence/clojure-machine-learning)

Hello world!

The "Hello world!" program in Hy is pretty basic:

```
(print "Hello world!")
```

Running it in IPython is similarly straightforward:

```
In [9]: %hylang (print "Hello world!")
Hello world!
```

For the language introduction, we will omit the IPython trappings and provide just the Hy when practicable.

Get used to parentheses

The first thing most people notice about Lisp (and Hy by extension) is how many parentheses it has. To some extent, this is a result of their placement. An ordinary Python program would have looked like this:

```
print("Hello world!")
```

The same number of parentheses, and only die-hard Python 2 users would complain about that!

The odd thing about Hy's parentheses is that they come before the function name and after the argument, rather than after the function name and around the arguments. This is the standard syntax for Lisp and all its dialects. The syntactic unit created by this form is called an *expression*, and every expression has the same form:

```
(<function> <arguments>)
```

In Hy, everything is an expression, so there will be a lot of parentheses. It can look awkward at first, but this simple syntax makes expression evaluation simple:

- Apply the function to the arguments to return the value of the expression
- There will only ever be one function

Arithmetic operations are in the wrong place

The code to add 1 and 1 is as follows:

```
(+ 1 1)
```

This follows the standard expression semantics: function first, arguments later (in this case, operator first and operands later). It is not Hy's fault that people use infix notation—consistency is a virtue in a programming language. A side benefit of this notation is that arithmetic operators can take an arbitrary number of operands:

```
(* 1 2 3 4)
```

This returns 24.

This should not be confused with a prefix version of stack arithmetic, however. The expression:

```
(* + + 1 2 3 4)
```

Is a syntax error. It breaks the second rule mentioned in the preceding list by having more than one function inside a single set of parentheses.

Function composition is everywhere

One can fix the previous example by using parentheses:

```
(* (+ (+ 1 2) 3) 4)
```

This will return 24. Evaluation proceeds from the inmost parentheses outward, so:

1. Add 1 and 2.
2. Add that result to 3.
3. Multiply that result by 4.
4. Return the value as the result of evaluating this expression.

There is a tendency in Lisp dialects to use function composition for control flow, rather than the more usual sequence-of-statements style found in object-oriented languages such as Python or Java, or imperative languages such as FORTRAN or C. Every language has a "natural" way of doing things. In Hy, function composition is more natural than stamen sequences.

Control structures in Hy

This does not mean that Hy lacks the full complement of control structures. They just look a little different.

Setting variable values

Hy provides the setv function to bind a value to a name. It works in a manner similar to Python's = operator.

In Python, we have this:

```
In [23]: x = 1 + 1

In [24]: x
Out[24]: 2
```

In Hy:

```
In [28]: %hylang (setv x (+ 1 2))

In [29]: x
Out[29]: 3
```

Note how the value of x was automatically exported from Hy to IPython.

Defining functions

Defining a function is a form of name binding, but the process gets a separate Hy function: `defn`. The basic syntax is as follows:

```
(defn <function name> [<args>] <list of expr>)
```

A simple variant on `Hello world!` will be illustrative:

```
In [31]: %%hylang
    ....: (defn hello [name]
    ....: (print (+ "Hello " name))
    ....: )
    ....:
```

As our first Hy program, it bears some examination:

- **Line 1**: Although the program is technically a one-liner, a cell magic makes it easier to type it using a human-readable formatting.

- **Line 2**: Our first function is `defn`. This will bind its first argument (the function name) to the second argument (the list of parameters) and the third argument (the list of expressions that makes up the function body). Readers versed in functional programming may notice a similarity to lambda calculus here, but that is beyond the scope of this book.

- **Line 3**: In this case, our list of expressions contains only a single (nested) expression. The `print` function will print its arguments. There is only one argument, and its return value is the string resulting from the concatenation of `"Hello "` and the parameter.

- **Line 4**: This is the closing parenthesis for the `defn` expression. All parentheses must match. Using multiple lines to match parentheses is a good habit for dealing with a problem that can easily become overwhelming.

Note that this definition carries over into the IPython world, with appropriate syntax:

```
In [32]: hello("bob")
Hello bob
```

if statements

`if` statements follow the same rules about expressions as every other part of Hy:

```
(if <bool_expr> <true_expr> <false_expr>)
```

Here, Hy will evaluate `<bool_expr>` first. If `<bool_expr>` evaluates to `true`, `<true_expr>` will be evaluated; otherwise, `<false_expr>` will be. For example:

```
In [7]: %%hylang
   ...: (import math)
   ...: (defn safesqrt [x]
   ...:     (if (< x 0)
   ...:         (math.sqrt (- 0 x))
   ...:         (math.sqrt x)
   ...:       )
   ...: )
   ...:

In [8]: safesqrt(-4)
Out[8]: 2.0
```
hy1.hy

For the complete code, you can refer to the code file named `hy1.hy` provided along with this book.

Conditionals

Hy even has the multiway conditional statement that Python lacks:

```
(cond [<bool_expr1> <expr1>] [<bool_expr2> <expr2>] … )
```

For example:

```
In [9]: %%hylang
   ...: (defn categorize [x]
   ...:   (cond
   ...:     [(< x 0) (print "negative")]
   ...:     [(= x 0) (print "zero")]
   ...:     [(> x 0) (print "positive")]
   ...:   )
   ...: )
   ...:

In [10]: categorize(52)
positive
```
hy2.hy

For the complete code, you can refer to the code file named `hy2.hy` provided along with this book.

Loops

Although it goes against the spirit of functional programming, loops are supported. For example:

```
In [12]: %hylang (for [i (range 10)] (print i))
0
1
2
3
4
5
6
7
8
9

In [13]: %hylang (for [i [1 2 3 4 5]] (print i))
1
2
3
4
5
```

Calling Python

All Python functions are available inside of Hy:

```
In [20]: def f(n):
    curr = n
    tmp = 0
    while curr != 1:
      tmp = tmp + 1
```

```
        if curr % 2 == 1:
            curr = 3 * curr + 1
        else:
            curr = curr/2
    return tmp
....:
```

In [21]: %hylang (f 35)

Out[21]: 13

And so are built-in Python functions and libraries:

In [28]: %%hylang

....: (setv f (open "hy1.hy"))

....: (print (.read f))

....:

This prints the contents of that file:

```
%%hylang
(import math)
(defn safesqrt [x]
  (if (< x 0)
    (math.sqrt (- 0 x))
    (math.sqrt x)
  )
)
```

Hy interoperates with Python in too many ways to list here, including list comprehensions, objects, and exceptions. It suffices to say that if you are already comfortable with Python and interested in branching out into a functional language, Hy is a good choice.

Summary

This chapter looked at some third-party tools that interoperate well with IPython: R, Octave, and Hy.

R is a language specialized for use in statistics and data visualization. It has several advantages, including a rich collection of libraries, a large user base skilled in statistics, easy graphics, and a syntax that allows the economic expression of statistical ideas. IPython can complement this with its huge collection of general-purpose libraries and a syntax that will be more familiar to most developers. At present, R and Python are struggling for supremacy in the data analysis realm—there is no reason they cannot work together.

Octave is another language specialized for numerical computing. Its initial draw is as an open source alternative to MATLAB. The two languages are highly compatible, providing access to a large library of already written MATLAB functions to the Octave user. Octave is particularly strong when working with matrices. Until recently, Octave did not come with a GUI, so IPython makes for a nice complement when visualization is required.

Hy is a dialect of Lisp that interprets/compiles to Python. Functional languages such as Lisp are an important part of the machine learning ecosystem, which is becoming increasingly important in big data analysis. Developers who are new to functional programming will find learning Hy easier than starting cold, given the interoperability between IPython and Hy.

The focus in this chapter was on multilanguage integration. In the next chapter, we will introduce third-party tools for data visualization.

7
Seeing Is Believing– Visualization

Although Python is an excellent language for scientific and numerical computing, it is somewhat less strong in terms of data visualization. IPython allows easy interoperation between Python (and other supported languages) and many third-party tools that can provide useful data analysis and graphing possibilities. This capability is another example of IPython's pragmatic philosophy of enabling the developer to use the best tool for the job.

While there are a great number of visualization libraries, this chapter will attempt to cover only a few of the more popular/interesting ones.

The following topics will be covered:

- Matplotlib
- Bokeh
- R
- Python-nvd3

Matplotlib

Matplotlib is a Python-based 2D plotting library. It works well with Python, and even better with IPython. It includes the `pyplot` module, which provides MATLAB-like functionality. Matplotlib functionality can be accessed both programmatically and interactively, from the IPython command line. The examples in this section will be run from the command line for ease of explication.

Starting matplotlib

Matplotlib should be installed along with most major IPython distributions. If yours does not include it, standard package installation procedures (for example, `pip install` or `sudo apt-get`) should suffice.

There are two ways to start up matplotlib: `matplotlib-only` or `pylab`.

The difference is that using `matplotlib-only` mode activates `matplotlib` interactive support but does not import anything into the namespace. `pylab` mode executes more imports and changes the namespace.

Once installed, `matplotlib-only` mode can be started either from the command line or by using the `%matplotlib` magic, as shown here:

```
(Ipython)-bash-4.1$ ipython --matplotlib
Python 3.4.3 |Anaconda 2.0.1 (64-bit)| (default, Oct 19 2015, 21:52:17)
Type "copyright", "credits" or "license" for more information.


IPython 4.0.1 -- An enhanced Interactive Python.
?         -> Introduction and overview of IPython's features.
%quickref -> Quick reference.
help      -> Python's own help system.
object?   -> Details about 'object', use 'object??' for extra details.
Using matplotlib backend: Qt4Agg


In [1]:
```

```
⊗ ⊖ ⊡   dipanjan@dipanjan-K53SD: ~

dipanjan@dipanjan-K53SD:~$ ipython --matplotlib
Python 2.7.11 |Anaconda 2.3.0 (64-bit)| (default, Dec  6 2015, 18:08:32)
Type "copyright", "credits" or "license" for more information.

IPython 3.2.0 -- An enhanced Interactive Python.
Anaconda is brought to you by Continuum Analytics.
Please check out: http://continuum.io/thanks and https://anaconda.org
?            -> Introduction and overview of IPython's features.
%quickref -> Quick reference.
help       -> Python's own help system.
object?    -> Details about 'object', use 'object??' for extra details.
GLib-GIO-Message: Using the 'memory' GSettings backend.  Your settings will not
be saved or shared with other applications.

(python:6628): Gtk-WARNING **: GModule (/usr/lib/x86_64-linux-gnu/gtk-2.0/2.10.0
/immodules/im-ibus.so) initialization check failed: GLib version too old (micro
mismatch)

(python:6628): Gtk-WARNING **: Loading IM context type 'ibus' failed

(python:6628): Gtk-WARNING **: GModule (/usr/lib/x86_64-linux-gnu/gtk-2.0/2.10.0
/immodules/im-ibus.so) initialization check failed: GLib version too old (micro
mismatch)

(python:6628): Gtk-WARNING **: Loading IM context type 'ibus' failed

(python:6628): Gtk-WARNING **: GModule (/usr/lib/x86_64-linux-gnu/gtk-2.0/2.10.0
/immodules/im-ibus.so) initialization check failed: GLib version too old (micro
mismatch)

(python:6628): Gtk-WARNING **: Loading IM context type 'ibus' failed
Using matplotlib backend: Qt4Agg

In [1]: █
```

Alternatively, there is a `%matplotlib` magic that will provide the same functionality:

```
In [1]: %matplotlib
Using matplotlib backend: Qt4Agg
```

Similarly, IPython can be started in `pylab` mode at the command line, as follows:

```
(Ipython)-bash-4.1$ ipython --pylab
Python 3.4.3 |Anaconda 2.0.1 (64-bit)| (default, Oct 19 2015, 21:52:17)
Type "copyright", "credits" or "license" for more information.
```

```
IPython 4.0.1 -- An enhanced Interactive Python.
?          -> Introduction and overview of IPython's features.
%quickref -> Quick reference.
help       -> Python's own help system.
object?    -> Details about 'object', use 'object??' for extra details.
Using matplotlib backend: Qt4Agg
```

And there is the `%pylab` magic; it will provide the same functionality:

```
In [1]: %pylab
Using matplotlib backend: Qt4Agg
Populating the interactive namespace from numpy and matplotlib
```

Entering `pylab` mode is equivalent to executing the following code:

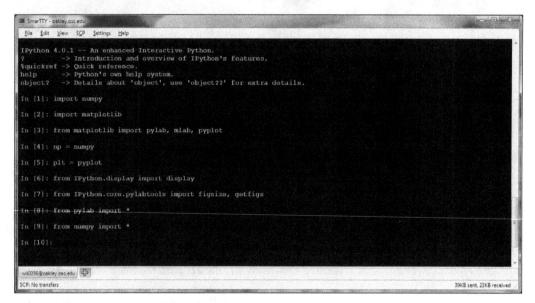

Care should be taken when using `pylab` mode. Although it can be convenient, these imports can shadow other defined functions, leading to surprising results. Examples in this section will use `pylab` mode unless specifically noted. Proper attention to detail should allow any code to be ported to/from either mode as desired.

An initial graph

As always with a new module, it is worth checking to see whether everything is working. From the IPython command line, issue the following commands:

```
In [2]: x = randn(90000)
```

```
In [3]: hist(x, 300)
Out[3]:
```

At this point, my command line printed two sorts of things:

- Two arrays and a list (the return values of the hist call)
- A stack trace (which went away when I deleted my matplotlib font cache in ~/.cache/matplotlib/fontList*.cache)

More to the point, it produced the following graph:

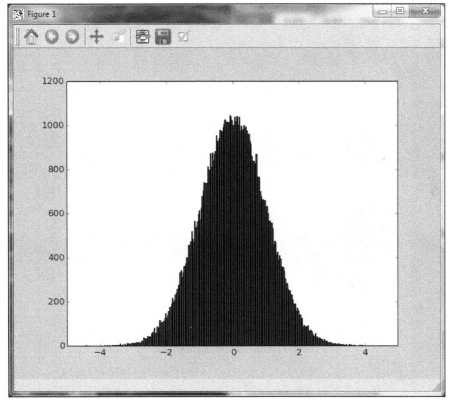

matplotlib1.gif

This code deserves some further description, as the first matplotlib example:

- **Line 1**: The `numpy.random.randn` function creates a one-dimensional array of 90,000 floating-point numbers; they follow a normal distribution with mean equal to `0` and variance equal to `1`.

- **Line 2**: The `hist` function accepts an array as an argument and computes and draws the histogram of the array. It takes many optional arguments; in this case, we have provided the number of bins to use.

Modifying the graph

It was easy to get the first graph up and running, but it could use some work. The first way to change things is to change/add parameters to the constructor. For example, suppose we execute this:

```
In [11]: hist(x, 300, orientation="horizontal", color="green")
```

It results in the following:

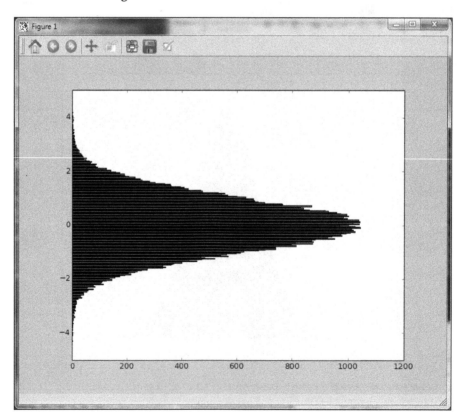

matplotlib2.gif

A little more usefully:

```
In [13]: hist(x, 300, cumulative=True)
```

The preceding line results in a cumulative histogram, like this:

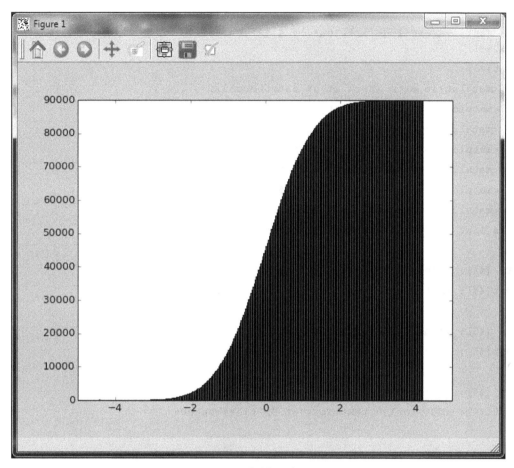

matplotlib3.gif

The complete list of parameters to the `hist` command can be found in the documentation maintained at *http://matplotlib.org*.

An even more useful feature is that the graph is redrawn every time a command that would change what is displayed is executed. Given our original histogram, we can issue a series of commands as follows:

```
In [42]: locs, labels = xticks()


In [43]: xticks(locs, ("-10%", "-6.7%", "-3.3%", "0", "3.3%", "6.7%",
"10%"))
Out[43]:
([<matplotlib.axis.XTick at 0x2b15e5bdcc88>,
  <matplotlib.axis.XTick at 0x2b15e5ba9710>,
  <matplotlib.axis.XTick at 0x2b15e5f09fd0>,
  <matplotlib.axis.XTick at 0x2b15e5fa4da0>,
  <matplotlib.axis.XTick at 0x2b15e5fa87f0>,
  <matplotlib.axis.XTick at 0x2b15e5fac240>,
  <matplotlib.axis.XTick at 0x2b15e5facc50>],
 <a list of 7 Text xticklabel objects>)


In [44]: xlabel("Percentage change")
Out[44]: <matplotlib.text.Text at 0x2b15e5bd8f98>


In [45]: ylabel("Number of Stocks")
Out[45]: <matplotlib.text.Text at 0x2b15e5bdc7f0>


In [46]: title("Simulated Market Performance")
Out[46]: <matplotlib.text.Text at 0x2b15e5beebe0>
```

code1.py

And we can see the resulting graph drawn as each command is issued:

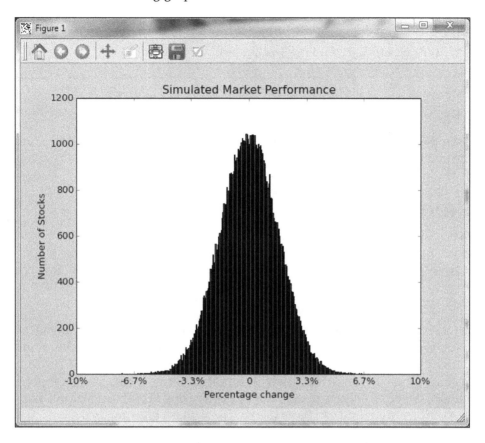

Controlling interactivity

While useful for interactive graphing, some commands can take time. If a number of changes need to be made in a row and the results are not needed until after all the changes are applied, the ioff() and ion() functions turn off/turn on interactive plotting. The ion() function should be followed by a call to plot() in order to update the display. Here is an example:

```
In [47]: ioff()


In [48]: title("Simulation")
Out[48]: <matplotlib.text.Text at 0x2b15e5beebe0>


In [49]: xlabel("Change Day Over Day")
```

```
Out[49]: <matplotlib.text.Text at 0x2b15e5bdc7f0>

In [53]: ion
Out[53]: <function matplotlib.pyplot.ion>

In [54]: plot()
Out[54]: []
```

This would result in changes to the diagram being delayed until the call to plot( ), at which point they all happen simultaneously.

Bokeh

Bokeh is a Python interactive visualization library that targets modern web browsers for presentation. Its goal is to provide elegant, concise construction of novel graphics in the style of D3.js and extend this capability with high-performance interactivity over very large or streaming datasets. Bokeh can help anyone who wants to quickly and easily create interactive plots, dashboards, and data applications.

For our purposes, Bokeh can be used to produce graphics that will be viewed from web browsers. Although it does not support the same sort of command-line interactivity as Matplotlib when used in this manner, the ability to produce durable images that are easily viewed remotely is important for purposes such as reporting. In addition, Bokeh's ability to generate web pages using HTML, JavaScript, and CSS means that the graph itself can be as interactive as those tools can make it.

A command-line-driven interactive approach is supported when using a Bokeh server, but this is beyond the scope of the current section.

Starting Bokeh

Bokeh can be installed as a standard IPython module using pip:

```
pip install bokeh
```

Once installed, the bokeh libraries can be accessed through a standard import statement:

```
In [1]: import bokeh
```

Bokeh is currently in constant flux. The version used in these examples did not include a %bokeh or %%bokeh magic, although one may become available.

An initial graph

The following code calls some basic Bokeh libraries to produce some IPython results and a graph:

```
In [1]: import numpy as np


In [2]: import bokeh.plotting as bp


In [3]: bp.output_file("bokeh1.html")


In [4]: x = np.linspace(0, 2 * np.pi, 1024)


In [5]: y = np.cos(x)


In [6]: fig = bp.figure( )


In [7]: fig.line(x, y)
Out[7]: <bokeh.models.renderers.GlyphRenderer at 0x2ac3cc1cde80>


In [8]: bp.show(fig)
```

The IPython results were the following:

```
ERROR: <path> :W-1001 (NO_DATA_RENDERERS): Plot has no data renderers:
Figure, ViewModel:Plot, ref _id: 3e2a57f0-8c52-463b-8e6b-5821ef6b04b8


In [9]: /usr/bin/xdg-open: line 402: htmlview: command not found
console.error:
  [CustomizableUI]
  Custom widget with id loop-button does not return a valid node
console.error:
  [CustomizableUI]
  Custom widget with id loop-button does not return a valid node
```

code2.py

These errors did not seem to prevent the desired effects. First off, a new browser opened and displayed a web page that contained this graph:

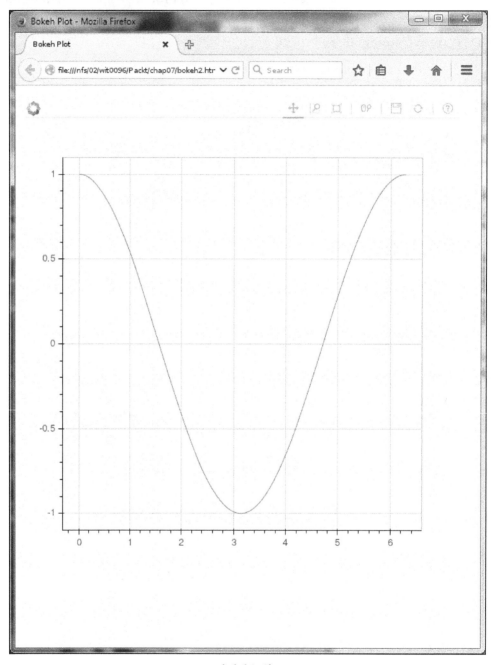

bokeh1.gif

It also produced a 748 KB-sized HTML file that produces the web page just shown.

This code deserves some further description, as it's our first Bokeh example:

- **Line 2**: The `bokeh.plotting` interface provides the `Figure` class. A `Figure` object acts as a container for all the required elements in a plot: lines, axes, glyphs, and so on.

- **Line 3**: The `output_file` function takes a filename as an argument. Bokeh then saves its output to this file in HTML format. Alternative output formats are as follows:

    ◦ `output_notebook`: Generates the output to be used in a Jupyter notebook

    ◦ `output_server`: Generates the output to be displayed through a Bokeh server

- **Line 6**: Here, we create a `Figure` object to put our graphical elements in. This comes with a host of default settings. Some will be discussed later, but for now, the basic window will suffice.

- **Line 7**: The `line` function takes two arguments—a list of x values and a list of y values—and creates a line by pairing them off. A line is a simple form of what Bokeh calls a glyph: a graphical element such as a line (straight or curved), a shape (for example, rectangle or annulus) or an image, among others. This line is now a part of the graph and will be displayed when the graph is. If desired, we can add more glyphs to this graph, but one is enough for this example.

- **Line 8**: The `show` method saves the current plot and (because this is an HTML-based plot) opens a web browser to display it. A related method is `save( )`, which will save a plot but not display it.

Modifying the graph

The preceding graph was about the simplest graph Bokeh could produce. It used many defaults that Bokeh provides for even the most basic graph. Even though the graph setup was primitive (a range of x values and the `cos` function), there is still a lot of functionality on the web page:

- The **Close All Plots** link works
- The icon in the upper left links to `bokeh.pydata.org`
- The icons in the upper right (**Pan, Box Zoom, Resize, Wheel Zoom, Preview/Save, Reset**, and **Help**) all work
- There are axes with appropriate scaling and labeling

Bokeh uses the `Figure` class as a container for the various parts that make up a graph. The previous example used a default `Figure`. More control over the graph can be obtained by passing parameters to the `Figure` constructor. Values set using this method apply to the entire graph, regardless of later additions of glyphs and so on.

We will also add some parameters to our line. This is a common feature of most Bokeh glyphs—the constructor has few required parameters and a larger set of optional parameters that can be overridden.

Here is the code for the new graph:

```
In [2]: import numpy as np


In [3]: import bokeh.plotting as bp


In [4]: bp.output_file("bokeh2.html")


In [5]: x = np.linspace(0, 2 * np.pi, 1024)


In [6]: y = np.cos(x)


In [7]: fig = bp.figure(title="simple line example", x_axis_label="x",
y_axis_label="y")


In [8]: fig.line(x, y, legend="cos(x)", color="red", line_width=2)
Out[8]: <bokeh.models.renderers.GlyphRenderer at 0x2ae1340cee80>


In [9]: bp.show(fig)
```

code3.py

With the resulting page:

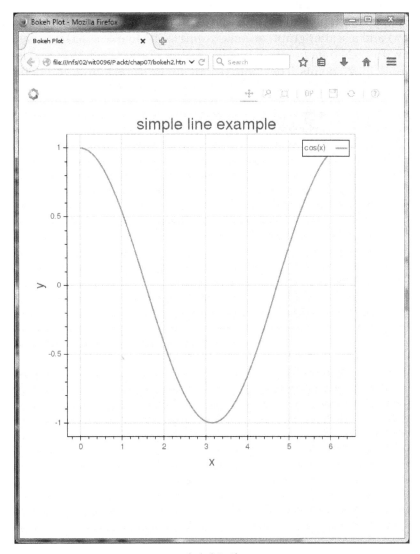

bokeh2.gif

Bokeh also supports placing multiple glyphs on the same graph. Using multiple glyphs is simple: just call the requisite method on the figure object and the appropriate type of glyph will be added to the graph. In this case, we have both a line for *cos(x)* and a scatter graph of *cos(x) * sin(x)*. The line of *cos(x)* is a standard red line graph with 1,024 data points, while the scatter graph of *sin(x) * cos(x)* is a green scatter graph with 20 points. They both belong to the same figure, and both appear on the resulting graph:

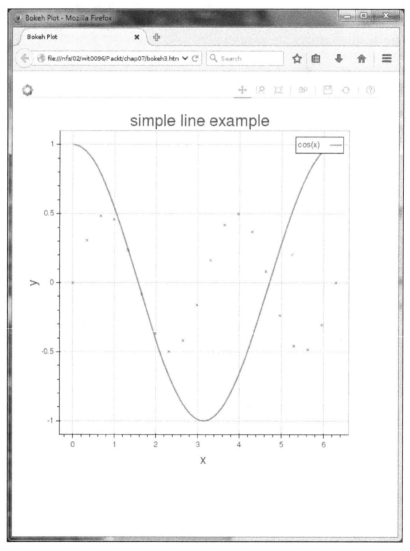

bokeh3.gif

The developer is free to play around with the graph while developing it. A graph may be displayed, and if additional glyphs are required, they may be added to the figure object by calling the appropriate method on the figure object from the IPython command line. At that point, the figure is changed, although the results of this change may not be saved until the next `save( )` or `show( )` command and will not be visible until the next `show( )` command.

Customizing graphs

The entire Bokeh toolbox is too large to describe in this section, but a few highlights will demonstrate its power.

Bokeh supports many types of glyph:

- Scatter markers (for scatter plots, including asterisks, crosses, diamonds, and many more)
- Straight lines
- Patches (polygonal shapes)
- Rectangles and ovals
- Images (including the ability to draw raw RGBA data)
- Wedges, arcs, and annulus shapes
- Other specialized curves

Bokeh also supports various types of axes:

- Categorical (enumerated, or custom numeric)
- Datetime (years, months, dates, and so on)
- Log-scaled
- Twin

Also supported are various annotations:

- Legends
- Box and span (to emphasize certain regions of a graph)

Interactive plots

An important feature of Bokeh is the ability to allow the user to interact with finished plots. This is accomplished in two ways:

- Built-in Bokeh functionality
- The ability to interface with JavaScript in the browser

Our example will involve the first option.

An example interactive plot

The following code displays two graphs side by side, and allows the user to select a set of points in one graph and see where the corresponding points lie in the other graph. The code introduces some new concepts, which will be discussed:

```
In [2]: import numpy as np

In [3]: import bokeh.plotting as bp

In [4]: import bokeh.models as bm

In [5]: bp.output_file("bokeh4.html")

In [6]: x = np.linspace(-2 * np.pi, 2 * np.pi, 100)

In [7]: y0 = np.cos(x)

In [8]: y1 = np.sin(x)

In [9]: mySource = bm.ColumnDataSource(data=dict(x=x, y0=y0, y1=y1))

In [10]: myTools = "box_select,lasso_select,help"

In [11]: left = bp.figure(tools=myTools, width=300, height=300,
title="Left")
```

```
In [12]: left.circle('x', 'y0', source=mySource)
Out[12]: <bokeh.models.renderers.GlyphRenderer at 0x2b47b457de80>


In [13]: right = bp.figure(tools=myTools, width=300, height=300,
title="Right")


In [14]: right.circle('x', 'y1', source=mySource)
Out[14]: <bokeh.models.renderers.GlyphRenderer at 0x2b47c2cb8940>


In [15]: p = bp.gridplot([[left, right]])


In [16]: bp.show(p)
```

code4.py

- **Line 4**: This allows us to use data models. It allows us to consider the three data vectors (x, y0, and y1) as a single data source that both windows can use.

- **Line 9**: This line creates a `ColumnDataSource` data model that will be shared between the windows. This sharing is what allows the actions in one window to be reflected in the other.

- **Line 10**: It is possible to create a list of tools that will be displayed in the graph. For this example, a subset of the usual will work.

- **Lines 11-12**: We create a figure to be the left graph and assign it a circle glyph for (x, y0) and our shared data source.

- **Lines 13-14**: We create a figure to be the right graph and assign it a circle glyph for (x, y1) and our shared data source.

- **Line 15**: A `gridplot` glyph is created, which contains the left and right glyphs.

The following graph is displayed. Note how the user can use a lasso tool to choose which points to examine. The chosen points are made bold, while the unchosen points are dimmer. This happens in real time as the points are selected by the user:

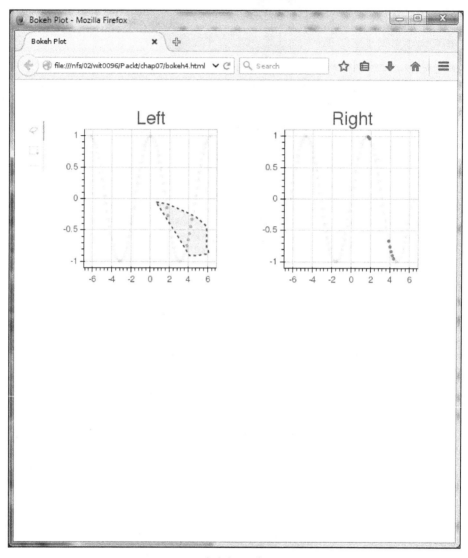

bokeh4a.gif

This selection persists after the user is done interacting with the graph:

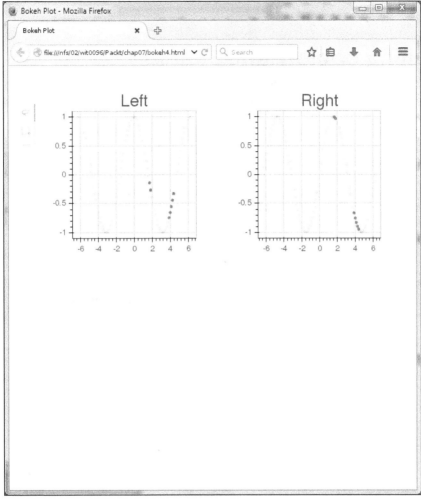

bokeh4b.gif

R

The previous chapter introduced some basic features of plotting in R. This section will introduce the ggplot2 library. ggplot2 is based on concepts from Leland Wilkinson's *The Grammar of Graphics*, a classic in the data visualization field. The goal of this book was to provide an underlying theory of graphical data display. The framework provided aims to provide a unified viewpoint in which various tools (scatter plots, bar charts, pie charts, and so on) can all be viewed as special cases of a more general concept of graphical data presentation.

For more information on ggplot2, see the home page for the project at http://ggplot2.org/ and the documentation at http://docs.ggplot2.org/current/index.html.

Installing ggplot2 and pandas

ggplot2 is an optional R package. It is possible that it is included in your R installation. If not, it can be installed easily enough in IPython using R magic:

```
In [12]: %%R
    ...: install_packages("ggplot2")
```

pandas is a data analysis library for Python. It contains many useful utilities, including the invaluable DataFrame class. It comes installed with the Anaconda distribution, or can be installed using pip:

```
pip install pandas
```

Using DataFrames

DataFrames are handy in that they are Python equivalents of R data frames. R uses data frames all over. Here is a simple example:

```
In [10]: %%R
    ....: x=c(1, 2, 3, 4)
    ....: y=c(2, 3, 5, 7)
    ....: df = data.frame(x, y)

In [11]: %%R
    ....: head(df)
    ....:
  x y
1 1 2
2 2 3
3 3 5
4 4 7
```

Note that df maintained its value even between invocations of the %%R magic. The built-in mtcars data is a data frame in R.

As a quick example of the usefulness of DataFrames, we will add a column to the built-in `mtcars` data frame to denote kilometers per gallon:

```
In [1]: %load_ext rpy2.ipython


In [2]: from rpy2.robjects import pandas2ri


In [3]: pandas2ri.activate()


In [4]: from rpy2.robjects import r


In [5]: df_cars = pandas2ri.ri2py(r['mtcars'])


In [6]: type(df_cars)
Out[6]: pandas.core.frame.DataFrame


In [7]: df_cars.describe()
Out[7]:
```

code5.py

The preceding code yields the following:

	mpg	cyl	disp	hp	drat	wt \
count	32.000000	32.000000	32.000000	32.000000	32.000000	32.000000
mean	20.090625	6.187500	230.721875	146.687500	3.596563	3.217250
std	6.026948	1.785922	123.938694	68.562868	0.534679	0.978457
min	10.400000	4.000000	71.100000	52.000000	2.760000	1.513000
25%	15.425000	4.000000	120.825000	96.500000	3.080000	2.581250
50%	19.200000	6.000000	196.300000	123.000000	3.695000	3.325000
75%	22.800000	8.000000	326.000000	180.000000	3.920000	3.610000
max	33.900000	8.000000	472.000000	335.000000	4.930000	5.424000

	qsec	vs	am	gear	carb
count	32.000000	32.000000	32.000000	32.000000	32.0000
mean	17.848750	0.437500	0.406250	3.687500	2.8125
std	1.786943	0.504016	0.498991	0.737804	1.6152
min	14.500000	0.000000	0.000000	3.000000	1.0000
25%	16.892500	0.000000	0.000000	3.000000	2.0000
50%	17.710000	0.000000	0.000000	4.000000	2.0000

75%	18.900000	1.000000	1.000000	4.000000	4.0000
max	22.900000	1.000000	1.000000	5.000000	8.0000

```
In [8]: df_cars.insert(11, "kpg", 1.609344 * df_cars['mpg'])

In [9]: df_cars.describe()
Out[9]:
```

	mpg	cyl	disp	hp	drat	wt \
count	32.000000	32.000000	32.000000	32.000000	32.000000	32.000000
mean	20.090625	6.187500	230.721875	146.687500	3.596563	3.217250
std	6.026948	1.785922	123.938694	68.562868	0.534679	0.978457
min	10.400000	4.000000	71.100000	52.000000	2.760000	1.513000
25%	15.425000	4.000000	120.825000	96.500000	3.080000	2.581250
50%	19.200000	6.000000	196.300000	123.000000	3.695000	3.325000
75%	22.800000	8.000000	326.000000	180.000000	3.920000	3.610000
max	33.900000	8.000000	472.000000	335.000000	4.930000	5.424000

	qsec	vs	am	gear	carb	kpg
count	32.000000	32.000000	32.000000	32.000000	32.0000	32.000000
mean	17.848750	0.437500	0.406250	3.687500	2.8125	32.332727
std	1.786943	0.504016	0.498991	0.737804	1.6152	9.699433
min	14.500000	0.000000	0.000000	3.000000	1.0000	16.737178
25%	16.892500	0.000000	0.000000	3.000000	2.0000	24.824131
50%	17.710000	0.000000	0.000000	4.000000	2.0000	30.899405
75%	18.900000	1.000000	1.000000	4.000000	4.0000	36.693043
max	22.900000	1.000000	1.000000	5.000000	8.0000	54.556762

Of course, the resulting DataFrame can be turned back into an R data frame and pushed back into R:

```
In [12]: r_df_cars = pandas2ri.py2ri(df_cars)

In [13]: %Rpush r_df_cars

In [14]: %%R
    ....: head(r_df_cars)
    ....:
```

	mpg	cyl	disp	hp	drat	wt	qsec	vs	am	gear	carb
kpg											
Mazda RX4 33.79622	21.0	6	160	110	3.90	2.620	16.46	0	1	4	4
Mazda RX4 Wag 33.79622	21.0	6	160	110	3.90	2.875	17.02	0	1	4	4
Datsun 710 36.69304	22.8	4	108	93	3.85	2.320	18.61	1	1	4	1
Hornet 4 Drive 34.43996	21.4	6	258	110	3.08	3.215	19.44	1	0	3	1
Hornet Sportabout 30.09473	18.7	8	360	175	3.15	3.440	17.02	0	0	3	2
Valiant 29.12913	18.1	6	225	105	2.76	3.460	20.22	1	0	3	1

An initial graph

Now we are ready to take a stab at a first graph using ggplot2.

First we will look at the code. This being the first graph using ggplot2, descriptions of important lines will follow:

```
In [1]: %load_ext rpy2.ipython
```

```
In [2]: from rpy2.robjects import pandas2ri
```

```
In [3]: pandas2ri.activate()
```

```
In [4]: from rpy2.robjects import r
```

```
In [5]: import pandas
```

```
In [6]: from rpy2.robjects.lib import ggplot2
```

```
In [7]: df_cars = pandas2ri.ri2py(r['mtcars'])
```

```
In [8]: wt = df_cars['wt']
```

```
In [9]: mpg = df_cars['mpg']
```

```
In [10]: type(mpg)
Out[10]: pandas.core.series.Series


In [11]: df_wtVsMpg = pandas.DataFrame()


In [12]: df_wtVsMpg['wt'] = wt


In [13]: df_wtVsMpg['mpg'] = mpg


In [14]: p = ggplot2.ggplot(df_wtVsMpg)


In [15]: type(p)
Out[15]: rpy2.robjects.lib.ggplot2.GGPlot


In [16]: p.plot()
```

code6.py

- **Lines 2-3**: These lines import and activate the new method of moving data to/from IPython/R. This is the preferred method since v0.16.0, at which point the `pandas.rpy` interface was deprecated and marked for removal in some future version.

- **Line 7**: This line actually imports R's `mtcars` data frame into a `panda` DataFrame.

- **Lines 8-10**: These lines illustrate the DataFrame's ability to be addressed as a Python dict and the type of the result.

- **Lines 11-13**: Here, we start out with an empty DataFrame and add columns dynamically.

The resulting graph appears as follows:

r1.gif

Admittedly, this was a lot of work to end up with such a disappointing result.

Modifying the graph

Luckily, this is not all that ggplot2 can do. A small addition to the code:

```
In [17]: p = ggplot2.ggplot(df_wtVsMpg) \
    ....: + ggplot2.aes_string(x = 'wt', y = 'mpg')


In [18]: p.plot( )
```

Results in a somewhat more satisfactory graph:

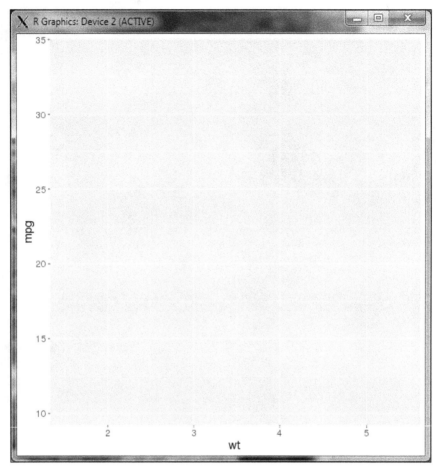

r2.gif

The difference lies in the addition of a layer consisting of an "aesthetic string":

```
+ ggplot2.aes_string(x = 'wt', y = 'mpg')
```

ggplot2 makes a distinction between the data (in this case, df_wtVsMpg) and how it is to be displayed. In our earlier graph, the data was present, but there was no information on what form the graph should take (for example, bar, line, or pie chart), how the data points should be represented (for example, x's or circles), or any of the other visual features of the graph. As such, ggplot2 just displayed a blank graph. With the addition of some aesthetic information – the x axis corresponds to the wt column and the y axis corresponds to the mpg column – ggplot2 is able to add some visual flair to the graph. In particular, it can label the axes, number the coordinates, and provide a nice little grid effect.

This graph is also a little underwhelming in that the data is not displayed. That can be remedied by adding another aesthetic element, a geometric object in this case:

```
In [19]: p = p + ggplot2.geom_point( )
```

```
In [20]: p.plot( )
```

Note the use of the + to add layers to a plot. The resulting graph is a scatter plot:

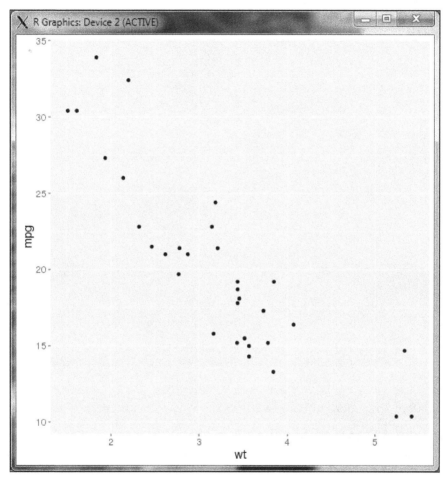

r3.gif

Adding a fit is easy enough—just add another geometry aesthetic:

```
ggplot2.geom_smooth(method = "loess")
```

And here is the resulting graph:

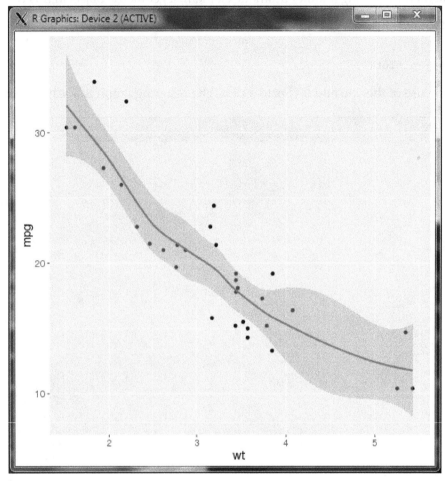

r4.gif

Unfortunately, there does not appear to be any way to easily remove a layer:

```
In [35]: p = p - ggplot2.geom_smooth(method = "loess")
--------------------------------------------------------------------------
---

TypeError                                 Traceback (most recent call
last)
<ipython-input-35-43aa876615bd> in <module>()
----> 1 p = p - ggplot2.geom_smooth(method = "loess")


TypeError: unsupported operand type(s) for -: 'GGPlot' and 'GeomSmooth'
```

So, adding another geometry just adds another layer:

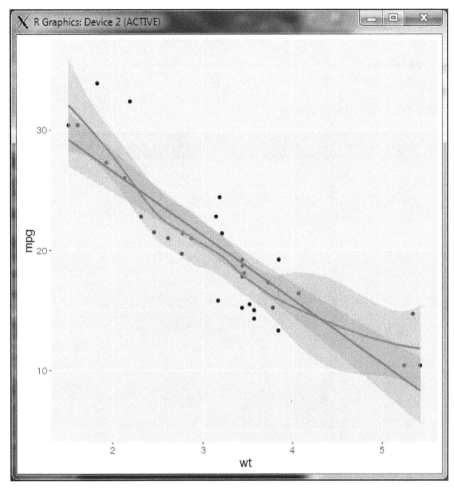

r5.gif

A different view

In the following example, we add a column to our previous data and show how the use of different aesthetic choices can produce an entirely different graph.

First, here's the code:

```
In [38]: df_wtVsMpg['cyl'] = df_cars['cyl']


In [39]: p2 = ggplot2.ggplot(df_wtVsMpg)
```

```
In [40]: p2 = p2 + ggplot2.aes_string(x="mpg", fill="factor(cyl)")

In [41]: p2 = p2 + ggplot2.geom_histogram( )

In [42]: p2.plot( )
```
code7.py

It produces the following graph:

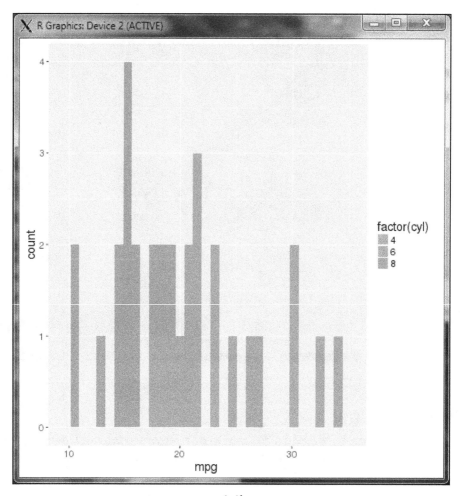

r6.gif

A great deal of learning to make good graphs with ggplot2 is learning the ins and outs of the sort of visual elements that can be added in layers.

Python-nvd3

Python-nvd3 is a wrapper around the NVD3 library. NVD3 is itself a layer on top of the D3.js library. This is from the NVD3 homepage (http://nvd3.org/):

> *"This project is an attempt to build re-usable charts and chart components for d3.js without taking away the power that d3.js gives you."*

Starting Python-nvd3

Python-nvd3 can be installed with the usual `pip install` command:

```
pip install python-nvd3
```

After this, one can check to make sure that it is available:

```
In [3]: import nvd3
loaded nvd3 IPython extension
run nvd3.ipynb.initialize_javascript() to set up the notebook
help(nvd3.ipynb.initialize_javascript) for options


In [4]: nvd3.__version__
Out[4]: '0.14.2'
```

An initial graph

The following code calls some basic Python-nvd3 libraries to produce an HTML file containing a graph:

```
In [1]: from nvd3 import scatterChart
loaded nvd3 IPython extension
run nvd3.ipynb.initialize_javascript() to set up the notebook
help(nvd3.ipynb.initialize_javascript) for options


In [2]: xs = [1, 2, 3, 4, 5]


In [3]: ys = [2, 3, 5, 7, 11]


In [4]: kwargs = {'shape': 'circle', 'size': '1'}


In [5]: chart = scatterChart(name='The first few primes', height=400,
width=400)
```

```
In [6]: chart.add_serie(name="Primes", x=xs, y=ys, **kwargs)

In [7]: output_file = open('nvd3-1.html', 'w')

In [8]: chart.buildhtml()

In [9]: output_file.write(chart.htmlcontent)
Out[9]: 1614

In [10]: output_file.close()
```

code8.py

When viewed in a browser, the output graph looks like this:

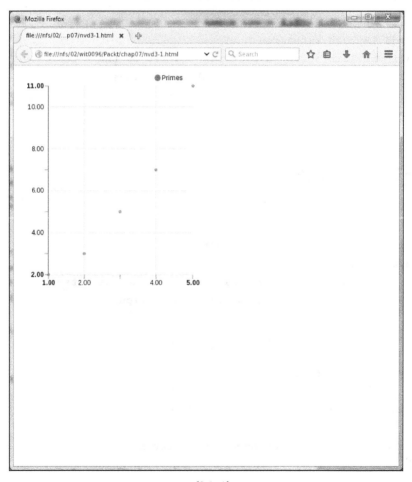

nvd3-1.gif

The resulting HTML page was 4 KB.

This code deserves some further description, being our first Python-nvd3 example.

- **Line 1**: Python-nvd3 supports a variety of different plot types, including the following:
    - ° `cumulativeLineChart`
    - ° `discreteBarChart`
    - ° `lineChart`
    - ° `lineWithFocusChart`
    - ° `linePlusBarChart`
    - ° `multiBarChart`
    - ° `multiBarHorizontalChart`
    - ° `pieChart`
    - ° `scatterChart`
    - ° `stackedAreaChart`

- **Line 4**: We need to set the graphical format of the data points. This is a JSON object, and we follow the Python convention of using `kwargs` as the variable name for keyword arguments.

- **Line 6**: We add our data to the chart. The data needs a name (which will show up in the legend), x and y values, and the arguments we set on line 4 to describe the points. A chart will support an arbitrary number of data series.

- **Line 7**: We would like to save the output to a file, so here we open one.

- **Line 8**: This tells Python-nvd3 to generate the HTML for our plot. By default, the generated text goes into the chart's `htmlcontent` field. Depending on your output method, this text can be handled in various ways.

- **Line 9**: The generated HTML is written to a file.

Under construction

Python-nvd3 is definitely still under construction. Even the examples provided by the project do not match up with either the provided graphs or the output generated by the latest version of IPython. It is not clear whether this is sloppy documentation, buggy software, or just the usual cross-platform problems. In any case, caution is warranted as the software develops.

Putting some tools together

Because Python-nvd3 is so well integrated with Python, it is easy to use data from other tools to generate plots. In the following code, we use pandas to grab some data out of R's `mtcars` dataframe and pass it along to Python-nvd3 for graphing:

```
In [2]: from nvd3 import scatterChart
loaded nvd3 IPython extension
run nvd3.ipynb.initialize_javascript() to set up the notebook
help(nvd3.ipynb.initialize_javascript) for options

In [3]: %load_ext rpy2.ipython

In [4]: from rpy2.robjects import pandas2ri

In [5]: pandas2ri.activate()

In [6]: from rpy2.robjects import r

In [7]: import pandas

In [8]: df_cars = pandas2ri.ri2py(r['mtcars'])

In [9]: wt = df_cars['wt']

In [10]: mpg = df_cars['mpg']

In [11]: kwargs = {'shape': 'circle', 'size': '1'}

In [12]: chart = scatterChart(name='Weight vs MPG', height=400,
width=800, y_axis_scale_min='0', show_legend='False')

In [13]: chart.add_serie(name="Cars", x=wt, y=mpg, **kwargs)

In [14]: output_file = open('nvd3-2.html', 'w')

In [15]: chart.buildhtml()

In [16]: output_file.write(chart.htmlcontent)
Out[16]: 3136

In [17]: output_file.close()
```

code9.py

This code produces the following graph:

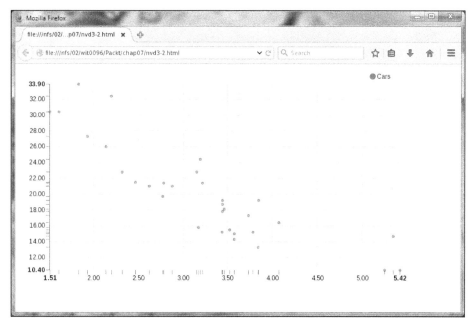

nvd3-2.gif

A different type of plot

One of the benefits of having a simple interface is that it is relatively easy to try out different views of the data. In this example, we look at the relative numbers of different engine sizes:

```
In [1]: from nvd3 import pieChart
loaded nvd3 IPython extension
run nvd3.ipynb.initialize_javascript() to set up the notebook
help(nvd3.ipynb.initialize_javascript) for options

In [2]: %load_ext rpy2.ipython

In [3]: xs = %R sort(unique(mtcars$cyl))

In [4]: ys = %R table(mtcars$cyl)

In [5]: chart = pieChart(name="Cylinders", color_category='category10',
height=500, width=400)
```

```
In [6]: chart.add_serie(x=xs.tolist(), y=ys.tolist())

In [7]: output_file = open('nvd3-3.html', 'w')

In [8]: chart.buildhtml()

In [9]: output_file.write(chart.htmlcontent)
Out[9]: 1630

In [10]: output_file.close()
```

code10.py

The preceding code produces the following plot:

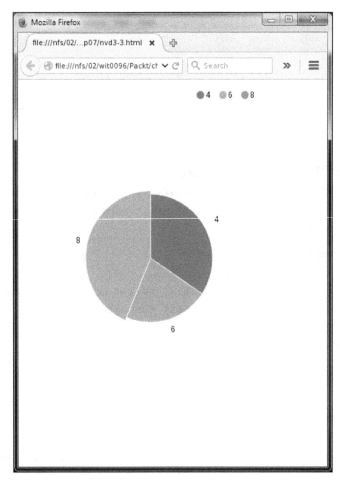

nvd3-3.gif

While this may look like a rather basic graph:

- The individual pie slices resize and change color when hovered over
- The colored dots at the top are buttons that can be used to turn on/off the display of the corresponding slice (and the pie itself is recalculated accordingly)

Overall, plotting in Python-nvd3 requires a minimal number of lines of code, most of which are in Python. This makes learning to use the package easier (and this should improve once the documentation catches up with the development). Perhaps more importantly, fewer lines of code mean quicker and easier development. During initial data exploration, the ability to create a large volume of different visualizations is more important than the quality of any graph in particular. Python-nvd3 provides a handy tool for such a situation.

Summary

Whether the project calls for interactive visuals created at the command line for immediate consumption, or a more off-line approach where results are expressed as an image that can be viewed at leisure, there is a tool that fits the need.

The degree to which various tools are integrated with IPython varies: R uses Rmagics to enable a mode in which the developer is virtually running an R interpreter, while Plotly prefers using Python as much as possible. Development in this area is rapid, and it seems likely that there will be an even greater degree of interoperability between different tools in the future, whether supported by the tools themselves or by new frameworks designed for that purpose.

To a large extent, the choice of which tool to use should come down to the one that the developer finds the easiest to use. Many good options are free, and the use of IPython to generate data makes it relatively easy to switch from one tool to another without loss of data.

Although seeing is believing, one should not believe everything they see. In the next chapter, we will talk about IPython's support for testing. Every project of any size should have an associated test suite, and the next chapter will discuss the tools available to make writing and running tests easier.

8
But It Worked in the Demo! – Testing

With the split from Jupyter went the need for specialized IPython testing tools. This does not reduce the need to test IPython programs, however. There are several testing frameworks for Python itself that fit neatly into this role. No one writes code expecting it to produce incorrect output, or bomb. Regardless, years of experience in the industry have demonstrated that good design is not enough. Programs need to be thoroughly tested before their results can be relied on. This is especially true for scientific and numeric systems, where errors can be subtle but their effects far-reaching. No one wants to repeat the Mars Climate Orbiter fiasco.

We will look at some of the more popular frameworks and discuss some issues that are particular to testing in a highly parallel/HPC environment.

The following topics will be covered:

- Unit testing
- unittest
- pytest
- nose2

Unit testing

While there are many types of testing (for example, acceptance testing, integration testing, and stress testing), this chapter will concentrate on unit testing. There are three reasons for this concentration:

1. Unit tests are more likely to be language-specific. While other test frameworks can treat code as a black box (for example, a GUI tester), unit tests are usually written using the same language as the system they are testing.

2. The day-to-day development of a system should include the writing of unit tests. For the audience of this book, unit tests should be the most familiar type.

3. It is the nature of most scientific and engineering code that a large amount of computation can occur before a comparatively simple, yet previously unknown, answer is produced. Unit testing is the type of testing that is most directly focused on the question, "Is that the right answer?"

 For ease of reference, we will refer to the part of the program being tested as "code", and the part of the program doing the testing as "tests" or "test cases".

A quick introduction

A unit test is code that exercises the functionality of other code. The standard unit of code under test is an individual function, and so unit tests look and act like function calls. The primary differences between unit tests and "normal" function calls are that the programmer knows the desired result and the function is being tested in isolation, not as a part of the system as it is designed to be run. This leads to two important features of unit test frameworks: assertions and environmental issues.

Assertions

A function can be viewed as a machine—you feed an input and the machine produces an output. The point of testing is to make sure you get the right output. This assumes that you know the right answer, at least for some inputs. An assertion is simply a statement that compares the actual answer with the known (correct) answer. If they match, the assertion passes. If not, it fails. A test passes only if all the assertions that it contains pass.

Environmental issues

When a function runs, it interacts with its environment in three phases: before it starts, while it is running, and after it finishes. We will outline each phase in turn.

Before it starts – setup

It is often the case that a particular function requires other parts of the system to be available before it can even begin. The other parts of the system (functions, objects, and so on) might require their own initialization and so on. The process of putting the system in a state from which the function to be tested can be called is called the setup phase (or just setup). The goal of setup is to put everything the function needs in a well-known, repeatable state before the function starts.

While it is running – mocks

The function may need to call other elements while it is running. If these elements can be relied on and are deterministic, nothing needs to be done. Most likely, these elements are also being tested and should not be relied on. In such a case, equivalent elements should be created that, while not functionally equivalent, at least implement the same interface and return acceptable results in a reliable, repeatable manner. These elements are often called mocks, as in mock objects or mock functions.

After it finishes – teardown

A function may make permanent changes to the environment that are undesirable in a testing situation. For example, a function may read in one database table, transform the data, and write the results to another table. While it is important to test this entire process, it is probably not acceptable for the data to remain in the table after the testing has been completed. The process of undoing any undesired, permanent changes is called teardown.

Writing to be tested

The flip side of knowing what value a function should return is that the function actually should return some value. There are entire classes of functions that do not return values, or for which the returned value is not that useful for testing. Consider a function called `display` that accepts a character as input and renders the character on a monitor.

If `display` does not return a value, it is impossible to write an `assert` statement to test it. It can be called, but without looking at the monitor, there is no way of knowing whether the character was displayed. At best, one could conclude that calling `display` does not crash.

If `display` does return a value, things are not much better. First off, it is not clear what meaningful value it could return. Maybe true for "it worked" and false for "it did not work"? That value can be tested at least. However, it will not resolve the underlying problem—perhaps, `display` returned true but the character was not actually displayed.

The takeaway from this short digression is that testing works better when the code to be tested is written in such a way as to make writing meaningful tests easier. The techniques for doing so can fill an entire book (and they have). Luckily, scientific and engineering code, with its emphasis on mathematical modeling, tends to naturally break down into testable functions.

unittest

unittest is the built-in (since version 2.1) testing framework for Python. It is modelled after the excellent JUnit framework for Java, and the xUnit testing frameworks in general. This makes for a clean, object-oriented style.

Important concepts

unittest supports the standard unit testing parts in a straightforward manner. The following concepts map onto functional elements:

- **Test case**: This is an individual test or group of tests. All tests in a test case belong to the same class and share a fixture.
- **Test fixture**: The functions required to do `setUp` and `tearDown` for all the test cases in a class.
- **Test suite**: This is a collection of test cases. Test cases in a test suite are meant to be run together.
- **Test runner**: This is a component that runs test suites and reports the results to the user.

Let's take a closer look at some code from earlier as an example:

```
def f(n):
    curr = n
    tmp = 1
    while curr != 1:
        tmp = tmp + 1
        if curr % 2 == 1:
```

```
        curr = 3 * curr + 1
    else:
        curr = curr/2
return tmp
```

hail1.py

This code accepts an integer as input, computes the corresponding hailstone sequence, and returns the length of that sequence. We would like to test this code to make sure that it gives the correct values. In this case, the values are known for up to very large values of *n*. Our source is sequence *A006577* in *The On-Line Encyclopedia of Integer Sequences* (`https://oeis.org/A006577`). We will be satisfied with checking the values for *0 < n < 11*:

```
import unittest
from hail1 import f

class TestHailStones(unittest.TestCase):

    def test_f(self):
        ans = [-1, 0, 1, 7, 2, 5, 8, 16, 3, 19, 6]
        for i in range(1, 11):
            print(i)
            self.assertEqual(f(i), ans[i])

if __name__ == '__main__':
    unittest.main()
```

test1.py

This code has some interesting features:

- **Line 1**: The `unittest` module must be imported, but it is standard.

- **Line 4**: All test cases inherit from the `unittest.TestCase` class.

- **Line 6**: Each test gets its own method. The method takes no parameters and produces no return value. It should start with `test`.

- **Line 7**: Lists start at `0`, but the hailstone sequences start at `1`, so a dummy value sits in slot `0`.

- **Line 10**: This is an instance of an `assert` statement. In this case, the `assert` will pass if `f(i) == ans[i]`, and will fail otherwise.

The `TestCase` class provides a great number of `assert` statements. The following are popular:

Assertion	Test
`assertEqual(x, y)`	`x == y`
`assertNotEqual(x, y)`	`x != y`
`assertTrue(x)`	`bool(x) is True`
`assertFalse(x)`	`bool(x) is False`
`assertIs(x, y)`	`x is y`
`assertIsNot(x, y)`	`x is not y`
`assertIsNone(x)`	`x is None`
`assertIsNotNone(x)`	`x is not None`
`assertIsIn(x, y)`	`x is in y`
`assertIsNotIn(x, y)`	`x is not in y`
`assertIsInstance(x, y)`	`isinstance(x, y)`
`assertIsNotInstance(x, y)`	`not isinstance(x, y)`
`assertIsNot(x, y)`	`x is not y`

More can be found at `https://docs.python.org/3.5/library/unittest.html`.

Running the test in verbose mode from the IPython command line results in the following output:

```
In [2]: %run test1.py -v
test_f (__main__.TestHailStones) ... 1
FAIL


======================================================================
FAIL: test_f (__main__.TestHailStones)
----------------------------------------------------------------------
Traceback (most recent call last):
  File "/nfs/02/wit0096/Packt/chap08/test1.py", line 10, in test_f
    self.assertEqual(f(i), ans[i])
AssertionError: 1 != 0


----------------------------------------------------------------------
Ran 1 test in 0.001s


FAILED (failures=1)
```

```
An exception has occurred, use %tb to see the full traceback.


SystemExit: True
```

The `assert` statement has failed. There must be a bug here. A quick look at the output shows that the `print` statement has printed out 1 (there are better ways of finding out which loop iteration failed, but this is simple and will work for now), so it must have failed for `f(1)`.

If more information is needed, the `%tb` magic will provide it:

```
In [3]: %tb
-----------------------------------------------------------------------
---
SystemExit                                Traceback (most recent call
last)
/nfs/02/kmanalo/envs/my_rpy2_zone/lib/python3.4/site-packages/IPython/
utils/py3compat.py in execfile(fname, glob, loc, compiler)
    181         with open(fname, 'rb') as f:
    182             compiler = compiler or compile
--> 183             exec(compiler(f.read(), fname, 'exec'), glob, loc)
    184
    185     # Refactor print statements in doctests.


/nfs/02/wit0096/Packt/chap08/test1.py in <module>()
     11
     12 if __name__ == '__main__':
---> 13     unittest.main()


/nfs/02/kmanalo/envs/my_rpy2_zone/lib/python3.4/unittest/main.py in __
init__(self, module, defaultTest, argv, testRunner, testLoader, exit,
verbosity, failfast, catchbreak, buffer, warnings)
     91         self.progName = os.path.basename(argv[0])
     92         self.parseArgs(argv)
---> 93         self.runTests()
     94
     95     def usageExit(self, msg=None):


/nfs/02/kmanalo/envs/my_rpy2_zone/lib/python3.4/unittest/main.py in
runTests(self)
```

```
    244            self.result = testRunner.run(self.test)
    245            if self.exit:
--> 246                sys.exit(not self.result.wasSuccessful())
    247
    248 main = TestProgram
```

SystemExit: True

In this case, it's not that interesting, but the information is there if needed.

A small fix should remedy this problem:

```python
def f(n):
    curr = n
    tmp = 0
    while curr != 1:
        tmp = tmp + 1
        if curr % 2 == 1:
            curr = 3 * curr + 1
        else:
            curr = curr/2
    return tmp
```

hail2.py

Along with a corresponding change to the test (normally, one would just change the original source, but this is clearer for instructional purposes):

```python
import unittest
from hail2 import f

class TestHailStones(unittest.TestCase):

    def test_f(self):
        ans = [0, 0, 1, 7, 2, 5, 8, 16, 3, 19, 6]
        for i in range(1, 11):
            print(i)
            self.assertEqual(f(i), ans[i])

if __name__ == '__main__':
    unittest.main()
```

test2.py

Now, running the test shows that everything works as expected:

```
In [4]: %run test2.py -v
test_f (__main__.TestHailStones) ... 1
2
3
4
5
6
7
8
9
10
ok

----------------------------------------------------------------------

Ran 1 test in 0.001s

OK
```

A test using setUp and tearDown

The previous test was straightforward—just include the right file and call the function to be tested. The function in question has no state, so there was nothing to set up or tear down. In this section, we will build a slightly more sophisticated test in which the tests and function require some initialization before they can be invoked, and need to be cleaned up afterward.

The example we will look at concerns random numbers. The class being tested is a simple iterative random number generator using the following formula:

$$x_{i+1} = (p_1 x_i + p_2) mod\ N$$

This is admittedly not the greatest random number generator. It is not completely terrible, however, depending on the choice of x, p1, p2, and N. It does have the advantage of being simple and easy to test. The code is as follows:

```
class MyRand(object):

    def set(self, p1, p2, x0, modulus):
```

```
        self.__p1 = p1
        self.__p2 = p2
        self.__x = x0
        self.__modulus = modulus

    def next(self):
        self.__x = (self.__p1 * self.__x + self.__p2) %
self.__modulus
        return self.__x

    def reset(self):
        self.__p1 = 2
        self.__p2 = 2
        self.__x = 2
        self.__modulus = 2
```

myrand.py

Our next test class is more elaborate than the previous one. We will apply a simple test: is the least significant digit of the "random" number evenly distributed over [0, 9]? Any generator failing this test would certainly fail more difficult tests, such as those in the Diehard Battery (found at http://stat.fsu.edu/pub/diehard/). The code is as follows:

```
import unittest
import numpy as np
import myrand
import scipy.stats
import sys
import random

class TestRandoms(unittest.TestCase):

    def setUp(self):
        print("Doing setUp")
        self.numVals = 10000
        self.vals = np.zeros((10), dtype=np.int32)
        self.randGen = myrand.MyRand( )

    def test_bad(self):
        print("Doing test_bad")
        x0 = 15
        p1 = 50
        p2 = 100
        modulus = 2217
```

```
        self.randGen.set(p1, p2, x0, modulus)
        for i in range(self.numVals):
            tmp = self.randGen.next( )
            tmp = tmp % 10
            self.vals[tmp] = self.vals[tmp] + 1

        chi2, p = scipy.stats.chisquare(self.vals)
        self.assertLess(p, 0.05)

    def test_better(self):
        print("Doing test_better")
        x0 = 79
        p1 = 263
        p2 = 71
        modulus = sys.maxsize
        self.randGen.set(p1, p2, x0, modulus)
        for i in range(self.numVals):
            tmp = self.randGen.next( )
            tmp = tmp % 10
            self.vals[tmp] = self.vals[tmp] + 1

        chi2, p = scipy.stats.chisquare(self.vals)
        self.assertGreater(p, 0.05)

    def test_builtin(self):
        print("Doing test_builtin")
        for i in range(self.numVals):
            tmp = random.randint(0, 9)
            self.vals[tmp] = self.vals[tmp] + 1

        chi2, p = scipy.stats.chisquare(self.vals)
        self.assertGreater(p, 0.05)


    def tearDown(self):
        print("Doing tearDown")
        self.randGen.reset( )


if __name__ == '__main__':
    unittest.main()
```

testrand.py

The output is simple:

```
In [1]: %run testrand.py
Doing setUp
Doing test_bad
Doing tearDown
.Doing setUp
Doing test_better
Doing tearDown
.Doing setUp
Doing test_builtin
Doing tearDown

.
----------------------------------------------------------------
Ran 3 tests in 0.172s

OK
```

The code itself contains some interesting features:

- **Line 10**: This overrides the setup method from `unittest.TestCase`. The setup function is run once before every test.

- **Line 11**: The `print` statements are included, so the output will show when `setUp`, the tests, and `tearDown` are executed. A production test suite would not include them.

- **Lines 12-14**: These lines contain the initialization functionality. The types of things found here are typical of a test run: constants, data structures to hold results, and object creation. While constants should generally be created only once per run (rather than before every test), that would complicate the example at this point.

- **Line 16**: Our first test uses some poor parameter choices for the random number generator. As such, when we apply a chi-squared test, the *pvalue* is too low to be acceptable.

- **Line 29**: Because we expect a poor result, we test for it.

Note that if the line were changed to this:

```
self.assertGreater(p, 0.05)
```

The output would change to the following:

```
In [2]: %run testrand.py
Doing setUp
Doing test_bad
Doing tearDown
Doing setUp
Doing test_better
Doing tearDown
.Doing setUp
Doing test_builtin
Doing tearDown
.
======================================================================
FAIL: test_bad (__main__.TestRandoms)
----------------------------------------------------------------------
Traceback (most recent call last):
  File "/nfs/02/wit0096/Packt/chap08/testrand.py", line 29, in test_bad
    self.assertGreater(p, 0.05)
AssertionError: 3.5277031043732684e-204 not greater than 0.05


----------------------------------------------------------------------
Ran 3 tests in 0.171s

FAILED (failures=1)
An exception has occurred, use %tb to see the full traceback.

SystemExit: True
```

There are some things worth pointing out about the program overall:

- The code contains several tests. There is no need to label the tests as such, as unittest assumes that every function starting with `test` is a test and will run it as such.

- The tests are run in alphabetical order regardless of their order in the source file. The official page at `https://docs.python.org/3.5/library/unittest.html` states:

    "The order in which the various tests will be run is determined by sorting the test method names with respect to the built-in ordering for strings."

One-time setUp and tearDown

unittest includes the ability for testers to specify unique functions that execute only once each at the beginning and the end of the lifetime of a testing class, as opposed to before and after every test. These methods must be named `setUpClass` and `tearDownClass` and must be implemented as class methods. For example, to initialize the `numVals` variable just once:

```
import unittest
import numpy as np
import myrand
import scipy.stats
import sys
import random

class TestRandoms(unittest.TestCase):

    @classmethod
    def setUpClass(cls):
        print("Doing setUpClass")
        cls.numVals = 10000

    def setUp(self):
        print("Doing setUp")
        self.vals = np.zeros((10), dtype=np.int32)
        self.randGen = myrand.MyRand()

    def test_bad(self):
        print("Doing test_bad")
        x0 = 15
        p1 = 50
        p2 = 100
        modulus = 2217
        self.randGen.set(p1, p2, x0, modulus)
        for i in range(TestRandoms.numVals):
            tmp = self.randGen.next()
            tmp = tmp % 10
```

```
                self.vals[tmp] = self.vals[tmp] + 1

            chi2, p = scipy.stats.chisquare(self.vals)
            self.assertLess(p, 0.05)

        def test_better(self):
            print("Doing test_better")
            x0 = 79
            p1 = 263
            p2 = 71
            modulus = sys.maxsize
            self.randGen.set(p1, p2, x0, modulus)
            for i in range(TestRandoms.numVals):
                tmp = self.randGen.next( )
                tmp = tmp % 10
                self.vals[tmp] = self.vals[tmp] + 1

            chi2, p = scipy.stats.chisquare(self.vals)
            self.assertGreater(p, 0.05)

        def test_builtin(self):
            print("Doing test_builtin")
            for i in range(TestRandoms.numVals):
                tmp = random.randint(0, 9)
                self.vals[tmp] = self.vals[tmp] + 1

            chi2, p = scipy.stats.chisquare(self.vals)
            self.assertGreater(p, 0.05)


        def tearDown(self):
            print("Doing tearDown")
            self.randGen.reset( )


    if __name__ == '__main__':
        unittest.main()
```

This generates the following output:

```
In [1]: %run testrand2.py
Doing setUpClass
Doing setUp
Doing test_bad
```

```
Doing tearDown
.Doing setUp
Doing test_better
Doing tearDown
.Doing setUp
Doing test_builtin
Doing tearDown
.
```

```
Ran 3 tests in 0.227s
```

```
OK
```

Decorators

It was somewhat awkward to use `assertLess` for one test and `assertGreater` for other tests. This is the sort of small inconsistency that can easily be overlooked, leading to bigger problems later on. Even worse, it might be caught and "corrected" only for that correction to cause the test to fail and lead to a lot of confused standing around as to why it was written that way in the first place.

This sort of thing happens all the time, especially when tests are not written before code.

Test-driven development

Test-driven development (TDD) is a software development process in which tests are written before code. This process allows them to be used as an automated means by which code can be checked against (at least some of) the requirements. The tests can also be used to ensure that future changes to the code do not break any already existing functionality.

In theory, all tests should be run and passed before the code is accepted. This is not always practical. To this end, unittest provides decorators to allow the tester to explicitly mark failing and skipped tests.

For example, our previous test can be decorated as follows:

```
@unittest.expectedFailure
def test_bad(self):
        print("Doing test_bad")
        x0 = 15
        p1 = 50
```

```
        p2 = 100
        modulus = 2217
        self.randGen.set(p1, p2, x0, modulus)
        for i in range(TestRandoms.numVals):
            tmp = self.randGen.next( )
            tmp = tmp % 10
            self.vals[tmp] = self.vals[tmp] + 1

        chi2, p = scipy.stats.chisquare(self.vals)
        self.assertGreater(p, 0.05)
```

This will result in all the tests passing, remove the inconsistency, and alert anyone examining the tests that we expect that test case to fail the same randomness test we expect the other test cases to pass.

The unittest framework provides several decorators of this sort:

Decorator	Description
`skip(reason)`	Skip this test because *reason*
`skipIf(cond, reason)`	Skip this test if `cond` is `true`
`skipUnless(cond, reason)`	Skip this test if `cond` is `false`
`expectedFailure`	If the test fails, it passes (and vice versa)

pytest

pytest is a unit testing framework that attempts to be more "Pythonic." An important goal of it was to minimize the amount of additional code that had to be written in unittest in order to make tests run. pytest has often been described as "no-boilerplate" testing due to its minimal setup requirements. The home page for the project can be found at `https://pytest.org/latest/index.html`.

Installation

pytest can be installed using `pip`:

```
pip install pytest
```

One can test the installation as follows:

```
(my_rpy2_zone)-bash-4.1$ py.test --version
This is pytest version 2.8.7, imported from …
```

It is easy to invoke from the command line:

```
(my_rpy2_zone)-bash-4.1$ py.test
============================================== test session starts ===
============================================
platform linux -- Python 3.4.4, pytest-2.8.7, py-1.4.31, pluggy-0.3.1
rootdir: …/chap08, inifile:
collected 0 items


============================================= no tests ran in 0.03
seconds ============================================
```

pytest will attempt to auto-locate tests according to rules that will be covered in a later section. In this case, none were found.

Back compatibility

It seems a shame to throw out all the work that was done on the tests from the previous sections. pytest will look for tests in files of the form test_*.py (and *_test.py). The laziest thing possible would be to just copy test1.py into test_1.py and see what happens:

```
(my_rpy2_zone)-bash-4.1$ cp test1.py test_1.py
(my_rpy2_zone)-bash-4.1$ py.test
============================================== test session starts ===
============================================
platform linux -- Python 3.4.4, pytest-2.8.7, py-1.4.31, pluggy-0.3.1
rootdir: …/chap08, inifile:
collected 1 items


test_1.py F


====================================================== FAILURES ========
============================================
_____ TestHailStones.test_f __
_____


self = <test_1.TestHailStones testMethod=test_f>

    def test_f(self):
```

```
        ans = [0, 0, 1, 7, 2, 5, 8, 16, 3, 19, 6]
        for i in range(1, 11):
            print(i)
>           self.assertEqual(f(i), ans[i])
E           AssertionError: 1 != 0


test_1.py:10: AssertionError
------------------------------------------------ Captured stdout call
--------------------------------------------------
1
================================================ 1 failed in 0.14 seconds
================================================
```

That was pretty neat. It automatically detected and was able to run a test suite that was written for unittest. But there is no guarantee that this will always work. The website at `http://pytest.org/latest/unittest.html` states:

> *"pytest has support for running Python unittest.py style tests. It's meant for leveraging existing unittest-style projects to use pytest features. Concretely, pytest will automatically collect unittest.TestCase subclasses and their test methods in test files. It will invoke typical setup/teardown methods and generally try to make test suites written to run on unittest, to also run using pytest. We assume here that you are familiar with writing unittest.TestCase style tests and rather focus on integration aspects."*

There are also tools such as **unittest2pytest** to help convert older tests over. There is no requirement that your project do so—unittest is a perfectly fine framework, likely to be supported for the indefinite future—but at least changing frameworks will not cause a massive loss of effort.

Test discovery

Because pytest does not require tests to be in classes that inherit from `unittest.TestCase`, it requires a more sophisticated approach to determining what is a test and what is not. It is hard to go wrong by putting all tests in files named `test_<something>.py` and naming the test functions themselves as `test_<function to be tested>`. The official rules (from `http://pytest.org/latest/goodpractices.html#test-discovery`) are a bit more complex:

- If no arguments are specified, then collection starts from `testpaths` (if configured) or the current directory. Alternatively, command-line arguments can be used in any combination of directories, filenames, or node IDs.

- recurse into directories, unless they match `norecursedirs`.
- `test_*.py` or `*_test.py` files, imported by their test package name.
- Test prefixed test classes (without an __init__ method).
- `test_` prefixed test functions or methods are test items.

Organizing test files

pytest allows test functions to be included in the same file as the functions to be tested. This has some advantages in that it makes it more likely that tests will be updated when functionality is, and makes the tests easy to find.

However, this is not a good idea for any but the smallest project, for several reasons:

- A good test suite can be several times the size of the code to be tested. Putting both in the same place obscures the code.
- It is often the case that different groups develop tests and code. Using different files makes for easier version control.
- Tests should not depend on how code is written, nor should code depend on how tests are structured. The easiest way to ensure this is to keep them completely separate.

When tests are no longer in the same file as code, it is important to keep them somewhere easy to find and associate with the code they test. A parallel directory structure is an easy way to achieve this:

```
pkg/
    __init__.py
    prog1.py
    ...
tests/
    test_prog1.py
    ...
```

Note the lack of an __init.py__ file in the tests directory. This provides an easier time for one of the test discovery rules listed previously. There is no requirement in pytest that things be mirrored this exactly; it is just a useful heuristic.

Assertions

pytest uses the assert statement found in Python. This obviates the need to remember all the different `assert*` methods from unittest. Consider the difference in readability between this:

```
self.assertEqual(f(i), ans[i])
```

And this line of code:

```
assert f(i) == ans[i]
```

In general, pytest tests are smaller in terms of lines of code. The `test2.py` test file can be rewritten under pytest as follows:

```
from hail2 import f

class TestHailStones():

    def test_f(self):
        ans = [0, 0, 1, 7, 2, 5, 8, 16, 3, 19, 6]
        for i in range(1, 11):
            print(i)
            assert f(i) == ans[i]
```

test_2.py

Here is the result:

```
In [2]: !py.test test_2.py
================================================ test session starts ===
================================================
platform linux -- Python 3.4.4, pytest-2.8.7, py-1.4.31, pluggy-0.3.1
rootdir: /nfs/02/wit0096/Packt/chap08, inifile:
collected 1 items


test_2.py .


================================================ 1 passed in 0.02 seconds
================================================
```

Even the results can be abbreviated with the -q command-line argument:

```
In [3]: !py.test -q test_2.py

.

1 passed in 0.01 seconds
```

A test using setUp and tearDown

unittest depends on overloading the `setUp` and `tearDown` functions from its parent class. As pytest drops the parent class, it needs a different mechanism. In fact, it has two: a classic xUnit-style and one using fixtures.

Classic xUnit-style

The following methods are provided to do setup and teardown:

Method	Effect
`setup_method(self, method)`	Called before every test method in a class
`teardown_method(self, method)`	Called after every test method in a class
`setup_function(function)`	Called before every test method in a module
`teardown_function(function)`	Called after every test method in a module

This makes rewriting our first random number test a breeze:

```
import numpy as np
import myrand
import scipy.stats
import sys
import random

class TestRandoms( ):

    def setup_method(self, mthd):
        print("Doing setUp")
        self.numVals = 10000
        self.vals = np.zeros((10), dtype=np.int32)
        self.randGen = myrand.MyRand( )

    def test_bad(self):
        print("Doing test_bad")
        x0 = 15
        p1 = 50
        p2 = 100
        modulus = 2217
        self.randGen.set(p1, p2, x0, modulus)
        for i in range(self.numVals):
            tmp = self.randGen.next( )
            tmp = tmp % 10
```

```
        self.vals[tmp] = self.vals[tmp] + 1

    chi2, p = scipy.stats.chisquare(self.vals)
    assert p > 0.05

def test_better(self):
    print("Doing test_better")
    x0 = 79
    p1 = 263
    p2 = 71
    modulus = sys.maxsize
    self.randGen.set(p1, p2, x0, modulus)
    for i in range(self.numVals):
        tmp = self.randGen.next( )
        tmp = tmp % 10
        self.vals[tmp] = self.vals[tmp] + 1

    chi2, p = scipy.stats.chisquare(self.vals)
    assert p > 0.05

def test_builtin(self):
    print("Doing test_builtin")
    for i in range(self.numVals):
        tmp = random.randint(0, 9)
        self.vals[tmp] = self.vals[tmp] + 1

    chi2, p = scipy.stats.chisquare(self.vals)
    assert p > 0.05


def teardown_method(self, mthd):
    print("Doing tearDown")
    self.randGen.reset( )
```

testrand_1.py

Here is the expected result:

```
In [7]: !py.test testrand_1.py
================================================= test session starts ===
================================================
platform linux -- Python 3.4.4, pytest-2.8.7, py-1.4.31, pluggy-0.3.1
rootdir: /nfs/02/wit0096/Packt/chap08, inifile:
```

```
collected 3 items

testrand_1.py F..

================================================== FAILURES ========
===================================================
_____ TestRandoms.test_bad __
_____

self = <testrand_1.TestRandoms object at 0x2b6610db1b38>

    def test_bad(self):
        print("Doing test_bad")
        x0 = 15
        p1 = 50
        p2 = 100
        modulus = 2217
        self.randGen.set(p1, p2, x0, modulus)
        for i in range(self.numVals):
            tmp = self.randGen.next( )
            tmp = tmp % 10
            self.vals[tmp] = self.vals[tmp] + 1

        chi2, p = scipy.stats.chisquare(self.vals)
>       assert p > 0.05
E       assert 3.5277031043732684e-204 > 0.05

testrand_1.py:28: AssertionError
------------------------------------------------ Captured stdout setup
-------------------------------------------------
Doing setUp
------------------------------------------------ Captured stdout call
-------------------------------------------------
Doing test_bad
======================================= 1 failed, 2 passed in 1.16
seconds =========================================
```

Being verbose

More information can be obtained by running pytest in verbose mode:

```
In [8]: !python -m pytest -v testrand_1.py
=================================================== test session starts ===
===========================================
platform linux -- Python 3.4.4, pytest-2.8.7, py-1.4.31, pluggy-0.3.1 --
/nfs/02/wit0096/envs/my_rpy2_zone/bin/python
cachedir: .cache
rootdir: /nfs/02/wit0096/Packt/chap08, inifile:
collected 3 items


testrand_1.py::TestRandoms::test_bad FAILED
testrand_1.py::TestRandoms::test_better PASSED
testrand_1.py::TestRandoms::test_builtin PASSED


========================================================= FAILURES ========
===========================================
_____ TestRandoms.test_bad __
_____


self = <testrand_1.TestRandoms object at 0x2ab6155f8e80>

    def test_bad(self):
        print("Doing test_bad")
        x0 = 15
        p1 = 50
        p2 = 100
        modulus = 2217
        self.randGen.set(p1, p2, x0, modulus)
        for i in range(self.numVals):
            tmp = self.randGen.next( )
            tmp = tmp % 10
            self.vals[tmp] = self.vals[tmp] + 1

        chi2, p = scipy.stats.chisquare(self.vals)
>       assert p > 0.05
```

```
E       assert 3.5277031043732684e-204 > 0.05


testrand_1.py:28: AssertionError
------------------------------------------------- Captured stdout setup
-----------------------------------------------

Doing setUp
------------------------------------------------- Captured stdout call
-----------------------------------------------

Doing test_bad
========================================= 1 failed, 2 passed in 0.82
seconds =========================================
```

Using fixtures

A function can be decorated as a pytest fixture. This fixture decoration can take a "scope" argument that specifies when the fixture should be called:

Scope	Effect
session	The function is executed once, at the beginning of the session
module	The function is executed once, at the beginning of the module
class	The function is executed once, at the beginning of the class
function	The function is executed before every test case

Our second random number testing class can then be rewritten as follows:

```python
import numpy as np
import myrand
import scipy.stats
import sys
import random
import pytest

class TestRandoms( ):

    @classmethod
    @pytest.fixture(scope="class")
    def setUpClass(cls):
        print("Doing setUpClass")
        cls.numVals = 10000

    @pytest.fixture(scope="function")
    def setUp(self, request):
```

```
        print("Doing setUp")
        self.vals = np.zeros((10), dtype=np.int32)
        self.randGen = myrand.MyRand( )
        self.numVals = 10000
        def tearDown(self):
            print("Doing tearDown")
            self.randGen.reset( )
        request.addfinalizer(tearDown)


    def test_bad(self, setUp, setUpClass):
        print("Doing test_bad")
        x0 = 15
        p1 = 50
        p2 = 100
        modulus = 2217
        self.randGen.set(p1, p2, x0, modulus)
        for i in range(self.numVals):
            tmp = self.randGen.next( )
            tmp = tmp % 10
            self.vals[tmp] = self.vals[tmp] + 1

        chi2, p = scipy.stats.chisquare(self.vals)
        assert p < 0.05


    def test_better(self, setUp, setUpClass):
        print("Doing test_better")
        x0 = 79
        p1 = 263
        p2 = 71
        modulus = sys.maxsize
        self.randGen.set(p1, p2, x0, modulus)
        for i in range(self.numVals):
            tmp = self.randGen.next( )
            tmp = tmp % 10
            self.vals[tmp] = self.vals[tmp] + 1

        chi2, p = scipy.stats.chisquare(self.vals)
        assert p > 0.05


    def test_builtin(self, setUp, setUpClass):
        print("Doing test_builtin")
        for i in range(self.numVals):
            tmp = random.randint(0, 9)
```

```
            self.vals[tmp] = self.vals[tmp] + 1

        chi2, p = scipy.stats.chisquare(self.vals)
        assert p > 0.05
```

testrand2.py

With appropriate editing (the `addfinalizer` line must be removed – in my environment, it produced a Python INTERNALERROR), it runs and produces the following output:

```
In [27]: !py.test -s testrand_2.py
================================================== test session starts ===
================================================
platform linux -- Python 3.4.4, pytest-2.8.7, py-1.4.31, pluggy-0.3.1
rootdir: /nfs/02/wit0096/Packt/chap08, inifile:
collected 3 items

testrand_2.py Doing setUpClass
Doing setUp
Doing test_bad
.Doing setUp
Doing test_better
.Doing setUp
Doing test_builtin
```

This code contains some interesting features:

- **Line 6**: The use of the pytest decorators requires importing the `pytest` module.
- **Line 11**: This is a fixture decorator. The scope is `class`, so it will be called only once for this class, before any of the tests are run. This is reflected in the output.
- **Line 16**: This fixture decorator has the `function` scope, and marks this function as one that should be run before every test function.
- **Line 22**: This is the definition of the `tearDown` function.
- **Line 25**: Here, the `tearDown` function is added to the request object as its finalizer. This will cause it to be called after the test has run.

Fixtures are even more flexible than this example can show. In particular, the various fixtures can be listed as parameters to only those functions that actually need them to run. It would be possible to define multiple fixtures, and each test case would use a different subset based on its requirements.

In addition, a fixture can have a return value that the test case can use. In the previous example, rather than setting fields in self, the setup could have created a new object with the appropriate values set as fields within it. This can help avoid namespace pollution.

There are too many decorators to cover in their entirety.

Skipping and failing

Decorators are also useful when a test should be skipped or is expected to fail.

The decorator for a test that should be unconditionally skipped is as follows:

```
@pytest.mark.skip(reason="…")
```

If the test should be conditionally skipped, the decorator is as follows:

```
@pytest.mark.skipif(<condition>, reason="…")
```

If the function is expected to fail, the decorator is as follows:

```
@pytest.mark.xfail
```

Monkeypatching

There are times when one wants to change the return value of a piece of code outside of the project's control. For example, an already existing test suite might always write its logs to a subdirectory of the current directory, but new guidelines require it to be written to the appropriate subdirectory of "/test". The current tests use os.getcwd() to obtain the current directory, from which the full path to the log file is created. One could always rewrite all the tests, but that would be a time-consuming and error-prone process, and would break in a few months when the logging policy changes again. The best fix would be to fool the already existing tests into thinking that the current directory was "/test", and leave them unchanged. There are only two problems:

- You do not have access to os.getcwd, nor can you change the old tests to use a different module
- Even if you could, other tests need an accurate return value from os.getcwd

The solution is to monkeypatch `os.getcwd`. A monkeypatch can set or delete the following:

- An attribute
- A dictionary item
- An environment variable
- Items in `sys.path`

The monkeypatch is used in a manner similar to a decorator object, except that the monkeypatch object is not explicitly declared; only its functions are called. Once a function that uses monkeypatch has ended, the settings obtained before it are invoked. Consider the following test (pseudo)code:

```
def test_func1( ):
    logdir = os.getcwd( ) + "/func1/loadtests"
    logfile = open(logdir + "/results1.log", "w")
    <do test things>
    logfile.close( )
```

This can be monkeypatched as follows:

```
@pytest.fixture(scope="function")
def change_cwd(monkeypatch):
    monkeypatch.setattr("os.getcwd", lambda: "/")

def test_func1(change_cwd):
    logdir = os.getcwd( ) + "/func1/loadtests"
    logfile = open(logdir + "/results1.log", "w")
    <do test things>
    logfile.close( )
```

The `change_cwd` function will tell monkeypatch to change the `os.getcwd` function into the lambda expression that is monkeypatch's second argument. Feeding `change_cwd` into `test_func1` ensures that the monkeypatch call is executed. Other test functions that do not require this modification to `os.getcwd` will simply not use `change_cwd` and will see normal functionality.

A monkeypatch is similar to the concept of a mock object. A mock object is a user-defined object that exposes the same interface as a different object but has a much simpler implementation. For example, when testing a function that reads data from a production database, it is usually undesirable to use actual production data. Instead, a stable set of test data should be used for every run to ensure that comparisons between runs are possible. In this case, a mock database object would be constructed. It would support (a subset of) the database operations, yet return the test data rather than connecting to the database servers and retrieving live data. A monkeypatch performs a similar function in that it replaces a fully functional value/function/object with a simplified implementation for testing.

nose2

The nose test framework started as a clone of pytest when pytest was at version 0.8. Its tagline is "nose extends unittest to make testing easier" (found at `http://nose.readthedocs.org/en/latest/`). All good things must come to an end, however; nose is currently in maintenance mode and it has been for several years.

As unittest only works on versions of Python 2.7 and greater, unittest2 was created as a backport for earlier versions. In addition to unittest's functionality, it also includes an improved API and better assertions. In effect, unittest2 is not only a backport but also a revision of unittest.

The changes to unittest were important enough that the successor to nose — imaginatively named nose2 — was based on the unittest2 plugins branch. From the home page:

> nose2 is the next generation of nicer testing for Python, based on the plugins branch of unittest2. nose2 aims to improve on nose by:
>
> Providing a better plugin API
>
> Being easier for users to configure
>
> Simplifying internal interfaces and processes
>
> Supporting Python 2 and 3 from the same codebase, without translation

Installation

nose2 can be installed using `pip`:

```
pip install nose2
```

One can test the installation by invoking the help functionality as follows:

```
(my_rpy2_zone)-bash-4.1$ python -m nose2 -h
usage: nose2 [-s START_DIR] [-t TOP_LEVEL_DIRECTORY] [--config [CONFIG]]
             [--no-user-config] [--no-plugins] [--plugin PLUGINS]
             [--exclude-plugin EXCLUDE_PLUGINS] [--verbose] [--quiet]
             [--log-level LOG_LEVEL] [-D] [--log-capture] [-F] [-B]
             [--coverage PATH] [--coverage-report TYPE]
             [--coverage-config FILE] [-C] [-h]
             [testNames [testNames ...]]
<more help>
```

It is easy to invoke from the command line using either Python –m, as shown previously, or the included nose2 script:

```
(my_rpy2_zone)-bash-4.1$ ./.local/bin/nose2


----------------------------------------------------------------------
Ran 0 tests in 0.000s


OK
```

nose2 will attempt to auto-detect tests using rules that will be discussed in a later section.

Back compatibility

It seems a shame to throw out all the work that was done on the tests from the previous sections. nose2 will try to run the tests written in unittest and pytest. The tests written in unittest run as expected. The pytest tests fail in spectacular and inscrutable ways:

```
(my_rpy2_zone)-bash-4.1$ ~/.local/bin/nose2 -v testrand_2

Doing setUpClass

testrand_2.TestRandoms.test_bad ... ERROR

Doing setUpClass
```

```
testrand_2.TestRandoms.test_better ... ERROR

Doing setUpClass

testrand_2.TestRandoms.test_builtin ... ERROR


======================================================================
ERROR: testrand_2.TestRandoms.test_bad
----------------------------------------------------------------------
Traceback (most recent call last):
  File "/nfs/02/kmanalo/envs/my_rpy2_zone/lib/python3.4/unittest/case.
py", line 58, in testPartExecutor
    yield
  File "/nfs/02/kmanalo/envs/my_rpy2_zone/lib/python3.4/unittest/case.
py", line 576, in run
    self.setUp()
  File "/nfs/02/wit0096/.local/lib/python3.4/site-packages/nose2/plugins/
loader/testclasses.py", line 210, in setUp
    self.obj.setUp()
TypeError: setUp() missing 2 required positional arguments: 'request' and
'setUpClass'


======================================================================
ERROR: testrand_2.TestRandoms.test_better
----------------------------------------------------------------------
Traceback (most recent call last):
  File "/nfs/02/kmanalo/envs/my_rpy2_zone/lib/python3.4/unittest/case.
py", line 58, in testPartExecutor
    yield
  File "/nfs/02/kmanalo/envs/my_rpy2_zone/lib/python3.4/unittest/case.
py", line 576, in run
    self.setUp()
  File "/nfs/02/wit0096/.local/lib/python3.4/site-packages/nose2/plugins/
loader/testclasses.py", line 210, in setUp
    self.obj.setUp()
TypeError: setUp() missing 2 required positional arguments: 'request' and
'setUpClass'


======================================================================
ERROR: testrand_2.TestRandoms.test_builtin
```

```
----------------------------------------------------------------
Traceback (most recent call last):
  File "/nfs/02/kmanalo/envs/my_rpy2_zone/lib/python3.4/unittest/case.
py", line 58, in testPartExecutor
    yield
  File "/nfs/02/kmanalo/envs/my_rpy2_zone/lib/python3.4/unittest/case.
py", line 576, in run
    self.setUp()
  File "/nfs/02/wit0096/.local/lib/python3.4/site-packages/nose2/plugins/
loader/testclasses.py", line 210, in setUp
    self.obj.setUp()
TypeError: setUp() missing 2 required positional arguments: 'request' and
'setUpClass'


----------------------------------------------------------------
Ran 3 tests in 0.001s


FAILED (errors=3)
```

nose2 seems to have a problem with pytest decorators. As pytest makes heavy use of decorators for all but the simplest tests, this would make porting tests from pytest to nose2 problematic. This is not necessarily a flaw in nose2—compatibility with pytest is not a stated goal—but it may have some impact on your choice of testing framework.

Test discovery

nose2 will look in the current directory and all qualifying subdirectories for modules that may contain tests. A directory qualifies if:

- It contains an __init.py__
- The directory name contains test (after being lowercased)
- The directory is named either lib or src

In each qualifying directory, nose2 will look for tests in every file that starts with test. The test files do not require the invocation of unittest.main( ), which our previous unittest-based tests did.

Running individual tests

Individual tests can be run by specifying the name of the module on the command line:

```
(my_rpy2_zone)-bash-4.1$ ~/.local/bin/nose2 -v test1
test_f (test1.TestHailStones) ... 1
FAIL


======================================================================
FAIL: test_f (test1.TestHailStones)
----------------------------------------------------------------------
Traceback (most recent call last):
  File "/nfs/02/wit0096/Packt/chap08/test1.py", line 10, in test_f
    self.assertEqual(f(i), ans[i])
AssertionError: 1 != 0


----------------------------------------------------------------------
Ran 1 test in 0.000s


FAILED (failures=1)
```

Do not specify the entire file name, or else an unhelpful error will be generated:

```
(my_rpy2_zone)-bash-4.1$ ~/.local/bin/nose2 -v test1.py
test1.py (nose2.loader.LoadTestsFailure) ... ERROR


======================================================================
ERROR: test1.py (nose2.loader.LoadTestsFailure)
----------------------------------------------------------------------
Traceback (most recent call last):
  File "/nfs/02/kmanalo/envs/my_rpy2_zone/lib/python3.4/unittest/case.
py", line 58, in testPartExecutor
    yield
  File "/nfs/02/kmanalo/envs/my_rpy2_zone/lib/python3.4/unittest/case.
py", line 580, in run
    testMethod()
  File "/nfs/02/wit0096/.local/lib/python3.4/site-packages/nose2/loader.
py", line 120, in testFailure
```

```
    raise exception
  File "/nfs/02/wit0096/.local/lib/python3.4/site-packages/nose2/plugins/
loader/parameters.py", line 118, in loadTestsFr
omName
    result = util.test_from_name(name, module)
  File "/nfs/02/wit0096/.local/lib/python3.4/site-packages/nose2/util.
py", line 106, in test_from_name
    parent, obj = object_from_name(name, module)
  File "/nfs/02/wit0096/.local/lib/python3.4/site-packages/nose2/util.
py", line 128, in object_from_name
    parent, obj = obj, getattr(obj, part)
AttributeError: 'module' object has no attribute 'py'


----------------------------------------------------------------------
Ran 1 test in 0.000s


FAILED (errors=1)
```

nose2 interprets the `.py` portion as specifying a module name. This can be useful when specifying a particular module but can lead to surprising results otherwise.

Assertions, setup, and teardown

As in pytest, nose2 uses the `assert` statement found in Python. It does not use the same fixture style as pytest, but it does support both a modified form of the classic xUnit-style setup and teardown along with its own set of fixtures.

 The testing features of nose2 are currently a little buggy when using testing classes. The examples that follow will use individual testing functions contained in modules, but they should otherwise work similarly to the previous examples.

Modified xUnit-style

Rather than simple setup and teardown functions distinguished by name, nose2 allows setup and teardown attributes on functions. We can rewrite our first random number generation test as follows:

```
import numpy as np
import myrand
import scipy.stats
```

```python
import sys
import random

numVals = 0
vals = 0
randGen = 0

def setup():
    print("Doing setUp")
    global numVals
    global vals
    global randGen
    numVals = 10000
    vals = np.zeros((10), dtype=np.int32)
    randGen = myrand.MyRand()

def test_bad():
    print("Doing test_bad")
    x0 = 15
    p1 = 50
    p2 = 100
    modulus = 2217
    randGen.set(p1, p2, x0, modulus)
    for i in range(numVals):
        tmp = randGen.next()
        tmp = tmp % 10
        vals[tmp] = vals[tmp] + 1

    chi2, p = scipy.stats.chisquare(vals)
    assert p > 0.05

def test_better():
    print("Doing test_better")
    x0 = 79
    p1 = 263
    p2 = 71
    modulus = sys.maxsize
    randGen.set(p1, p2, x0, modulus)
    for i in range(numVals):
        tmp = randGen.next()
        tmp = tmp % 10
        vals[tmp] = vals[tmp] + 1

    chi2, p = scipy.stats.chisquare(vals)
```

```
        assert p > 0.05

    def test_builtin():
        print("Doing test_builtin")
        for i in range(numVals):
            tmp = random.randint(0, 9)
            vals[tmp] = vals[tmp] + 1

        chi2, p = scipy.stats.chisquare(vals)
        assert p > 0.05

    def teardown():
        print("Doing tearDown")
        randGen.reset( )

    test_bad.setup = setup
    test_bad.teardown = teardown
    test_better.setup = setup
    test_better.teardown = teardown
    test_builtin.setup = setup
    test_builtin.teardown = teardown
```

testrand_nose2_2.py

Admittedly, using global variables is not a recommended practice, but without classes, drastic measures are called for. The important feature to notice is at the end. Here, the `setup` and `teardown` methods are assigned as attributes to the actual tests. There is some flexibility here: the `setup` attribute may be named `setup`, `setUp`, or `setUpFunc`, and the `teardown` attribute may be named `teardown`, `tearDown`, or `tearDownFunc`.

This may feel like an odd way to do things compared to simply declaring functions with the prescribed names, but it provides a lot of the flexibility that decorators do: if a particular test does not need setup or teardown, or different tests need different setups/teardowns, they can be assigned here.

The results are as expected:

```
(my_rpy2_zone)-bash-4.1$ ~/.local/bin/nose2 -v testrand_nose2_1
testrand_nose2_1.FunctionTestCase (test_bad) ... Doing setUp
Doing test_bad
Doing tearDown
FAIL
```

```
testrand_nose2_1.FunctionTestCase (test_better) ... Doing setUp

Doing test_better

Doing tearDown

ok

testrand_nose2_1.FunctionTestCase (test_builtin) ... Doing setUp

Doing test_builtin

Doing tearDown

ok


======================================================================
FAIL: testrand_nose2_1.FunctionTestCase (test_bad)
----------------------------------------------------------------------
Traceback (most recent call last):
  File "/nfs/02/wit0096/Packt/chap08/testrand_nose2_1.py", line 33, in
test_bad
    assert p > 0.05
AssertionError


----------------------------------------------------------------------

Ran 3 tests in 0.184s


FAILED (failures=1)
```

Using decorators

nose2 provides two decorators in the `nose2.tools.decorators` module that are
helpful in `setup` and `teardown`:

Decorator	Effect
`with_setup(setup)`	Runs the `setup` function before each test
`with_teardown(teardown)`	Runs the `teardown` function after each test

This allows us to rewrite the previous tests as follows:

```
import numpy as np
import myrand
import scipy.stats
import sys
import random
```

```
import nose2.tools.decorators

numVals = 0
vals = 0
randGen = 0

def setup():
    print("Doing setUp")
    global numVals
    global vals
    global randGen
    numVals = 10000
    vals = np.zeros((10), dtype=np.int32)
    randGen = myrand.MyRand( )

def teardown():
    print("Doing tearDown")
    randGen.reset( )

@nose2.tools.decorators.with_setup(setup)
@nose2.tools.decorators.with_teardown(teardown)
def test_bad():
    print("Doing test_bad")
    x0 = 15
    p1 = 50
    p2 = 100
    modulus = 2217
    randGen.set(p1, p2, x0, modulus)
    for i in range(numVals):
        tmp = randGen.next( )
        tmp = tmp % 10
        vals[tmp] = vals[tmp] + 1

    chi2, p = scipy.stats.chisquare(vals)
    assert p > 0.05

@nose2.tools.decorators.with_setup(setup)
@nose2.tools.decorators.with_teardown(teardown)
def test_better():
    print("Doing test_better")
    x0 = 79
    p1 = 263
    p2 = 71
    modulus = sys.maxsize
```

```
        randGen.set(p1, p2, x0, modulus)
        for i in range(numVals):
            tmp = randGen.next( )
            tmp = tmp % 10
            vals[tmp] = vals[tmp] + 1

        chi2, p = scipy.stats.chisquare(vals)
        assert p > 0.05

    @nose2.tools.decorators.with_setup(setup)
    @nose2.tools.decorators.with_teardown(teardown)
    def test_builtin():
        print("Doing test_builtin")
        for i in range(numVals):
            tmp = random.randint(0, 9)
            vals[tmp] = vals[tmp] + 1

        chi2, p = scipy.stats.chisquare(vals)
        assert p > 0.05
```

The expected results are as follows:

```
(my_rpy2_zone)-bash-4.1$ ~/.local/bin/nose2 -v testrand_nose2decs_1
testrand_nose2decs_1.FunctionTestCase (test_bad) ... Doing setUp
Doing test_bad
Doing tearDown
FAIL
testrand_nose2decs_1.FunctionTestCase (test_better) ... Doing setUp
Doing test_better
Doing tearDown
ok
testrand_nose2decs_1.FunctionTestCase (test_builtin) ... Doing setUp
Doing test_builtin
Doing tearDown
ok


======================================================================
FAIL: testrand_nose2decs_1.FunctionTestCase (test_bad)
----------------------------------------------------------------------
```

```
Traceback (most recent call last):
  File "/nfs/02/wit0096/Packt/chap08/testrand_nose2decs_1.py", line 40,
in test_bad
    assert p > 0.05
AssertionError


----------------------------------------------------------------

Ran 3 tests in 0.277s


FAILED (failures=1)
```

Plugins

An important feature of the move from nose to nose2 was the implementation of an improved plugin API. Plugins provide additional functionality and allow third parties to extend nose2. A complete list of all plugins would be outside of the scope of this book, and would be incomplete by the time it went to press in any case. An example should suffice to demonstrate the power of plugins.

Generating XML with the junitxml plugin

Although nose2 generates test results to stdout by default, large test suites can be too much for one person to watch the results scroll by on a screen. In this case, it can be helpful for each test to generate output in a standardized format. The xUnit family has popularized XML as this format, so many test reporting tools expect it as input.

In order to output XML, the junitxml plugin can be invoked as follows:

```
(my_rpy2_zone)-bash-4.1$ ~/.local/bin/nose2 -v --plugin nose2.plugins.
junitxml --junit-xml testrand_nose2decs_1
```

The output consists of two streams:

- The usual output, sent to stdout
- An XML file (nose2-junit.xml), created in the directory the test was run in

In this case, the resulting XML file contained the following:

```
<testsuite errors="0" failures="1" name="nose2-junit" skipped="0"
tests="3" time="0.258">
  <testcase classname="" name="test_bad" time="0.093808">
    <failure message="test failure">Traceback (most recent call
last):
  File "/nfs/02/wit0096/Packt/chap08/testrand_nose2decs_1.py",
line 40, in test_bad
    assert p &gt; 0.05
AssertionError
</failure>
    <system-err />
  </testcase>
  <testcase classname="" name="test_better" time="0.096404">
    <system-err />
  </testcase>
  <testcase classname="" name="test_builtin" time="0.066199">
    <system-err />
  </testcase>
</testsuite>
```

nose2-junit.xml

The junitxml plugin can be loaded and configured using nose2's standard configuration file mechanisms, as can any other plugin. The configuration files (or file) used follow a standard .ini format. nose2 as a whole is very configurable, and each plugin has its own set of options. There is no standard set of options for all plugins — interested developers are referred to each plugin's documentation for details.

A plugin API is provided so that the developer can write project-specific plugins if desired. This opens up the nose2 architecture relative to nose, as there is no central approval bottleneck for plugins.

Summary

The single most important property a running program can have is being correct. Too often, testing is left until the end of development, where it is either skipped entirely or rushed through because the project is late. This is especially true for scientific and engineering code, where lives might be at stake. Even exploratory code needs to be tested so that sound decisions can be based on it. No code should be accepted into the project repository without its associated unit tests. As such, testing should be made as easy as possible for developers.

While IPython supports many wonderful visualization tools that can provide visual feedback on results, there is no replacement for thorough unit testing. This chapter outlined the basics of unit testing—setup, test, and teardown—and showed how three different frameworks implemented these concepts. The decision of which framework to use is up to the project team.

In the next chapter, we will look at support for another often neglected component of professional-grade software: documentation. We will discuss the various audience documentation is written for, the types of information important to each, formatting options, and the tools available to make producing documentation relatively painless.

9
Documentation

"Real programmers don't comment their code. If it was hard to write, it should be hard to understand.

Real Programmers don't do documentation. Documentation is for those who can't figure out the listing."

– Legendary

The days of the hero coder toiling away in the darkness for 36 hours straight to produce the perfect code are drawing to a close. Although that still happens (and is fun to do), at the end of the day, most code is written for other people to use, fix, and extend. In order to do this, people other than the original author need to be able to understand what the code does and how.

These groups fall into three classes, each with its appropriate genre of documentation:

Group	Genre
Users	User manuals and sales pamphlets
External developers	Interface definitions, APIs, and docstrings
Maintenance coders	Inline comments and docstrings

Documentation required by users is outside the scope of this book. This chapter will focus on the documentation needs of external developers and maintenance coders, and how developers can produce that documentation with minimal pain.

The following topics will be covered in this chapter:

- Inline comments
- Docstrings
- reStructuredText
- Docutils
- Sphinx

Inline comments

We will use the term "inline comment" to refer to all comments that are meant for maintenance coders and will never be visible to anyone not reading the source code.

Inline comments start with a # sign and continue up to the end of the line. They may not occur within a string literal. No characters within an inline comment are interpreted.

Python does not support block comments. Rumors to the effect that triple double-quotes (" " ") can be used to comment out multiple lines are to be disbelieved. While that will often work, what actually happens is that Python looks at the included lines as one multiline string. As a string, the included lines are not interpreted. A string literal is created instead. As this new literal is not assigned to a variable, it is immediately garbage-collected.

In addition to this strange behavior, triple double-quotes are used for docstrings. Using them for both purposes can be confusing, which is what we set out to avoid in the first place.

Using inline comments

The "official" guide for Python style is PEP 0008 (found at `https://www.python.org/dev/peps/pep-0008/`). To the extent that code can be said to be self-documenting, this guide provides a standard set of suggestions for stylistic consistency that can help further that goal. The section on comments in particular contains some useful recommendations:

- Comments should match code. If the code changes, make sure that the comments reflect it.
- Comment in complete sentences.

- Block comments should be at the same indentation level as the code they apply to. Each line should start with a # sign and a single space.
- Comments should rarely be used on the same line as code.

Function annotations

Function annotations and type hints can be considered a type of inline comment. Function annotations originated in PEP 3107, which provided a syntax for adding arbitrary metadata annotations to Python functions. From the definition (`https://www.python.org/dev/peps/pep-3107/`):

> *"Because Python's 2.x series lacks a standard way of annotating a function's parameters and return values, a variety of tools and libraries have appeared to fill this gap. (...) This PEP aims to provide a single, standard way of specifying this information, reducing the confusion caused by the wide variation in mechanism and syntax that has existed until this point."*

Syntax

Function annotations apply to two sorts of things: parameters and return values.

Parameters

For parameters, an annotation is indicated by a colon, in a manner similar to that of marking a default value by an equal to sign, like this for example:

```
def foo(x: "int >= 0"):
```

Both an annotation and a default value can be indicated by placing them sequentially, as follows:

```
def foo(x: "int >= 0" = 0):
```

Informally, parameters can be described like this:

```
identifier [: expression] [= expression]
```

Here, both the annotation and the default value are optional.

Return values

The return value of the function can be annotated by following the parameter list with `->` and an expression. Here is an example:

```
def foo(x: "int >= 0" = 0) -> "seemingly random integer" :
    return 42
```

Semantics

Function annotations are completely optional. They allow static association of arbitrary Python expressions with parts of a function. The annotations are held in the function's __annotations__ attribute, like this:

```
In [5]: def foo(x: "int >= 0" = 0) -> "seemingly random integer" :
    return 42
...:

In [6]: foo.__annotations__
Out[6]: {'return': 'seemingly random integer', 'x': 'int >= 0'}
```

There is no standard semantics for the annotations. They serve two purposes: documentation for the coder and as inputs to third-party tools. Of course, each tool has its own standards and provides different semantics.

Type hints

Of course, the first and the most popular use of function annotations was to denote parameter and return types. This is practically the only use case listed in PEP 3107. It took 8 years, but eventually a PEP came along to provide some standard definitions. This is PEP 0484. From the definition (https://www.python.org/dev/peps/pep-0484/):

> *"PEP 3107 introduced syntax for function annotations, but the semantics were deliberately left undefined. There has now been enough 3rd party usage for static type analysis that the community would benefit from a standard vocabulary and baseline tools within the standard library.*
>
> *This PEP introduces a provisional module to provide these standard definitions and tools, along with some conventions for situations where annotations are not available."*

The PEP does not require annotations, nor does it specify (or forbid) any particular framework for processing them. In particular, *no type checking happens at either compile time or runtime*, unless a third-party tool does it. Also, in particular, annotations do not change the fact that Python is a dynamically typed language.

Syntax

Type hints use the same syntax and apply to the same things as function annotations. The major extension is that they allow the annotation to be a class. The full rule set is complicated, but the following hints should cover the most common cases:

- Built-in classes
- User-defined classes
- Types in the `types` module
- Abstract base classes
- Special constructs, including `None`, `Any`, `Union`, `Tuple`, and `Callable`

A great deal of the PEP is devoted to special cases and complex types, including generics, covariance and contravariance, forward references, and stub files.

Semantics

Like PEP 3107, there is no standard semantics associated with type hints. The goal instead was to provide a standard that third-party tools could work with. To the extent that type hints have a semantics, it is the one provided by the tool they are used with, not by the Python language itself. From the definition:

> *"This PEP aims to provide a standard syntax for type annotations, opening up Python code to easier static analysis and refactoring, potential runtime type checking, and (perhaps, in some contexts) code generation utilizing type information."*

An influential tool in the formation of the standard was mypy (`http://mypy-lang.org/`). The purpose of **mypy** is to provide a static type checker for Python. While the merits of static type checking in documentation and debugging can be debated, it is nice to have the option.

Docstrings

A Python docstring is a string literal. It can occur as the first statement in a module or as the first statement following the definition of a function, method, or class. The docstring becomes the __doc__ special attribute of that thing. Its purpose is to provide a more free-form way to document part of a program.

Example

The following code provides docstrings for an abbreviated version of an earlier test suite:

```
"""
This is an abbreviated version of my random number generator test
suite.

It uses the pytest framework.  It does not do much in this form.
"""

import numpy as np
import scipy.stats
import random

class TestRandoms( ):
    """
    This is the main class.

    Normally it would hold all the tests, plus and setup and
tearDown fixtures.
    """
    def test_builtin(self):
        """
        Test the built-in random number generator on 10000
numbers.
        """
        num_tests = 10000
        vals = [0 for i in range(10)]
        for i in range(num_tests):
            tmp = random.randint(0, 9)
            vals[tmp] = vals[tmp] + 1

        chi2, p = scipy.stats.chisquare(self.vals)
        assert p > 0.05

def foo( ):
    """ I just needed a function outside of a class as an
example"""
    pass
```

code1.py

The docstring can be accessed by using Python's built-in `help` function. The results are displayed in the standard help fashion (that is, as if viewing a text file with `less`) and are as follows:

```
In [4]: import code1
```

```
In [5]: help(code1)
Help on module code1:
```

```
NAME
    code1 - This is an abbreviated version of my random number generator
test suite.
```

```
DESCRIPTION
    It uses the pytest framework.  It does not do much in this form.
```

```
CLASSES
    builtins.object
        TestRandoms


    class TestRandoms(builtins.object)
     |  This is the main class.
     |
     |  Normally it would hold all the tests, plus and setup and teardown
fixtures.
     |
     |  Methods defined here:
     |
     |  test_builtin(self)
     |      Test the built-in random number generator on 10000 numbers.
     |
     |  ----------------------------------------------------------------
-----
     |  Data descriptors defined here:
     |
     |  __dict__
     |      dictionary for instance variables (if defined)
     |
```

```
 |  __weakref__
 |      list of weak references to the object (if defined)


FUNCTIONS
    foo()
        I just needed a function outside of a class as an example


FILE
    /nfs/02/wit0096/Packt/chap09/code1.py
```

Docstrings for individual parts can be accessed by naming them.

Here, we access help for the class:

```
In [6]: help(code1.TestRandoms)


Help on class TestRandoms in module code1:


class TestRandoms(builtins.object)
 |  This is the main class.
 |
 |  Normally it would hold all the tests, plus and setup and teardown
fixtures.
 |
 |  Methods defined here:
 |
 |  test_builtin(self)
 |      Test the built-in random number generator on 10000 numbers.
 |
 |  ----------------------------------------------------------------
--
 |  Data descriptors defined here:
 |
 |  __dict__
 |      dictionary for instance variables (if defined)
 |
 |  __weakref__
 |      list of weak references to the object (if defined)
```

Next, we access `help` for a method within the class:

```
In [6]: help(code1.TestRandoms.test_builtin)


Help on function test_builtin in module code1:


test_builtin(self)
    Test the built-in random number generator on 10000 numbers.
```

And we can get help for the independent function as follows:

```
In [7]: help(code1.foo)


Help on function foo in module code1:


foo()
    I just needed a function outside of a class as an example
```

Inheriting docstrings

If a class inherits from a parent class, the parent class' docstring will become a part of the child class'. Here is another example from an earlier test suite:

```
"""
This is my hailstone unit test suite.

It uses the unittest framework.  Admittedly, it does not do much.
"""

import unittest
from hail1 import f

class TestHailStones(unittest.TestCase):
    """
    The main class for testing the hailstone sequence generator.
    """

    def test_f(self):
        """currently the only test in this suite."""
        ans = [0, 0, 1, 7, 2, 5, 8, 16, 3, 19, 6]
        for i in range(1, 11):
            print(i)
```

```
                    self.assertEqual(f(i), ans[i])

def foo( ):
    """
    An independent function.

    I needed another function to illustrate the docstring for a
function that was not a member of a class.
    """
    pass
```

code2.py

It produces the following (abbreviated) output:

In [10]: import code2

In [11]: help(code2)

Help on module code2:

NAME
    code2 - This is my hailstone unit test suite.

DESCRIPTION
    It uses the unittest framework. Admittedly, it does not do much.

CLASSES
    unittest.case.TestCase(builtins.object)
        TestHailStones

    class TestHailStones(unittest.case.TestCase)
     | The main class for testing the hailstone sequence generator.
     |
     | Method resolution order:
     | TestHailStones
     | unittest.case.TestCase
     | builtins.object
```
```

```
|

|   Methods defined here:

|

|   test_f(self)
|       currently the only test in this suite.

|

|   ----------------------------------------------------------------
-----

|   Methods inherited from unittest.case.TestCase:

|

|   __call__(self, *args, **kwds)

|

|   __eq__(self, other)

|

|   __hash__(self)

|

|   __init__(self, methodName='runTest')

|       Create an instance of the class that will use the named test
|       method when executed. Raises a ValueError if the instance
does
|       not have a method with the specified name.

|

|   __repr__(self)

|

|   __str__(self)

|

|   addCleanup(self, function, *args, **kwargs)

|       Add a function, with arguments, to be called when the test is
|       completed. Functions added are called on a LIFO basis and are
|       called after tearDown on test failure or success.

|

|       Cleanup items are called even if setUp fails (unlike
tearDown).
```

```
 |
 |    addTypeEqualityFunc(self, typeobj, function)
 |
Add a type specific assertEqual style function to compare a type.

 |
 |        This method is for use by TestCase subclasses that need to
register
 |        their own type equality functions to provide nicer error
messages.
 |
 |        Args:
 |            typeobj: The data type to call this function on when both
values
 |                are of the same type in assertEqual().
 |            function: The callable taking two arguments and an
optional
 |                msg= argument that raises self.failureException
with a
 |                useful error message when the two arguments are
not equal.
 |
 |    assertAlmostEqual(self, first, second, places=None, msg=None,
delta=None)
```

Note how the documentation for the `unittest.TestCase` class is included without additional effort.

Recommended elements

PEP 0257 documents the conventions associated with docstrings. From the standard (`https://www.python.org/dev/peps/pep-0257/`):

> *"The aim of this PEP is to standardize the high-level structure of docstrings: what they should contain, and how to say it (without touching on any markup syntax within docstrings). The PEP contains conventions, not laws or syntax."*

While there is no requirement that developers should follow these guidelines, third-party tools (such as Docutils and Sphinx) may rely upon them to extract features from docstrings.

The PEP divides docstrings into two families: one-liners and multiline. Although both follow the rules for docstrings in general, each has its own recommended syntax and semantics.

One-line docstrings

These are for obvious cases or when a great deal of code can be concisely described. One-liners are similar to inline comments in that they are terse and targeted at fellow developers.

Syntax

These should fit in one line (72 characters). The beginning triple double-quotes and the ending quotes should be on the same line. If used to document a class, a single blank line may follow. Otherwise, there should be no blank lines either before or after the docstring.

Semantics

A phrase should end in a period. The phrase should be imperative ("Do X") rather than a description ("Does X"). It should not simply restate the signature of a function—a tool can determine the signature statically or through introspection. Also, the docstring should provide information that cannot be algorithmically derived. If type hints are not used, it can contain the return type of the function as this is not discoverable through introspection.

Multiline docstrings

Multiline docstrings are meant to provide a more elaborate description than a one-liner. Whereas a one-liner often carries information about a type and density similar to inline comments, a multiline docstring is meant to explain bigger, more complex chunks of code to people outside of the development team.

Syntax

A multiline docstring should start out with a line containing either the three double-quotes followed by a one-line summary, or the three double-quotes by themselves and followed on the next line by the summary line. In either case, the summary line has a function similar to that of a one-line docstring. A blank line should follow the summary, then a series of explanatory comments. The closing triple double-quotes should follow on their own line. The opening and closing quotes should be aligned to the body of the entity that is being described. The leftmost lines in the docstring should be indented at the same level as the triple quotes. Other lines may be indented further.

As with any standard that allows variations, there are several groups that promote different versions:

- Google weighs in its Python Style Guide at `https://google.github.io/styleguide/pyguide.html#Comments`

- numpy has its own recommendations at `https://github.com/numpy/numpy/blob/master/doc/HOWTO_DOCUMENT.rst.txt#docstring-standard`

- Epydoc prefers docstrings at `http://epydoc.sourceforge.net/manual-docstring.html`

Finally, your team should pick a multiline docstring syntax that works for it and the tool (or tools) it uses to generate documentation.

Semantics

A multiline docstring should provide enough information for an interested party to use the thing it is documenting. It is not enough to just describe its name and purpose. The potential user should, by reading the docstring, understand the following:

- The API
- The inputs
- Functionality
- The output (or outputs)
- The error conditions
- The relationship with other parts of the system
- Example uses

The API

This is important for classes and modules. This docstring for a module should describe all classes, exceptions, and functions that are exported by that module. The docstring for a class should describe its public interface and instance variables. The descriptions should be brief (a single line is good enough) — more details will be provided by the docstrings for the individual parts.

Inputs

These are especially important for scripts (command-line arguments and options) and functions (parameters). Users should be able to specify complete, valid inputs, which means describing:

- The names of the inputs
- Their types

- Their ranges
- Optional versus required

Functionality

These are important for scripts and functions. Users should understand what relationship the inputs have with the outputs without being told (more than necessary) about the mechanism used to achieve the results. This means using plain English to describe what the function does. If there is a simple mathematical expression that the function implements, this is a good place to include it. This is probably the hardest part of the comment to write.

Outputs

These are important for scripts and functions. The number and types of outputs should be listed. Any side effects should also be described.

Error conditions

Possible conditions that could result in an error should be listed. Errors fall under two categories: silent errors and noisy errors.

Noisy errors are those that result in thrown exceptions or error codes being set. All thrown exceptions should be documented. Any variables or data structures used to signal errors (for example, `errno`) should also be documented.

Silent errors are those in which the code appears to function normally, but in fact is producing invalid results. For example, many numeric algorithms produce meaningful results over only a subset of otherwise legal inputs.

In either case, users should be presented with enough information to:

- Avoid error conditions (when possible)
- Detect error conditions (whether by catching an exception or by checking for an error code)
- Recover from an error (for example, retrying, or using an alternate method)

Relationship with other parts of the system

This is important primarily for classes, modules, and public interfaces. Object-oriented systems consist of a myriad of interacting parts. Some of these parts are internal to the system and some are external. The docstring should describe how the current part relates to other parts.

An important relationship is that of dependency. One part can depend on another part logically (through inheritance or composition), functionally (for example, by being imported), or temporally (perhaps, one part performs the setup required for another part to function correctly). All dependencies should be documented.

Another important relationship is being a part of the same pattern. Design patterns are becoming increasingly important and dictating the existence of various mechanisms. If a class is part of the implementation of a pattern, this should be documented.

Example uses

As useful as an English description is, there is no substitute for a few examples. There are entire operating systems where the only useful documentation is in the form of examples.

Example

We will take an example from Rosetta Code, the Python implementation of the Chinese Remainder Theorem (`http://rosettacode.org/wiki/Chinese_remainder_theorem#Python`). Our implementation will be modified in two ways. First, it will use a class rather than the functions shown so that a full range of commenting conventions can be demonstrated. Second, it will be brought up to Python 3 from 2.7:

```
"""Company boilerplate goes here.
```

Suppose `n1, ..., nk` are positive integers that are pairwise coprime. Then, for any given sequence of integers `a1, ..., ak`, there exists an integer x solving the following system of simultaneous congruences.

```
x ≡ a1 mod n1
x ≡ a2 mod n2
...
x ≡ ak mod nk
```

A full explanation of the theorem can be found at `https://en.wikipedia.org/wiki/Chinese_remainder_theorem`.

```
Attributes:
    None


Dependencies:
```

```
        functools
"""


import functools


class CRT:
```

"""The Chinese Remainder Theorem method for solving a system of linear congruences.

This class has no __init__ method. As such, there are no arguments required to construct an instance. Without class or instance variables, all objects of this class are stateless.

```
        Args:
                None


        Attributes:
                None


        Example:
                An example is provided in the main guard corresponding to the
system:
                x ≡ 2 mod 3
                x ≡ 3 mod 5
                x ≡ 2 mod 7


        """


        def chinese_remainder(self, n, a):
```

"""Use the existence construction form of the CRT to compute the solution.

```
        First, calculate the product of all the modulos (b1, n2, …, nk)
as prod
                For each i, calculate prod/n_i as p
                Sum up each ai * the multiplicative inverse of ni mod p


        Args:
                n: a list of modulos (n1, n2, …, nk)
```

```
                a: a list of congruences (a1, a2, …, ak)


        Returns:
            The smallest integer solution to the system of congruence
equations defined
            by a and n.


        Error conditions:
            When len(n) == len(a), a solution always exists.
            When len(a) > len(n), any additional a's are ignored.
            When len(n) > len(a), behavior is deterministic but
erroneous.
        """
        sum = 0
        prod = functools.reduce(lambda a, b: a*b, n)

        for n_i, a_i in zip(n, a):
            p = prod / n_i
            sum += a_i * self.__mul_inv(p, n_i) * p
        return int(sum % prod)


    def __mul_inv(self, a, b):
        """Calculate the multiplicative inverse of b mod a."""
        b0 = b
        x0, x1 = 0, 1
        if b == 1:
            return 1
        while a > 1:
            q = a / b
            a, b = b, a%b
            x0, x1 = x1 - q * x0, x0
        if x1 < 0:
            x1 += b0
        return x1


if __name__ == '__main__':
    n = [3, 5, 7]
```

```
    a = [2, 3, 2]
    crt = CRT( )
    print(crt.chinese_remainder(n, a))
```

The result is as follows:

```
In [22]: help(CRT)


Help on class CRT in module __main__:


class CRT(builtins.object)
 |  The Chinese Remainder Theorem method for solving a system of linear
congruences.
 |
 |  Notes:
 |      This class has no __init__ method.  As such, there are no
arguments required
 |      to construct an instance.
 |
 |      Without class or instance variables, all objects of this class
are stateless.
 |
 |  Args:
 |      None
 |
 |  Attributes:
 |      None
 |
 |  Example:
 |      An example is provided in the main guard corresponding to the
system:
 |          x ≡ 2 mod 3
 |          x ≡ 3 mod 5
 |          x ≡ 2 mod 7
 |
 |  Methods defined here:
 |
```

```
|   chinese_remainder(self, n, a)
|       Use the existence construction form of the CRT to compute the
solution.
|
|       First, calculate the product of all the modulos (b1, n2, …, nk)
as prod
|       For each i, calculate prod/n_i as p
|       Sum up each ai * the multiplicative inverse of ni mod p
|
|       Args:
|           n: a list of modulos (n1, n2, …, nk)
|           a: a list of congruences (a1, a2, …, ak)
|
|       Returns:
|           The smallest integer solution to the system of congruence
equations defined
|           by a and n.
|
|       Error conditions:
|           When len(n) == len(a), a solution always exists.
|           When len(a) > len(n), any additional a's are ignored.
|           When len(n) > len(a), behavior is deterministic but
erroneous.
|
|   ----------------------------------------------------------------
--
|   Data descriptors defined here:
|
|   __dict__
|       dictionary for instance variables (if defined)
|
|   __weakref__
|       list of weak references to the object (if defined)
```

Note that the docstring for the private method, __mul_inv, is not included.

reStructuredText

One could say a lot of things about the preceding example (in particular, that there are more lines of comments than code), but it would be difficult to say that the end result is aesthetically pleasing. In particular, compared to the output of a program using Javadoc, this documentation looks rather plain. In order to remedy this shortcoming, it was decided that a more sophisticated way of specifying and generating documentation was needed.

History and goals

Jim Fulton of Zope invented StructuredText as a simple markup language. It is similar to WikiWikiWebMarkup but simpler. Problems with both the specification and the implementation led to David Goodger creating a revised version, called reStructuredText. His goals for the language were that it should be:

- Readable
- Unobtrusive
- Unambiguous
- Unsurprising
- Intuitive
- Easy
- Scalable
- Powerful
- Language-neutral
- Extensible
- Output-format-neutral

This led to the publication of PEP 0287 (`https://www.python.org/dev/peps/pep-0287/`).

Customers

Any documentation system has three groups of customers: developers, automated document generation software, and readers. Each of them has different requirements and limitations.

Developers have to write the documentation. As a class, developers hate typing, and hate typing anything that is not code even more. Any attempt to force them to write great swathes of comments will result in a failed standard. So much so that if documentation can be generated from code, it should be. Any additional comments should be easy to create with a standard keyboard and minimal additional markup.

The document generation software turns the characters produced by the developers into documents to be consumed by outside readers. This generally consists of a transformation from the markup language used by the developers into a more human-readable format. For example, the Javadoc written by developers can automatically be transformed into HTML that readers can view in a browser. This transformation can include the addition of both aesthetic (for example, colors and formatting) and functional (for example, hyperlinks) properties. It is important for the document generation software that the markup used by the developers be powerful and structured enough to support this transformation.

Readers consume the end result of this transformation. Readers may or may not be developers, but they expect the documentation to be structurally well organized. The documentation should be easy to read, and it should be easy to find what one is looking for. Note that readers often do not have access to the original source and might not be able to read the original markup if it were to be available.

There is an important tension in this division between developers and readers. Simply put, readers want as much documentation as possible, and in a structured form. Developers will write as little documentation as they can get away with and will use as little structure as possible.

The solution

The solution that reStructuredText adopted was to use a two-fold process: a simple markup language coupled with powerful documentation generation software. The markup is reStructuredText and the software is Docutils. The basic process is simple:

1. The developer writes docstrings in plain text using the reStructuredText conventions.

2. Docutils is applied to the resulting code + comments document to generate documentation in an external format (for example, HTML or LaTeX).

3. The reader consumes the resulting document in the appropriate viewer.

We will later take a look at Sphinx, a documentation generation program that builds upon and extends reStructuredText and Docutils.

Overview

The basic syntax of reStructuredText is that of regular text, with special conventions associated with certain usages. This is in contrast with, say, HTML, in which metadata is associated with text through the use of angle brackets. For example, in HTML a bulleted list might look like this:

```
<ul>
  <li>Python</li>
  <li>Java</li>
  <li>Ruby</li>
</ul>
```

In reStructuredText, it would look like the following:

```
* Python
* Java
* Ruby
```

An important difference is that while HTML (and its relatives, such as XML) allows nested tags, reStructuredText does not allow nested markup. While this is ordinarily not an issue, it does come up from time to time.

What follows is a listing of some of the more important usages.

Paragraphs

A paragraph is a chunk of text separated by one or more blank lines. The left edge of paragraphs should line up. If a paragraph is indented relative to other paragraphs, it is treated as a quote.

The reStructuredText looks as follows:

```
It turns out Abraham Lincoln never said

    Never trust anything you read on the Internet.

It was Benjamin Franklin
```

This produces HTML output which is displayed as follows:

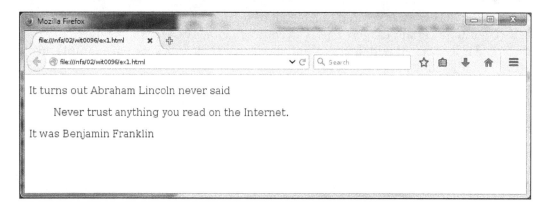

Text styles

Text in italics should be surrounded by asterisks (*):

```
Use italics for *emphasis*.
```

Text in bold uses two asterisks (**):

```
Using a **goto** statement is a bold move in structured programming.
```

Unfortunately, there is no easy way to make text both italicized and bold.

For the most part, reStructuredText is pretty smart in knowing when something is markup and when it should be left alone. For example, consider these strings:

```
x = 5*6
x = 5*6*7
```

The asterisk is not interpreted as making the 6 italicized.

Surrounding text with double back quotes (``) forces it to be a fixed-space literal—all special characters between the quotes are left uninterpreted. Individual characters that would otherwise be interpreted as markup can be escaped using a backslash (\).

Literal blocks

If there is a need to have an entire paragraph included as a literal block (that is, exactly as it is, without any interpretation of markup characters or indentation within the paragraph), then a paragraph containing only two colons indicates that the following indented or quoted text should be taken literally. This can be useful when citing code or explaining markup conventions.

From the documentation (`http://docutils.sourceforge.net/docs/user/rst/quickref.html#literal-blocks`):

```
::

    Whitespace, newlines, blank lines, and
    all kinds of markup (like *this* or
    \this) are preserved by literal blocks.
```

Lists

There are three types of lists: enumerated, bulleted, and definition. Enumerated lists are those in which the elements are counted in some manner. Bulleted lists use the same character to denote every item. Definition lists are used to lay out term-definition pairs.

Enumerated lists

An enumerated list uses a counter and a delimiter. The counter is generally a number, letter, or Roman numeral. The delimiter is one of a period, a right bracket, or two brackets. reStructuredText is flexible in terms of which is chosen. In any case, the counter and the delimiter come before the text of the list item.

Here is an example of some enumerated lists:

```
1. Start out *emphatically*
2. And get **bolder** as the list goes on

A. Here we use a letter to count

a. Even lower-case letters work
    i. One can use different counters on indented lists

I) And mix up delimiters
   with a multi-line comment

   and a blank line in the middle.

(D) One can even start numbering non-sequentially.
```

rst2.txt

It results in the following web page:

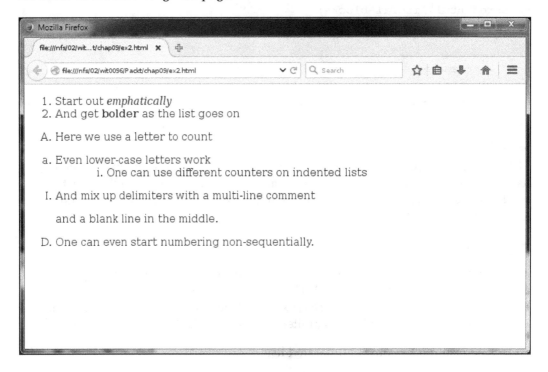

Bulleted lists

Bulleted lists work just like enumerated lists, except that:

- The only allowed counters are -, +, and *
- There is no delimiter

Bulleted lists support the usual rules for indentation.

Definition lists

A definition list is just a series of term-definition pairs. The term is on the first line and the definition is in the following paragraph, which is indented. Here is an example:

```
do
    a deer, a female deer
re
    a drop of golden sun
mi
    a name i call myself
fa
```

```
        a long long way to run
    so
        a needle pulling thread
```

rst3.txt

It results in the following:

Hyperlinks

The hyperlink markup creates a link to a URL in the browser. The syntax is as follows:

```
<citation>
.. _<hyperlink-name>: <link-block>
```

An example will make things clear:

```
Buy my book at Packt_.

.. _Packt: https://www.packtpub.com/
```

rst4.txt

It results in the following web page:

Sections

The preceding markup should suffice for most developers, for most documentation. Should more in-depth documentation be required, reStructuredText provides the ability to break documents into sections using section headers. This is accomplished by creating a single line of text consisting entirely of a single repeated character (the underline). The previous line becomes the section header (the overline). The underline and the overline must be of the same length. All sections that use the same underline are at the same level. Any section beneath a section with a different underline is at a lower level than that section.

Here is an example:

```
Chapter 1 Main Title
--------------------


Section 1.1 An Important Subject
```

```
==================================

Subsection 1.1.1 A Special Case

~~~~~~~~~~~~~~~~~~~~~~~~~~~~~~~~

Section 1.2 Another Important Subject

======================================

Chapter 2 Conclusions

---------------------
```

This is what it yields:

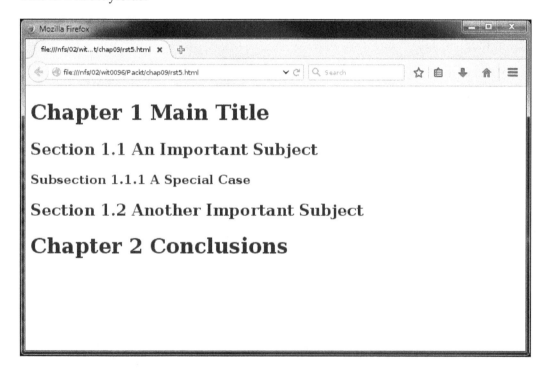

Docutils

Docutils is a suite of utilities for transforming text files that contain reStructuredText into other formats, including HTML, XML, and LaTeX. It is meant to bridge the gap between what users want to read (aesthetically pleasant formats) and what programmers can easily type (plain text). Docutils falls into two broad categories: libraries (to do behind-the scenes parsing and manipulation) and frontend tools (which use libraries to produce a particular output format).

Installation

Docutils can be installed using `pip`:

```
pip install docutils
```

This will install a number of scripts, including the important transformation scripts. The author's installation is included:

- `rst2html.py`
- `rst2latex.py`
- `rst2man.py`
- `rst2odt_prepstyles.py`
- `rst2odt.py`
- `rst2pseudoxml.py`
- `rst2s5.py`
- `rst2xetex.py`
- `rst2xml.py`
- `rstpep2html.py`

Usage

These scripts can be used from the command line. They expect an input from `stdin` and produce the output in `stdout`:

```
./rst2html.py <infile> > <outfile>
```

Documenting source files

Unfortunately, unlike Javadoc, Docutils cannot take a `.py` file full of Python code and automatically extract the docstrings from it in order to generate documentation. There is a tool called Epydoc that will do this, but the project has been inactive since 2009. A team could write a script to attempt to extract just the docstrings, but there is a better solution. It will be outlined in the next section.

Sphinx

Sphinx is a documentation generation tool. It began as a way to produce Python documentation, but it is branching out to other languages, notably C/C++. It can produce output in several formats, including HTML, LaTeX, ePub, man pages, and plain text, among others. It accepts reStructuredText and builds upon the Docutils suite, adding a few pieces of markup along the way.

Installation and startup

Sphinx can be installed using `pip`:

```
pip install sphinx
```

Installation will add several scripts to the path. The first one we will examine is named `sphinx-quickstart`. It will set up a prompt the user for information and then a source directory, a configuration file, and some skeleton files:

```
bash-4.1$ sphinx-quickstart
Welcome to the Sphinx 1.3.6 quickstart utility.


Please enter values for the following settings (just press Enter to
accept a default value, if one is given in brackets).


Enter the root path for documentation.
> Root path for the documentation [.]: docs


You have two options for placing the build directory for Sphinx output.
Either, you use a directory "_build" within the root path, or you
separate
"source" and "build" directories within the root path.
```

```
> Separate source and build directories (y/n) [n]: y
```

```
Inside the root directory, two more directories will be created; "_
templates"
for custom HTML templates and "_static" for custom stylesheets and other
static
files. You can enter another prefix (such as ".") to replace the
underscore.
> Name prefix for templates and static dir [_]:
```

```
The project name will occur in several places in the built documentation.
> Project name: Chap09
> Author name(s): Thomas Bitterman
```

```
Sphinx has the notion of a "version" and a "release" for the
software. Each version can have multiple releases. For example, for
Python the version is something like 2.5 or 3.0, while the release is
something like 2.5.1 or 3.0a1.  If you don't need this dual structure,
just set both to the same value.
> Project version: 0.1
> Project release [0.1]:
```

```
If the documents are to be written in a language other than English,
you can select a language here by its language code. Sphinx will then
translate text that it generates into that language.
```

```
For a list of supported codes, see
http://sphinx-doc.org/config.html#confval-language.
> Project language [en]:
```

```
The file name suffix for source files. Commonly, this is either ".txt"
or ".rst".  Only files with this suffix are considered documents.
> Source file suffix [.rst]:
```

```
One document is special in that it is considered the top node of the
"contents tree", that is, it is the root of the hierarchical structure
```

of the documents. Normally, this is "index", but if your "index"
document is a custom template, you can also set this to another filename.
> Name of your master document (without suffix) [index]:

Sphinx can also add configuration for epub output:
> Do you want to use the epub builder (y/n) [n]:

Please indicate if you want to use one of the following Sphinx
extensions:
> autodoc: automatically insert docstrings from modules (y/n) [n]: y
> doctest: automatically test code snippets in doctest blocks (y/n) [n]:
> intersphinx: link between Sphinx documentation of different projects
(y/n) [n]:
> todo: write "todo" entries that can be shown or hidden on build (y/n)
[n]:
> coverage: checks for documentation coverage (y/n) [n]:
> pngmath: include math, rendered as PNG images (y/n) [n]:
> mathjax: include math, rendered in the browser by MathJax (y/n) [n]:
> ifconfig: conditional inclusion of content based on config values (y/n)
[n]:
> viewcode: include links to the source code of documented Python objects
(y/n) [n]:

A Makefile and a Windows command file can be generated for you so that
you
only have to run e.g. `make html' instead of invoking sphinx-build
directly.
> Create Makefile? (y/n) [y]:
> Create Windows command file? (y/n) [y]: n

Creating file docs/source/conf.py.
Creating file docs/source/index.rst.
Creating file docs/Makefile.

Finished: An initial directory structure has been created.

You should now populate your master file docs/source/index.rst and create
other documentation

```
source files. Use the Makefile to build the docs, like so:

   make builder
```

where "builder" is one of the supported builders, e.g. html, latex or linkcheck.

Possibly, the two most important answers are concerned with autodoc and Makefile. The autodoc is the Sphinx extension that knows how to extract docstrings from Python files. This is a must for easy documentation of code. Makefile generation is optional. When true, Sphinx will create a Makefile to generate the output. The result is that the documentation generation will look like this:

```
make <builder>
```

Rather than this:

```
sphinx-build -b <builder> <source-dir> <build-dir>
```

Here, <builder> is one of the output formats that Sphinx supports. Popular builders are HTML, ePub, LaTeX, man, XML, and JSON. A complete list can be found at http://www.sphinx-doc.org/en/stable/builders. html?highlight=builders#module-sphinx.builders.

When sphinx-quickstart is complete, the following directory/file hierarchy comes into existence:

```
(my_rpy2_zone)-bash-4.1$ ls -R docs

docs:
build   Makefile   source


docs/build:


docs/source:
conf.py   index.rst   _static   _templates


docs/source/_static:


docs/source/_templates:
```

Specifying the source files

At this point, one could run `make html`, but no source files would be included.

The first step is to add the path to the source file to this project's configuration. In the "source" directory under the project root `sphinx-quickstart` created a `conf. py` file. It is a full-fledged Python file with the ability to execute arbitrary code that is run once at build time. It contains all possible configuration values. Default values are present but commented out. In order to add our source files to the locations that Sphinx will grab files from, the following line will suffice:

```
sys.path.insert(0,"/path/to/dir")
```

There is a spot for this after the first comment block after the imports.

The next step is to specify the names and locations of the Python files to generate the source for. In the "source" directory under the project root `sphinx-quickstart` created an `index.rst` file. It should look like this:

```
.. Chap09 documentation master file, created by
   sphinx-quickstart on Wed Mar  9 10:51:38 2016.
   You can adapt this file completely to your liking, but it should at
least
   contain the root `toctree` directive.


Welcome to Chap09's documentation!
====================================


Contents:


.. toctree::
   :maxdepth: 2




Indices and tables
==================


* :ref:`genindex`
* :ref:`modindex`
* :ref:`search`
```

Each of the lines has a special meaning to Sphinx, but for now, we just want to add a module to the list of things to be documented. A minor addition using the `automodule` directive will do it:

```
.. toctree::
   :maxdepth: 2


.. automodule:: crt1
```

Now change the directory to the project root and start the build:

```
bash-4.1$ make html
sphinx-build -b html -d build/doctrees    source build/html
Running Sphinx v1.3.6
making output directory...
loading pickled environment... not yet created
building [mo]: targets for 0 po files that are out of date
building [html]: targets for 1 source files that are out of date
updating environment: 1 added, 0 changed, 0 removed
reading sources... [100%] index
looking for now-outdated files... none found
pickling environment... done
checking consistency... done
preparing documents... done
writing output... [100%] index
generating indices... genindex py-modindex
writing additional pages... search
copying static files... done
copying extra files... done
dumping search index in English (code: en) ... done
dumping object inventory... done
build succeeded.

Build finished. The HTML pages are in build/html.
```

The resulting HTML page shows a nicely formatted version of the docstring for the module:

This is missing documentation for the class, so that can be added to `index.rst` using the `autoclass` directive as such:

```
.. toctree::
   :maxdepth: 2

.. automodule:: crt1

.. autoclass:: CRT
```

This results in the following page:

This Page

Show Source

Quick search

Go

Enter search terms or a
module, class or function
name.

Welcome to Chap09's documentation!

Contents:

Company boilerplate goes here.

Suppose n1, ..., nk are positive integers that are pairwise coprime. Then, for any given sequence of integers a1, ..., ak, there exists an integer x solving the following system of simultaneous congruences.

$x \equiv a1 \bmod n1 \quad x \equiv a2 \bmod n2 \quad ... \quad x \equiv ak \bmod nk$

A full explanation of the theorem can be found at https://en.wikipedia.org/wiki/Chinese_remainder_theorem

Attributes:
　None

Dependencies:
　functools

class `crt1.`**CRT**
　The Chinese Remainder Theorem method for solving a system of linear congruences.

　Notes:
　　This class has no __init__ method. As such, there are no arguments required to construct an instance.

　　Without class or instance variables, all objects of this class are stateless.

　Args:
　　None

　Attributes:
　　None

　Example:
　　An example is provided in the main guard corresponding to the system: $x \equiv 2 \bmod 3 \quad x \equiv 3 \bmod 5 \quad x \equiv 2 \bmod 7$

Indices and tables

- Index
- Module Index
- Search Page

This is missing documentation for the `chinese_remainder` method, so that can be added to `index.rst` using the `automethod` directive:

```
.. toctree::
   :maxdepth: 2


.. automodule:: crt1
```

```
.. autoclass:: CRT
```

```
.. automethod:: CRT.chinese_remainder
```

The result is as follows:

Welcome to Chap09's documentation!

Contents:

Company boilerplate goes here.

Suppose n1, ..., nk are positive integers that are pairwise coprime. Then, for any given sequence of integers a1, ..., ak, there exists an integer x solving the following system of simultaneous congruences.

x ≡ a1 mod n1 x ≡ a2 mod n2 ... x ≡ ak mod nk

A full explanation of the theorem can be found at https://en.wikipedia.org/wiki/Chinese_remainder_theorem

Attributes:
    None
Dependencies:
    functools

class crt1.**CRT**

The Chinese Remainder Theorem method for solving a system of linear congruences.

Notes:
    This class has no __init__ method. As such, there are no arguments required to construct an instance.

    Without class or instance variables, all objects of this class are stateless.

Args:
    None
Attributes:
    None
Example:
    An example is provided in the main guard corresponding to the system: x ≡ 2 mod 3 x ≡ 3 mod 5 x ≡ 2 mod 7

CRT.**chinese_remainder**(*n, a*)

Use the existence construction form of the CRT to compute the solution.

First, calculate the product of all the modulos (b1, n2, ..., nk) as prod For each i, calculate prod/n_i as p Sum up each ai * the multiplicative inverse of ni mod p

Args:
    n: a list of modulos (n1, n2, ..., nk) a: a list of congruences (a1, a2, ..., ak)
Returns:
    The smallest integer solution to the system of congruence equations defined by a and n.
Error conditions:
    When len(n) == len(a), a solution always exists. When len(a) > len(n), any additional a's are ignored. When len(n) > len(a), behavior is deterministic but erroneous.

Indices and tables

- Index
- Module Index
- Search Page

©2016, Thomas Bitterman. | Powered by Sphinx 1.3.6 & Alabaster 0.7.7 | Page source

While flexible, this can be tedious and error-prone. One solution is to use the `:members:` attribute, like this:

```
.. toctree::
   :maxdepth: 2

.. automodule:: crt1
    :members:
```

Another is to use the `sphinx-apidoc` tool. The purpose of `sphinx-apidoc` is to extract the docstrings from the source files and produce `.rst` files from them. Consider this example:

```
bash-4.1$ sphinx-apidoc -o docs .
```

It will create a set of `.rst` files:

```
Creating file docs/code1.rst.
Creating file docs/code2.rst.
Creating file docs/crt1.rst.
Creating file docs/hail1.rst.
Creating file docs/modules.rst.
```

The files themselves are not much to look at, but they can be fed into Sphinx or other documentation tools that are expecting reStructuredText for further processing. This is especially handy when using tools that cannot extract docstrings on their own.

Summary

While inline comments and type notations are useful for developers who will be working on the code base, external parties need more extensive documentation, and need it in a more attractive format than reading the source (this is especially true when they do not have access to the source). This need for documentation must be balanced against the understandable reluctance of developers to spend a great deal of time and energy producing anything but code.

Python's solution is to employ a lightweight markup language, reStructuredText, and a toolchain (Docutils, Sphinx) to transform reStructuredText into a more aesthetically attractive format (for example, HTML or LaTeX).

Aesthetics are not everything, however. Documentation must contain useful information in order to be worth using. Various guidelines (PEP 0008, PEP 3107, PEP 0484, PEP 0257, Google, NumPyDoc, and others) have come into being to provide advice. A production project should settle for a set of guidelines before coding starts and stick to it. Documentation is one of those areas where even foolish consistency is better than none.

In the next chapter, we will take a quick tour of the Jupyter notebook. Jupyter provides a flexible framework to make available not just documentation but the code itself.

10
Visiting Jupyter

A major strength of IPython is its interactive nature. It expresses this interactive nature in three modalities: as a terminal, through a graphical console, and as a web-based notebook. Most of this book has centered on the terminal, with a few graphical examples using a Qt-based console. In this chapter, we will look at using IPython as part of a web-based notebook.

The following topics will be covered:

- Introduction
- Installation and startup
- The Dashboard
- Creating a notebook
- Working with cells
- Graphics
- Format conversion

Command lines have had a long and useful tradition in software development. It is only recently, as GUIs have become ubiquitous, that alternative development environments have become viable choices.

One important family of alternatives is the **Integrated Development Environment (IDE)** – built for coders, by coders. The functionality in IDEs centers on programming tasks: writing, compiling, running, and debugging code. Important members of this family include Microsoft Visual Studio, Eclipse, and Xcode.

The scientific community came up with a different metaphor – the notebook. The important tasks for scientists are different from those for programmers:

- Conducting experiments
- Gathering and recording data
- Analyzing data
- Collaboration with colleagues
- Creating demos
- Sharing results

Before computers, it was the job of the laboratory notebook to handle these tasks. A lab notebook has the benefit of being both structured and flexible. The structure comes from the notebook itself, where the pages are broken down into individual elements (lines or spreadsheet-like cells). The flexibility comes from the experimenter, who can fill in each cell with whatever is required – data, explanation, a graph, and so on. In a notebook, as opposed to an IDE, code is just one piece of the puzzle, no more or less important than the others are.

The need for an IPython-based notebook was evident from the early days of the project. On December 21, 2011, IPython 0.12 was released. It contained the first version of the IPython notebook, created by Fernando Perez, physicist and *Benevolent Dictator For Life* of the Jupyter project. As he explains in his history of the project (`http://blog.fperez.org/2012/01/ipython-notebook-historical.html`), the initial design of IPython itself was guided by his experiences with Mathematica and Sage (both scientifically-inclined, notebook-style applications).

As time went on, more features were added to IPython. Each feature required additional code to implement, and the repository became larger over time. Eventually, the IPython project grew to the point where it became clear that it was really several different projects sharing (parts of) a codebase. Broadly speaking, the major components were:

- The command line interface
- The REPL protocol
- The language kernel
- The notebook

Chapter 6, Works Well with Others – IPython and Third-Party Tools provides some examples of how splitting the command line interface from the kernel by using the REPL protocol as an intermediary allows the same interface to be used with different languages.

Chapter 3, Stepping Up to IPython for Parallel Computing, provides some details on how splitting out the kernel and REPL protocol enabled a parallel architecture to emerge.

This chapter will provide some examples of the power of the notebook, and how it relates to the other components. The move from the IPython notebook to the Jupyter project was probably the biggest of the reorganizations, and has been called *The Big Split.* For an in-depth look at the reasons for *The Big Split,* and details regarding its effect on various package structures, see `https://blog.jupyter.org/2015/04/15/the-big-split/`.

Installation and startup

Jupyter can be installed using `pip`:

```
pip install jupyter
```

It can be started like this:

```
(my_rpy2_zone)-bash-4.1$ ipython notebook
```

```
[I 10:38:27.193 NotebookApp] Serving notebooks from local directory: /nfs/02/wit0096
```

```
[I 10:38:27.193 NotebookApp] 0 active kernels
```

```
[I 10:38:27.193 NotebookApp] The Jupyter Notebook is running at: http://localhost:8888/
```

```
[I 10:38:27.193 NotebookApp] Use Control-C to stop this server and shut down all kernels (twice to skip confirmation).
```

```
/usr/bin/xdg-open: line 402: htmlview: command not found
```

```
console.error:
```

```
  [CustomizableUI]
```

```
  Custom widget with id loop-button does not return a valid node
```

```
console.error:
```

```
  [CustomizableUI]
```

```
  Custom widget with id loop-button does not return a valid node
```

```
1457711201438   addons.update-checker   WARN    Update manifest for {972ce4c6-7e08-4474-a285-3208198ce6fd} did not contain an updates property
```

Note that this has started an HTML server (called the Jupyter Notebook App) on port `8888`. It may also (depending on your platform) start a browser pointed at `http://localhost:8888`. If not, manually start a browser and point it there. Jupyter can only access files in the directory it was started in (and its subdirectories), so take care to start it where it can access your notebook files.

When a notebook is started, an instance of the kernel associated with it is also started. A list of these can be seen under the **Running** tab, for instance:

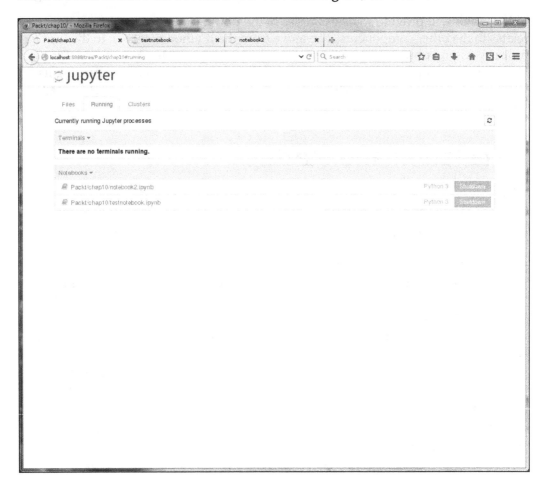

Closing the browser neither stops the Jupyter Notebook App nor stops the kernels. A kernel can be stopped using either of the following two methods:

- Using the menu item **File | Close and Halt** from the notebook page
- Using the **Shutdown** button in the **Running** tab

The Jupyter Notebook App itself can only be stopped by issuing the *Ctrl + C* command in the terminal in which the app was started, and then either answering y to a prompt, or typing *Ctrl + C* again.

The Dashboard

When you are ready to start working with a notebook, choosing the **Files** tab should display the following:

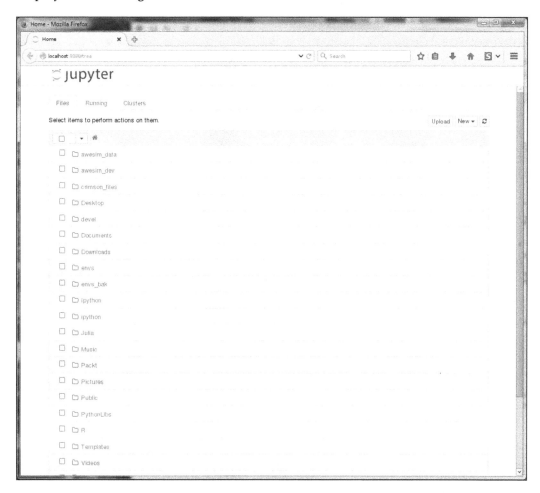

This is the Jupyter Notebook Dashboard. It looks like a file explorer because that is one of the things the Dashboard does – it allows access to notebook files. Opening a `"Hello world!"` notebook in the Dashboard results in the following:

A notebook file is a JSON text file with a `.ipynb` extension. The notebook file for the preceding example, `HelloWorld.ipynb`, is as follows:

```
{
  "cells": [
    {
      "cell_type": "code",
      "execution_count": 1,
      "metadata": {
```

```json
      "collapsed": false
    },
    "outputs": [
     {
      "name": "stdout",
      "output_type": "stream",
      "text": [
       "Hello world!\n"
      ]
     }
    ],
    "source": [
     "print(\"Hello world!\")"
    ]
   }
  ],
  "metadata": {
   "kernelspec": {
    "display_name": "Python 3",
    "language": "python",
    "name": "python3"
   },
   "language_info": {
    "codemirror_mode": {
     "name": "ipython",
     "version": 3
    },
    "file_extension": ".py",
    "mimetype": "text/x-python",
    "name": "python",
    "nbconvert_exporter": "python",
    "pygments_lexer": "ipython3",
    "version": "3.4.4"
   }
  },
  "nbformat": 4,
  "nbformat_minor": 0
}
```

Creating a notebook

Of course, no one writes a notebook in JSON – it is just used as a text format for persistence and interchange. The Dashboard can be used to create notebooks. In the upper-right section of the interface is a dropdown box that provides options to create new notebooks:

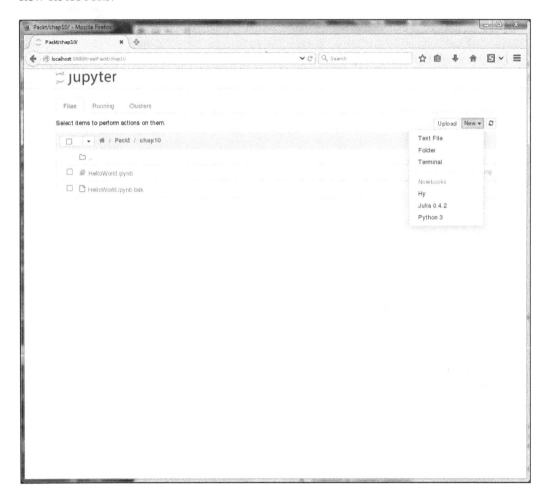

Note that a notebook need not use Python; in this case Hy and Julia are also options. Once chosen (we will use Python 3 for this example), a new tab is created in which the following web page is displayed:

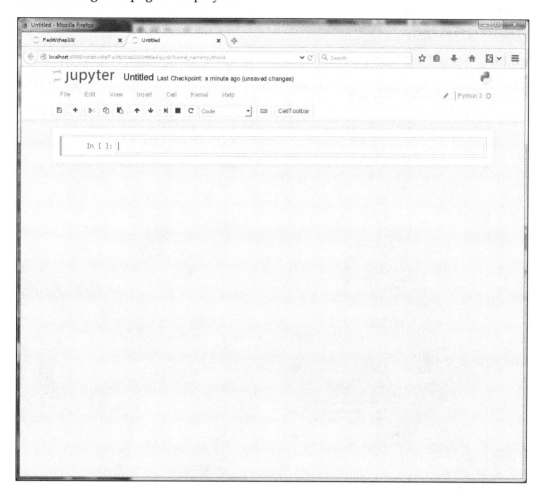

Note the green outline around the cell. This indicates that the editor is in *edit* mode. This mode is used to enter text into cells. There is also *command* mode, which is used to issue commands to the notebook as a whole.

At this point, we can enter our code into the cell, resulting in the notebook previously discussed, without having to edit any JSON.

Interacting with Python scripts

A simple way to take Python code that already exists and bring it into a notebook is to use the %load magic in a cell:

```
%load <filename>.p
```

Running this cell will load the contents of <filename>.py into the current cell:

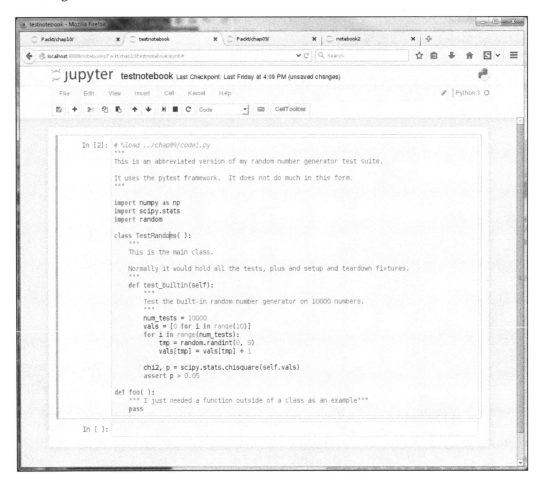

Running the cell again does not run the script – the point of using %load was simply to include the script on the page, not execute it.

Using the `%run` magic runs the script and inserts its output into the notebook as the output of that cell:

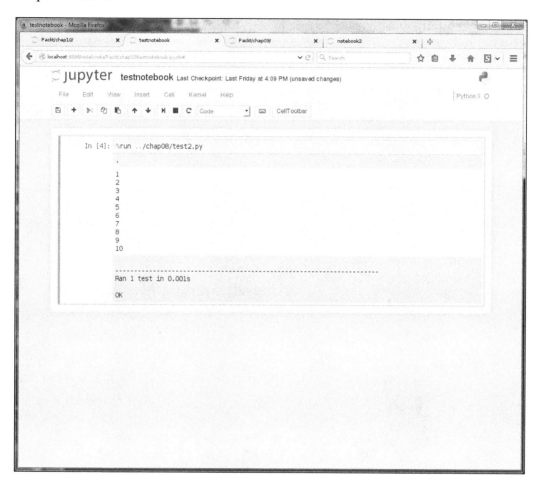

Using a notebook with tests

A notebook full of calls to test functions can be a convenient and attractive way to maintain a test suite and records of its results over time.

Of course, if the only thing a notebook did was to allow one to display the output of programs on a web page, it would be of limited usefulness. The real power of Jupyter comes into focus when working with individual cells.

Working with cells

Individual cells function very much like the IPython command line, with the slight change that hitting *Enter* does not cause the cell to be executed, but instead creates a new line to be typed on. In order to execute a cell, there are many options:

- *Alt + Enter* runs the current cell and inserts a new one below
- *Ctrl + Enter* runs the current cell and does not create a new cell
- The **Cell** menu item contains a list of ways to run cells, including **Run All**

The result of cell execution is very similar to what would be expected from the command line, for example:

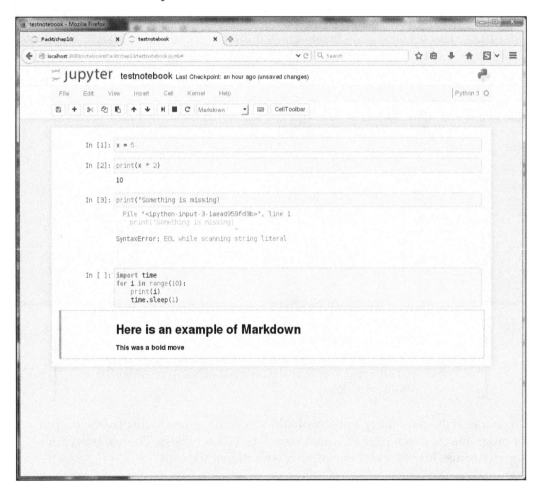

Note that the bottom cell contains Markdown text (`http://daringfireball.net/projects/markdown/`) rather than Python code. Markdown is a plain text formatting syntax meant to be easily convertible to HTML. Why docstrings are in reStructuredText and notebook cells are in Markdown is a mystery. Luckily, they are fairly similar.

Fixing the error in cell 3 allows the code in the next cell to run, which highlights a neat feature: the notebook displays results as they become available. For the previous code, that means the numbers 0 through 9 will appear in order on the web page, one per second.

Cell tricks

Cells work a little differently than a command line, so some care should be exercised to avoid seemingly strange behavior. In the following sections, we outline some of the differences and ways in which they can be leveraged to harness the power of the notebook paradigm.

Cell scoping

Although cells appear to be self-contained, they actually belong to the same session. Such features as variable scope and loaded libraries carry over from cell to cell.

Cell execution

A cell must be executed for its contents to have any effect. It is easy to declare a variable in *cell A*, reference it in *cell B*, then execute *cell B* without executing *cell A*. This will result in a `NameError`, as the variable in *cell A* is not defined until *cell A* is executed.

Restart & Run All

The vagaries of cell execution can be confusing – development can involve uncoordinated changes to several cells at a time. Rather than guessing which cells to re-run and in what order, there is a menu item at **Kernel | Restart & Run All** that will clear the results of any previous executions, clear all output, and run all cells, starting at the top and working down to the last one. This execution will stop if any cell throws an error.

Following this pattern leads to a natural ordering of cells not too dissimilar to the way code is structured in a standard script – dependencies at the top, followed by code that uses the dependencies. Once the initial strangeness of the cell idea is overcome, developers should find working with a notebook familiar.

Magics

Cells support both line and cell magics. Line magics can occur anywhere that is syntactically valid. Cell magics must be the first element in a cell.

Cell structure

Not all cells are created the same. We saw in the previous example how some cells held code, while other cells held Markdown. Each cell has a type, and the type of a cell determines what happens when it is executed.

Code cells

A code cell holds code. By default, the language used is Python, but support for a great number of languages (such as R and Julia) is already in place, and more are being added. Code cells work more like IDEs that use simple command lines, and include multiline capability, syntax highlighting, tab completion, cell and line magics, and support for graphical output.

Each code cell is associated with a kernel. When a code cell is executed, that code is sent to the kernel for execution, with the result being displayed in the notebook as the output for that cell.

Markdown cells

Markdown cells hold plain text that conforms to the Markdown standard. Markdown cells also support LaTeX notation: $...$ for inline notation and $$...$$ for equations meant to stand on their own. The Markdown portion is translated into HTML, while the LaTeX portions are handled by MathJax (a JavaScript display engine that supports a large subset of LaTeX).

Raw cells

A raw cell is uninterpreted – anything typed into a raw cell is not processed by any engine, and arrives in the output unchanged. This allows the developer to, for example, provide code examples in the output without worrying that they will be interpreted by the notebook.

Heading cells

Heading cells are special cases of the Markdown section notation. A header cell is plain text, and should begin with 1-6 octothorpes (#), followed by a space and then the title of the section. Each additional octothorpe specifies a deeper section level.

Jupyter is moving away from heading cells – in fact, the version used for this chapter popped up a warning about using them that stated: **Jupyter no longer uses special heading cells. Instead, write your headings in Markdown cells using # characters**. The previous uses of heading cells for internal links and table of contents generation appear to be in flux at this time.

Being graphic

It would be a waste of time and energy to just use a web browser as a command line. The primary purpose of Jupyter is its usage as a lab notebook, which requires the ability to display visual information. To this end, an important feature of Jupyter is its seamless integration with the graphical capabilities of a browser.

This section will provide examples of using the plotting software from *Chapter 7, Seeing Is Believing – Visualization* in Jupyter. For the most part, displaying plots in Jupyter is easier done than said, with only minor modifications required to specify output to the notebook rather than IPython.

Using matplotlib

The key to using matplotlib in a notebook is the `%matplotlib inline` magic. It should be the first line in the cell. For example:

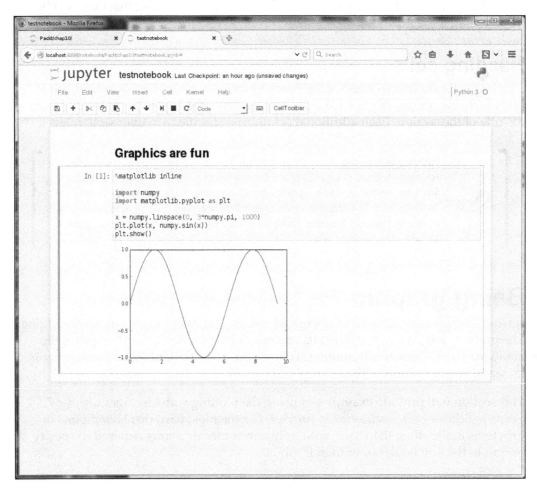

The first cell (which prints **Graphics are fun**) is Markdown; the second cell creates the plot shown.

Using Bokeh

The key to making Bokeh work with the notebook is to use the `output_notebook(` `)` method instead of `output_file( )`. For example, the following screenshot shows how to transform an earlier plot:

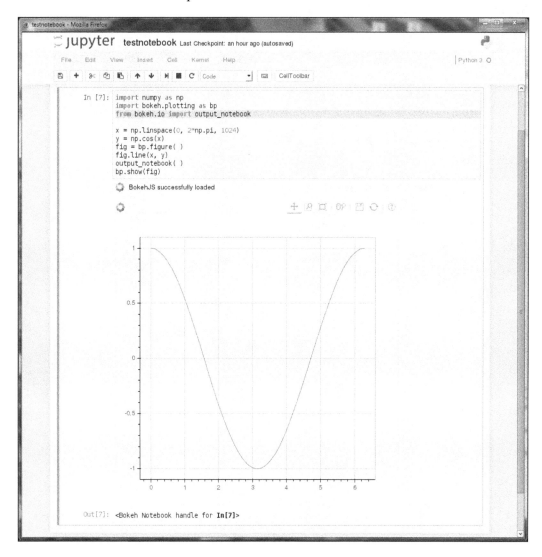

Using R

The important thing when using R is that all the work should be done in R (or at least the part that actually displays the plot). If not, the plot will open in a separate window, rather than in the notebook. The %%R cell magic is the right tool for the job. In particular, the plot should be printed out, rather than using the plot( ) function. For example:

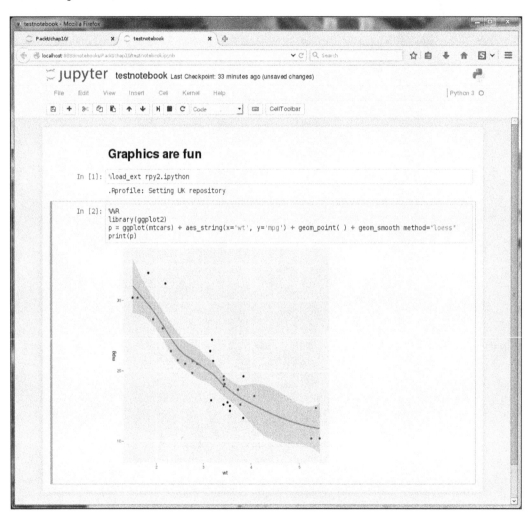

Using Python-nvd3

Using nvd3 within Jupyter will explain the meaning of that obscure warning message from earlier:

```
In [3]: import nvd3
loaded nvd3 IPython extension
run nvd3.ipynb.initialize_javascript() to set up the notebook
help(nvd3.ipynb.initialize_javascript) for options
```

It is, if anything, even easier than writing the output to a file. The chart object can be invoked to display itself in the notebook. For example:

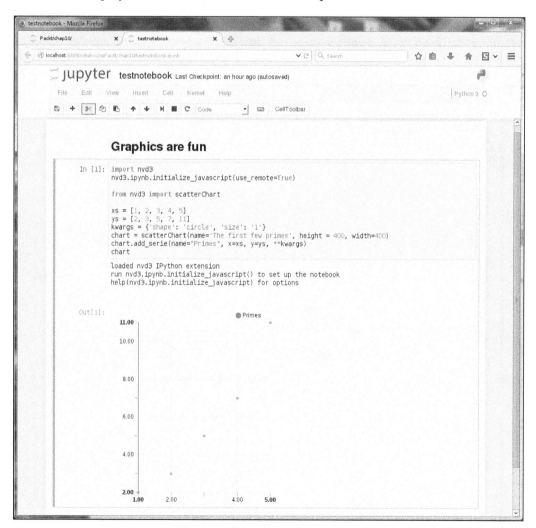

Format conversion

The Jupyter project includes a tool for format conversion called **nbconvert**. It is easy to invoke from the command line:

```
jupyter nbconvert <file>.ipynb
```

It leaves the original `<file>.ipynb` alone and produces as output `<file>.html`. For example, we can transform a previous example as follows:

```
(Ipython)-bash-4.1$ jupyter nbconvert notebook2.ipynb

[NbConvertApp] Converting notebook notebook2.ipynb to html

[NbConvertApp] Writing 214390 bytes to notebook2.html

(Ipython)-bash-4.1$ ls

HelloWorld.ipynb   img7.png   notebook2.html   notebook2.ipynb
testnotebook.ipynb
```

This results in a 214K HTML file that displays as:

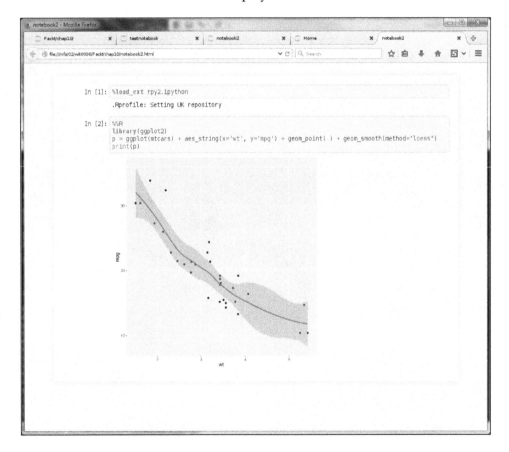

Note that the HTML preserves the full text of the code used to produce the plot, just in a read-only format. This can be important when using Jupyter as a method of disseminating research results, as readers can see the actual code used to produce the graph.

Other formats

HTML is the default format for nbconvert. The complete syntax is:

```
jupyter nbcomvert -to <format> <notebook file>
```

Where `<format>` is described in this table:

Format	Details
html	Enables additional arguments: • `--template full` (close to interactive view) • `--template basic` (simplified HTML)
latex	Enables additional arguments: • `--template article` (derived from Sphinx's howto template) • `--template report` (includes table of content and chapters) • `--template basic`
pdf	Generates PDF via LaTeX, so supports same templates
slides	Generates a Reveal.js HTML slideshow
markdown	Generates Markdown text
rst	Generates reStructuredText
script	Converts the notebook to an executable script, depending on what kernel was used
notebook	Used to invoke preprocessors without changing the notebook's format

nbconvert also supports the creation of custom exporters, which allow the developer to define conversions to any format desired.

nbviewer

The Jupyter project also provides nbviewer, a web service that allows requesters to view notebook files as static HTML files. In effect, nbviewer runs nbconvert on demand, sending the results out across an HTTP(s) connection. nbconvert can be run as a service on a project's own site, or a public instance can be used, as long as the notebook file itself has a publicly-accessible URL. There are even plugins for most major browsers that will run nbviewer on a URL that points to a notebook. Not every member of the potential audience will have IPython/Jupyter/every other kernel installed, but at least the results will be accessible.

Summary

The Jupyter Notebook is a flexible tool that excels in presenting scientific results, especially those comprised of a mixture of text, code, graphics, and computer-generated plots. It consists of two parts: the notebook format and the Dashboard.

The notebook format is a JSON text string. JSON is a lightweight, flexible text protocol that makes it easy to share notebooks between collaborators.

The Dashboard contains all the tools required to build a notebook. At this level, a notebook is a series of cells, each of which contain either Markdown text, code, or raw text. Markdown is a simple text format that provides enough power to build useful HTML pages. Code cells can be written in any language that has a kernel which Jupyter supports (66+ at the last count), although the most popular language continues to be IPython. Raw text is for text that should not be converted before display.

Between these cell types, the developer has the ability to produce high-quality documents for external consumption through the Notebook. Jupyter also supports the conversion of notebooks into other formats, including HTML, PDF, and LaTeX, among others. nbviewer allows for notebooks to be dynamically converted to HTML so that they can be viewed by users without Jupyter or other required software.

In the next chapter, we will take a look at where IPython is likely to go in the future. Its past has been eventful (as evidenced by the major shakeup surrounding the split with Jupyter) and its future promises to contain even more change. We will look at several important trends in scientific and high performance computing and how they may affect IPython and related projects.

11
Into the Future

IPython has come a long way since 2001, when Fernando Perez decided he wanted a better interactive environment than vanilla Python provided. In the best open source tradition, he wanted some functionality so he wrote some code to do it. This process has continued to the present day and the future of IPython looks to be filled with even more activity. In this chapter, we will attempt to situate IPython within the broader development ecosystem and try to guess where the future will take it. We start out at the project level and take a look at Jupyter and IPython, then take a look at the near future and the effect increasing parallelism will have on the field, and finally broaden our scope to consider the future of scientific software development in general.

The following topics will be covered:

- Some history
- The Jupyter project
- IPython
- The rise of parallelism
- Growing professionalism
- Summary

Some history

Some systems spring fully-conceived from a theoretical backing – Lisp is pretty much just a working out of John McCarthy's 1960 paper, *Recursive Functions of Symbolic Expressions and Their Computation by Machine, Part I.*

IPython is not such a system. In 2001, Fernando Perez was a graduate student at the University of Colorado in Boulder. He was not a computer science major, he was a physics graduate student who needed to program and wanted a better tool. As a physicist, his idea of "better" was different from what a computer scientist might have envisioned. In particular, the formative influences on the young IPython was tools designed primarily for data analysis and presentation: Mathematica (`http://www.wolfram.com/mathematica/`) and Sage (`http://www.sagemath.org/`).

Perez has stated that IPython is "meant to be a highly configurable tool for building problem-specific interactive environments," which provides a key to its history and future directions.

Initial efforts came at the problem from two directions. On one hand, there were a couple of Python extensions that already existed – IPP (by Janko Hauser) and LazyPython (by Nathan Gray). On the other hand, Perez had his own ideas about what should be implemented. In the end, IPython was born through a merger of code from IPP, LazyPython, and Perez's own efforts.

At this point development slowed down. A few stabs at making a notebook were made. Some consideration was given to merging with Sage, but in the end the projects went their own ways. In 2009, the first full-time developer was funded. His first task was a refactoring of the entire codebase, which was at that point still a mash of IPP, LazyPython, and Perez's original code. No new functionality was added, but development could move forward more easily on the newly clean code.

2010 was an important year. The first big development was the move to an architecture based on ZeroMQ. The adoption of ZeroMQ allowed for two important architectural advances: separation between the frontend and the interpreter, and support for parallelism.

Separating the frontend and backend was huge on several fronts. Perhaps most importantly, it meant that implementing a notebook was simple(r): the Notebook became just another interface to the Python kernel on the back end. On the flip side, the command-line interface was free to connect to a kernel that supported any language, not just Python. IPython was moving from "a better Python shell" to "a multi-interface, multi-language platform." Work proceeded quickly at this point: the remainder of 2010 saw the development of a command-line interface, a Qt console, integration into Python Tools for Visual Studio, and a prototype web notebook. 2011 saw the prototype turned into a fully-working version, and IPython 0.12 was released.

At this point, most of the basic functional parts of IPython were in place. The first IPython book, Cyrille Rossant's Learning IPython for *Interactive Computing and Data Visualization* (`https://www.packtpub.com/big-data-and-business-intelligence/learning-ipython-interactive-computing-and-data-visualization`) was released in April of 2013. IPython 1.0 followed shortly in August of 2013 and added nbconvert among a host of fixes. IPython 2.0 came out in April 2014 and added interactive HTML widgets. IPython 3.0 followed in February of 2015 and formalized support for non-Python kernels.

It was at this point that the codebase got too big to handle. The decision was made to break it up into two major sections. In one section went all the language-agnostic components (the Notebook, the Qt console, nbconvert, all the non-Python kernels, and so on). These moved into a new project called Jupyter. The Python-specific components (the shell, the Python kernel, and the parallel architecture) remained in the IPython project.

Here is a quote from the IPython homepage (`http://ipython.org/`):

> *"IPython is a growing project, with increasingly language-agnostic components. IPython 3.x was the last monolithic release of IPython, containing the notebook server, qtconsole, etc. As of IPython 4.0, the language-agnostic parts of the project: the notebook format, message protocol, qtconsole, notebook web application, etc. have moved to new projects under the name Jupyter. IPython itself is focused on interactive Python, part of which is providing a Python kernel for Jupyter."*

The Jupyter project

This reorganization of code is reflected in the hierarchy of projects that produce it: IPython is now an official subproject of the Jupyter project. IPython is Kernel Zero, in some sense the reference kernel, but in the end just one kernel among many. There are still some sections of code that are shared between the projects and need to be separated, but this is a relatively simple technical issue.

Even after the codebases became completely separate, Jupyter will constrain the future of IPython due to requirements for continued compatibility. Although IPython can be used as an independent tool (as this book attempts to demonstrate), its role in the Jupyter project greatly increases its user base.

At first glance, this would seem impossible. The Jupyter project is large and contains more subprojects than could be comfortably listed here (see `http://jupyter.readthedocs.org/en/latest/subprojects.html` for a complete list), making any attempt at staying compatible a nightmare. Luckily, many subprojects are completely independent of IPython. Not all, however, and some are worth discussing in detail because of their impact on IPython's future.

The Notebook

The Jupyter Notebook is the primary cause for the Big Split. Looking back over the release notes for the versions of IPython before 4.0, it is clear that a great number of the improvements were being made to the notebook component rather than the Python-specific features, or even the underlying architecture.

The Notebook itself is so big it has subprojects of its own:

- The document format (and its API, nbformat)
- nbconvert
- nbviewer

The Notebook's primary function is information display – the computation is left to the kernels – so it seems unlikely that compatibility issues will arise at this level. The notebook provides more functionality than just display, however, and more functionality is being added all the time, so the opportunity for compatibility issues to arise will persist.

The console

The console is a command-line interface that can communicate with any kernel that follows the Jupyter interactive computing protocol. It is not clear why a new terminal interface was needed, instead of just using IPython's terminal now that it is language-independent. They certainly look the same from a user's perspective. They may actually be the same, just with some IPython-specific code swapped out for Jupyter-compatible code. The documentation explains how to start and use the console, but not how it is related to IPython, if at all. A quick search on the web is no help, with some sites even claiming that the console is the new IPython.

Jupyter Client

The Jupyter Client package is a Python API used to start, manage, and communicate with kernels. IPython also follows this standard for its kernels. It specifies the messaging protocol that all kernels must adhere to in order to communicate with the notebook. The IPython kernel will certainly continue to adhere to this specification as the reference kernel for Jupyter.

The future of Jupyter

Although Fernando Perez is *Benevolent Dictator For Life*, and there is a Steering Committee of 10 members, Jupyter is an open source project using a revised BSD license. As such, there is no authoritative list of things to do. Instead, there are varying levels of "officialness."

Official roadmap

At the first level are the mainline subprojects at the Jupyter GitHub site: `https://github.com/jupyter`. A high-level roadmap is held at `https://github.com/jupyter/roadmap`. The following table presents some highlights:

Feature	Description	Details
JupyterLab	Initially a new page in the existing notebook web app that allows multiple plugins in the same browser tab	Potentially a replacement for the current notebook interface. A major project.
ipywidgets	Interactive widgets that tie together code in the kernel and JavaScript/CSS/HTML in the browser	Improved styling. General refactoring. Compartmentalization of JavaScript.
JupyterHub	Manages and proxies multiple instances of the single-user Jupyter notebook server	Configuration enhancements. Sharing and collaboration.
IPython		Comparatively mature, so few major changes planned.

At a finer level of detail are the bugs listed under the **Issues** tag and the new features under the **Pulls** tag.

Next in line appear to be the **Jupyter Enhancement Proposals (JEPs)** (`https://github.com/jupyter/enhancement-proposals`). According to the documentation (`http://jupyter.readthedocs.org/en/latest/contrib_guide_bugs_enh.html`) these are similar to bug requests in that the submitter hopes someone else does the work. At present, there are only four Enhancement Proposals on the site. There are four pull requests. None of them appear to be prominent parts of the Roadmap.

Official subprojects

Official subprojects are considered part of the Jupyter project and are hosted on the Jupyter GitHub organization. This includes support and maintenance along with the rest of the Jupyter project. New subprojects come into existence in one of two manners: direct creation or incorporation.

Direct creation

Any Steering Committee member can create a new Subproject in Jupyter's GitHub repository. The only requirement is consensus among the other Steering Committee members.

Incorporation

Projects that have existed and been developed outside the official Jupyter organization, but wish to join, can be incorporated. At the very least, a software project should be well-established, functional, and stable before considering incorporation.

According to the official site (`https://github.com/jupyter/governance/blob/master/newsubprojects.md`) the following criteria are used to determine suitability for incorporation:

- Have an active developer community that offers a sustainable model for future development
- Have an active user community
- Use solid software engineering with documentation and tests hosted with appropriate technologies (*Read the Docs* and *Travis* are examples of technologies that can be used)
- Demonstrate continued growth and development
- Integrate well with other official Subprojects
- Be developed according to the Jupyter governance and contribution model that is documented here
- Have a well-defined scope
- Be packaged using appropriate technologies such as `pip`, `conda`, `npm`, `bower`, `docker`, and so on

If the criteria are met, the potential Subproject's team should submit a pull request against the `jupyter/enhancement-proposals` repository. The Steering Council will evaluate the request.

It is not clear exactly what the relationship is between a **Proposal For Incorporation** (**PFI**) and a Jupyter Enhancement Proposal. It is clear how they are conceptually different:

- A JEP is a suggestion for enhancement (for example, *Issue #6* proposes adding more debugging/profiling/analysis tools to the Notebook). The suggestion itself is just that – a suggestion, not a solution.

- A PFI concerns an already-existing project that provides new functionality.

Yet both PFIs and JEPs are handled in the same repository. GitHub reports minimal activity in this repository.

Incubation

Incubation is the process a Subproject follows when it is not ready to be accepted as part of the Jupyter project yet. Incubation is for projects that are not mature enough for consideration as Subprojects yet. The criteria are:

- Significant unanswered technical questions or uncertainties that require exploration

- Entirely new directions, scopes, or ideas that haven't been vetted with the community

- Significant, already existent code bases where it is not clear how the Subproject will integrate with the rest of Jupyter

The goal of the incubation process is to allow interesting ideas to be explored quickly and exposed to a wide audience of potentially interested developers. As such, the process is lightweight compared to official incorporation.

The instructions state that new incubation proposals should involve a pull request to the `jupyter-incubator/proposals` repository. There are none at present. It appears that once a proposal is accepted its proposal is deleted and a new repository is created for it. Sometimes the original proposal remains in the **Code** tab of the proposals repository.

A description of some of the subprojects currently under incubation is as follows:

Name	Description
Dashboards Server	Renders Jupyter Notebooks as interactive dashboards outside the Jupyter Notebook server
Declarative Widgets	Extensions to widgets
Sparkmagic	A set of tools for working with Spark clusters
Dynamic Dashboards	Enables the layout and presentation of grid-based dashboards from notebooks
Kernel Gateway Bundlers	A collection of bundlers that convert, package, and deploy notebooks as standalone HTTP microservices
SciPy Trait Types	Trait types for NumPy, SciPy, and friends, used to (optionally) enforce strict typing

On March 9, 2016, it was announced that the incubating Jupyter Kernel Gateway project was accepted as an official Jupyter project.

External incubation

As an open source project, anyone is free to start up his or her own repository and commit code in whatever manner they see fit. The Jupyter organization calls this external incubation. The only consideration for these projects is that to move from external incubation to official incubation they will have to adopt the licensing, organizational, and other criteria required to be part of the Jupyter project.

IPython

> *"IPython is comparatively mature, and there are consequently fewer major changes planned."*

> *– The Jupyter project*

Despite its maturity, there is still a lot of work to be done on IPython. The official GitHub repository (`https://github.com/ipython`) lists 933 open issues for the core of IPython, not including popular modules such as `ipyparallel`, `ipykernel`, and `nbconvert`.

The repository also contains a wiki with a roadmap (`https://github.com/ipython/ipython/wiki/Roadmap:-IPython`). Unfortunately, the roadmap has not been updated since 2014.

IPython used a system of **IPython Enhancement Proposals** (**IPEPs**) similar to Python Enhancement Proposals (PEPs) in order to organize ongoing projects. A list can be found at `https://github.com/ipython/ipython/wiki/IPEPs:-IPython-Enhancement-Proposals`. While an interesting historical document, no IPEP has been modified since 2014. The sole exception is a note in IPEP 29 (project governance) stating that the document is now being maintained as part of project Jupyter.

A number of IPEPs are still marked as "Active", including proposals that would allow for custom messages and the implementation of concurrent futures (PEP 3148) in `ipyparallel`. Given the generally abandoned look of the site, however, it is difficult to tell what the status of the IPEPs might be.

Current activity

The Big Split seems to have scrambled a lot of the more formal development coordination mechanisms such as the IPEP/JEP repositories and associated pull requests. The codebase itself continues to be healthy, but the associated documentation has not kept up (for example, the wiki has not been updated since prior to the release of 3.0, over a year ago).

The breakdown in formal management methods has not stopped progress on IPython. Much of the current development is being coordinated in a more informal manner. The IPython-dev mailing list in particular is useful (`https://mail.scipy.org/mailman/listinfo/ipython-dev`).

 Useful news and insight on some important scientific Python packages can be found by subscribing to the mailing lists provided at `https://mail.scipy.org/mailman/listinfo`.

The rise of parallelism

It is commonplace to remark that a cell phone has more computing power than the Apollo rocket that sent the astronauts to the Moon. It is somewhat less common to hear that the cell phone also costs a lot less. How did this happen? It required the interplay of economics and technology to bring the development community to its current position.

In the beginning, computers were big, slow, and expensive. Programmers were rare and highly skilled. It was worth spending a programmer's time to save a computer's time. This is the era of mainframes, assembly language, and Fortran.

As time went on, computers got faster and cheaper. Programmers became somewhat less rare, but still commanded a premium. At some point, it became more cost-effective to spend the computer's time to save some programmer time. This is the era of PCs and high-level languages.

For a time, things were good. Computers were always getting faster, and memory was always getting bigger. There was no need to write efficient code because the next generation of computers could always handle bad code faster than this generation could handle good code. As a bonus, the underlying hardware was changing so fast that users threw out or replaced many programs after a short lifespan. Why put effort into writing good code when the hardware would run it fast and the user would throw it away in any case? Good code is expensive to write and the return was not there.

Then the good times came to a halt.

The megahertz wars end

Eventually processors stopped getting faster, or at least stopped getting faster as fast as they had previously. Physical limitations were preventing the development of denser circuits and higher clock speeds. A graph shows the stalling out of increased CPU speeds:

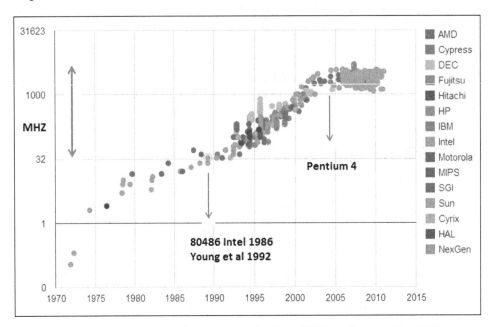

The preceding image is by Newhorizons msk - For CPU scaling study, CC0, https://en.wikipedia.org/w/index.php?curid=38626780.

The answer was to add more computing cores to the chip, rather than trying to make a single core go faster. Each core would run at the same speed, but each additional core meant that more than one instruction could be carried out in any given clock cycle. Theoretically, this meant that a 4-core machine could run programs four times as quickly as a single core machine, as it could execute four instructions per cycle rather than one.

The problem

While true in theory, the promised speedups were not observed in practice. This has left the development community in a bind. Three trends have coincided to stifle progress.

First, there is an ever-increasing number of cycles available for computation. This would not normally be a problem but the cycles are structured in parallel, so that existing programs cannot take advantage of them without significant rework by programmers. This has driven demand for an ever-increasing number of programmers to write programs that can take advantage of the new multi-core architectures.

Second, the number of programmers is not growing to meet the demand. Limited success toward increasing the size of the programmer pool has been achieved through efforts to make programming more accessible, but any progress is running up against the third trend.

Third, parallel programming is harder than serial programming. Many current programmers find it difficult, and it is more difficult to teach to new programmers.

A parallel with the past

To some extent, the current problem has parallels in the crisis that occasioned the development of Fortran all those years ago. Fortran came into existence because two factors collided:

- The increasing complexity of writing larger systems in machine or assembly language. Computers were being looked to in order to solve an increasing number of problems, and the programs required were growing beyond what those languages could support.

- Computers were getting faster. If the code could be written, the cycles were available to run it. There was just no economically feasible way to do it, given the difficulty of low-level programming.

Initial solutions were piecemeal and pragmatic. At the lowest level, CPU instruction sets became more complex to allow for more sophisticated operations. Assembly languages (and the associated assemblers) grew in complexity to match.

In the end, the breakthrough did not come from creating increasingly baroque assembly-language hacks. A new conceptual framework was needed. The genius of Fortran (and COBOL) was to discover that framework: the compiler. With a compiler, the additional cycles provided by technological advances can be used to help tame the increased complexity of growing systems.

Not everyone was immediately convinced by this idea. Using a compiler means giving up control over exactly what code is being executed. For developers used to determining exactly where every byte was stored and when every instruction would be executed, this was a major break from a paradigm that had worked well for decades. Even worse, the code generated by compilers tended to use more memory and run more slowly than code written by hand. Why, when systems were getting bigger, would one want them to be even more bloated and slower?

In the end, compilers (and the high-level languages they enable) won out over hand-coded assembly for all but the most demanding applications. The code that compilers generated became better and better, to the point that only highly skilled specialists can compete. More importantly, high-level languages opened the field to more concise, sophisticated ways to express algorithms. It turned out that using some cycles to help build the program was more important than using those cycles to make the program run faster.

The present

This brief history lesson is included because the author believes it illustrates the state of the parallel/HPC field at present. In particular, the parallel "revolution" is at the stage prior to the invention of the compiler. Consider the similarities.

Problems are getting bigger and harder

HPC problems are getting larger. Consider the "NSF Advisory Committee for Cyberinfrastructure Task Force on Grand Challenges Final Report (2011)" (`https://www.nsf.gov/cise/aci/taskforces/TaskForceReport_GrandChallenges.pdf`). This report defined **Grand Challenges** (**GC**) as "fundamental problems of science and engineering, with broad applications, whose solution would be enabled by high-performance computing resources." Although the time frame for solutions to GCs is measured in decades rather than years, they are selected because of their relevance to applications. The breakthroughs involved in a solution to any GC would be expected to have important immediate economic impacts.

Here are some examples of a few GCs listed in the report:

- Global climate change prediction
- Virtual product design
- High-temperature superconductors
- Simulation of complex multiscale, multiphysics, multi-model systems
- Large-scale simulation-based optimization
- Exascale computing
- New numerical algorithms

Computers are becoming more parallel

At lower levels of computing (PCs, most enterprises), parallel computing is being driven by chip manufacturers. Each new version of the x86 architecture seems to include more cores, and GPUs are stretching the definition of "core" itself. For the most part, this has not had a great impact on most uses of the PC: e-mail, web surfing, word processing, and the like. The primary class of application that can use all this power is games. Games have traditionally led the other sectors of PC applications in terms of utilizing the platform, so this is not unexpected.

The cutting edge of parallelism is in HPC. There is a race on in the HPC community to be the first to exascale computing. Exascale computing refers to a computing system capable of sustained calculation of at least one exaFLOPs (1,018 floating point operations per second). The only practical way to achieve this is to build a massively parallel machine. There is enough money behind the effort:

- The U.S. National Strategic Computing Initiative is an executive order funding research into exascale computing
- The European Union is funding the CRESTA, DEEP, and Mont Blanc projects
- The RIKEN Institute in Japan is planning an exascale system for 2020
- The U.S.'s Intelligence Advanced Research Projects Activity organization is working on cryogenic technology to enable exaflop machines based on superconducting technologies
- India's Centre for Development of Advanced Computing is hoping to build an exascale machine by 2017

Clouds are rolling in

Another approach to parallelism is the cloud. While less tightly coupled than the traditional HPC architecture, a cloud can provide many more processing units at any given time. This architecture is a good fit for algorithms that can be structured so that communication between processors is minimal. Many clouds also have the benefit that they are publically accessible and relatively cheap to use (especially compared to the cost of running a supercomputer center). Some notable public clouds include:

- Amazon Web Services (`https://aws.amazon.com/`)
- Google Cloud Platform (`https://cloud.google.com/`)
- Microsoft Azure (`https://azure.microsoft.com`)

While IPython already provides a solid basis for parallel computing in a traditional architecture (see *Chapters 3, Stepping Up to IPython for Parallel Computing* and *Chapter 4, Messaging With ZeroMQ and MPI* for details), there are efforts underway to support the new cloud platforms. While there is no official distribution for a cloud architecture at present, the following pages should provide enough information for the curious to get an instance of IPython/Jupyter up-and-running on a cloud:

- Amazon Web Services (EC2): `https://gist.github.com/iamatypeofwalrus/5183133`
- Google Cloud Platform (using a Dataproc cluster): `https://cloud.google.com/dataproc/tutorials/jupyter-notebook`
- Azure: `https://azure.microsoft.com/en-us/documentation/articles/virtual-machines-linux-jupyter-notebook/`

There is no Big Idea

One quintillion operations a second is a lot of computing power. There are some algorithms (the embarrassingly parallel ones such as brute-force cryptography and genetic algorithms) that can use that sort of power without special treatment. Most other algorithms need to be adapted to use these many parallel computing units. Currently, there is no well understood, widely accepted way, analogous to a compiler for serial programs, to write such parallel programs. Several approaches are actively being pursued.

Pragmatic evolution of techniques

It is not that no one can program in parallel at all. There is a wide variety of tools available: monitors, semaphores, threads, shared memory models, data flow dependency analysis, MPI, and so on. These tools and concepts do represent progress in writing software that can take advantage of parallel architectures.

The difficulty comes from their patchwork nature. Knowing which tool applies when and how to use it is more of an art than a science. The situation is analogous to the end of the assembly language era: some developers can do amazing things with these tools, but not many, and it is becoming apparent that continued ad hoc progress will not be enough.

Better tools

Another approach is to empower the programmer by giving them better tools. This approach has synergies with the pragmatic evolution approach, in that new techniques often require new tools to make them easy to work with, and new tools can spur the development of new techniques. There are multiple sections in the Grand Challenges paper devoted to tools. The paper calls out several in particular, including compilers, debuggers, and development environments.

IPython has one foot squarely planted in this approach. To use IPython (with Python) is to sacrifice some level of performance for other benefits: a high level of abstraction, multi-language support, a friendly IDE, and all the other features detailed in this book. It is in some way a bet – the cycles spent running IPython will outweigh the ones lost to a less efficient final product. Given that the power of the tools available is the difference between creating a working product at all, and producing one that doesn't work, this looks to be a safe bet.

To the extent that IPython is a tool for interactive parallel computing, its future looks secure, if unclear. The future is secure to the extent that, as new techniques are developed, IPython (and the Jupyter organization as a whole) is well situated to integrate them into itself. It is unclear in that no one knows what techniques will be developed in the future.

Because of the ongoing growth in parallel computing, learning IPython is not a matter of memorizing some syntax and working through a few koans. IPython will grow and evolve over the next few decades in a way that will require developers to regularly update their knowledge of the field, in addition to adopting new versions of the tool.

The Next Big Idea

It may be that, between evolving new techniques and improving tools, the community will arrive at a satisfactory framework for developing parallel systems. If history is any guide, however, an entirely new paradigm (similar to the change from hand-coding assembly language to compiling a high-level language) will be needed.

As an example, consider Notre Dame de Paris. In outline, it sounds a great deal like a software project:

Source image: https://commons.wikimedia.org/wiki/File:Notre_Dame_dalla_Senna.jpg

Notre Dame was built over the course of ~182 years (1163 AD - ~1345 AD) under at least four different architects. It was in continuous use from its earliest days, despite ongoing construction. Although there was a plan at the outset, important features (including some of the famous flying buttresses) were added over time as construction difficulties uncovered a need for them. It is a remarkable feat of engineering.

What makes it even more remarkable is that, in a very real sense, nobody involved really understood what they were doing. The underlying physical laws that justified the architectural decisions were not understood until Newton, almost 350 years later. Until Newton, all architectural knowledge was a result of trial and error – decisions about wall thickness, height, the ability to bear loads, arch height/width, and all other structural parameters were made based on the accumulated results of past experiment and the architect's own judgement.

This does not make their decisions wrong – obviously, they could build quite large, stable, and aesthetically pleasing buildings. What it does mean is that they had strict limits to what they could accomplish. As buildings got larger, there were fewer previous examples to rely on, and the costs of failure grew.

Software development for massively parallel machines shares this problem. We have a lot of experience building smaller parallel systems, and some for larger degrees of parallelism, but the problems (and the costs of failure) are growing. What the field needs is something similar to the Principia – a unified theory of parallel programming. We need the Next Big Idea.

Until the Next Big Idea comes along, the scientific software development community can advance by adopting some practices from the field of software engineering.

Growing professionalism

> *"A scientist builds in order to learn; an engineer learns in order to build."*
>
> *– Fred Brooks*

What scientists do and what engineers do is different. Scientists are concerned with extending knowledge, engineers with applying it. When a scientist builds something, its purpose is fulfilled when the desired knowledge is gained – at that point, the useful life of the object is over. When an engineer builds something, a long useful lifetime is the purpose of applying the knowledge.

Much scientific software is written by scientists for scientific purposes. It is no surprise that it is often considered expendable once the knowledge it was written to produce has been extracted. While this approach produces immediate results, other researchers in the field who would also wish to use the software often find it difficult to use, maintain, and extend.

As problems and budgets get larger, funding agencies are starting to require that software be developed so that its lifetime is longer than a single project. This enables the cost of writing the software to be recouped over multiple projects. Writing software with such a lifetime takes more of an engineering mindset, and belongs to the field of software engineering. We take a brief look at the National Science Foundation's approach in the next section.

The NSF

The National Science Foundation has published a vision for the future of software development under the title *Cyberinfrastructure Framework for 21st Century Science and Engineering (CIF21)* (see `http://www.nsf.gov/funding/pgm_summ.jsp?pims_id=504730`). From the document:

> *The overarching goals of CIF21 are:*
>
> > *Develop a deep symbiotic relationship between science and engineering users and developers of cyberinfrastructure to simultaneously advance new research practices and open transformative across opportunities all science and engineering fields.*
> >
> > *Provide an integrated and scalable cyberinfrastructure that leverages existing and new components across all areas of CIF21 and establishes a national data infrastructure and services capability.*
> >
> > *Ensure long-term sustainability for cyberinfrastructure, via community development, learning and workforce development in CDS&E and transformation of practice.*

(Emphasis and wording in the original).

The vision as a whole is very broad, and includes several key strategies:

- Forming communities to identify common needs and set standards between scientific domains
- Training and retaining a qualified workforce in scientific computing
- Conducting foundational research in cyberinfrastructure itself
- Building a sustainable infrastructure (both physical and organizational) to support progress and collaboration

The key for our purposes is "leverages existing and new components," and "long-term sustainability for cyberinfrastructure." Under CIF21, the NSF will expect quality in all phases of the development process, from analysis and design through implementation and including testing and documentation. This is from the Vision Statement (`http://www.nsf.gov/cise/aci/cif21/CIF21Vision2012current.pdf`):

> *"Investments will also target domain-specific programming to establish paradigms for verification, validation, uncertainty quantification, and provenance to ensure trustworthy and reproducible scientific findings."*

The only way to ensure this sort of quality is to create and maintain extensive test suites and documentation (both internal and external). As this book has demonstrated, IPython (and Python with it) contains tools to ease the writing of test suites and documentation. As a tool for programmers, IPython provides both the flexibility of interactive development and the ability to test and document the results.

Software Infrastructure for Sustained Innovation

The CIF21 initiative is large enough that it requires several programs to implement its various goals. The program that focuses on software development is the *Software Infrastructure for Sustained Innovation - SSE & SSI* (aka SI2, see `http://www.nsf.gov/funding/pgm_summ.jsp?pims_id=503489&org=NSF`). This is from the site:

> *"NSF has established the Software Infrastructure for Sustained Innovation (SI2) program, with the overarching goal of transforming innovations in research and education into sustained software resources that are an integral part of the cyberinfrastructure... NSF expects that its SI2 investment will result in trustworthy, robust, reliable, usable and sustainable software infrastructure that is critical to achieving the CIF21 vision and will transform science and engineering while contributing to the education of next-generation researchers and creators of future cyberinfrastructure."*

In his keynote talk at the 2016 SI2 PI Workshop, Rajiv Ramnath, Program Director of SI2, made the following points:

Software (including services) essential for the bulk of science:

> *About half the papers in recent issues of Science were software-intensive*

> *Research becoming dependent upon advances in software*

> *Wide range of software types: system, applications, modeling, gateways, analysis, algorithms, middleware, libraries*
>
> *Significant software-intensive projects across NSF: e.g. NEON, OOI, NEES, NCN, iPlant, etc.*

And:

> *Software is not a one-time effort, it must be sustained:*
>
> *Development, production, and maintenance are people intensive*
>
> *Software life-times are long vs hardware*
>
> *Software has under-appreciated value*

See `http://cococubed.asu.edu/si2_pi_workshop_2016/ ewExternalFiles/2016-PI-Meeting-PD-Presentation-2016-02-15-20-49- Compressed.pdf` for the entire presentation.

Both of these points support the primary strategy of the SI2 project, to *Enable A Sustainable Software-Enabled Ecosystem for Advancing Science.*

Put another way, the community should start treating software the same way it treats any other experimental apparatus because so much science is riding on it. For software to be useful in the way that, say, a Bunsen burner is useful, it should meet several criteria:

Criteria	Description	IPython's role
Trustworthiness	The program should be correct	Supports testing at all levels. Easy visualization of results.
Transparency	Others should be able to inspect and verify the program	Internal documentation support.
Reproducibility	Others should be able to run the same program on the same data and obtain the same result	IPython is supported on many platforms. Support for external documentation. Jupyter is built for reproducibility by providing both data and code.
Maintainability	A program should be easy to update as the environment around it changes	Support for unit and regression testing.
Extendibility	It should be easy to add additional functionality over time	Support for unit and regression testing, modules, object orientation.

Criteria	Description	IPython's role
Longevity	The useful life of the program should be long	IPython/Jupyter has a large and active user and developer community.

Summary

IPython belongs to the Jupyter project. From their inception, both IPython and Jupyter have been very opportunistic and pragmatic about their features – if a feature seemed like a good idea to the Steering Committee, it became part of the project. This has both good and bad aspects. On the good side, any useful advance in programming is likely to be incorporated into the project. On the down side, it makes predicting where the project is going difficult. About the only sure bet is that the project will continue to be active, given its large and growing popularity.

The technological and economic infrastructure supporting coding means that further advances in performance and scaling will result from increased reliance on parallel computing, whether the tightly coupled traditional architecture, or the more loosely coupled cloud style. In either case, IPython is well situated to follow the field as it advances.

In a wider view, scientific computing is reaching the end of disposable code: the phase where a small group of gifted developers could hack together enough code to get a result and then toss it and write a completely new system to compute the next result. The results are too important, the systems are too big, and the dollar amounts too high, to support this model at the highest level any longer.

This is to some extent a reflection of the crisis looming in software. We are coming to the limits of the systems that can be built using our current techniques. Even the most professional, best-funded software organizations (such as Microsoft and Google) routinely struggle to put out large products without too many serious bugs (and open source is not the answer).

Until someone discovers the Next Big Thing in software development, scientific software has room to grow in terms of system size and quality. It can only do this by adopting software engineering techniques from professional software development houses. In order to adopt these techniques, the right tools are needed. It has been the goal of this book to show that IPython is indeed a valuable tool that can aid scientific software developers in the production of better, more professional code.

Index

Symbols

K

kernel 45
Kill GIL 60

L

lists
  about 289
  bulleted 290
  definition lists 290, 291
  enumerated 289
LoadBalancedView
  about 146
  data movement 147
  imports 147
load balancing 82

M

magic commands
  about 38
  custom magic commands, creating 39
  Cython 40
  debugging 38
  documentation 38
  IPython, configuring 41
  logging 38
  OS equivalents 38
  other languages, working with 38
  profiling 38
  working with code 38
MapReduce
  about 77, 78
  scatter and gather 78
  sophisticated method 79, 80
map_sync
  using 66
markdown cells 320
markdown text
  URL 319
Mathematica
  URL 330
Matplotlib
  about 182
  graph, modifying 186-189
  initial graph 185, 186

interactivity, controlling 189, 190
  starting 182-184
  URL 187
  using 322
Message Passing Interface (MPI)
  about 107
  broadcasting 110
  configuration, changing 112
  Hello World 108
  master 113
  point-to-point communication 109
  process control 113
  rank and role 108
  reduce 110-112
  URL 74
  work, dividing 112, 113
  work, parceling out 113
messaging, use cases
  about 117
  heartbeat 118
  IOPub 119
  registration 117
Microsoft Azure
  URL 342
MIMD (Multiple Instruction Multiple
      Data stream) 80
MIT (Expat) license
  URL 171
monkeypatching 249-251
Monte Carlo simulation 84
MPMD (Multiple Program Multiple
      Data stream) 80-82
mp.pool.AsyncResult class
  about 130
  example program, various methods
      used 131, 132
  results, obtaining 130
multi-core machines 60
multiple processors
  using 61
multiprocessing.pool.Pool class
  about 127
  blocking methods 127
  example program, various methods
      used 128-130
  nonblocking methods 128
  results, obtaining 128

U

unittest
about 224-228
decorators 236, 237
one-time setUp 234, 235
one-time tearDown 234, 235
test case 224
test fixture 224
test runner 224
test, setUP used 229-234
test suite 224
test, tearDown used 229-234
URL 239
unittest2pytest 239
unit testing
about 222, 223
assertions 222
environmental issues 222
mocks 223
setup 223
teardown 223

V

View class
about 138
DirectView object 140
LoadBalancedView 146
Python functions, calling 138
view attributes 138

X

x86 assembly language
URL 3

Z

ZeroMQ
about 93
and IPython 115
client 96
discussion 98
features 105
issues 105
messaging patterns 97
pairwise 97
sample program 93
server 93-96
socket types 115
URL 93-95
ZeroMQ, issues
about 105
discovery 106, 107
startup and shutdown 105, 106

www.ingramcontent.com/pod-product-compliance
Lightning Source LLC
Chambersburg PA
CBHW062047050326
40690CB00016B/3011